Locational Analysis of Firms' Activities from a Strategic Perspective

Toshiharu Ishikawa
Editor

Locational Analysis of Firms' Activities from a Strategic Perspective

Springer

Editor
Toshiharu Ishikawa
Institute of Economic Research
Chuo University
Hachioji, Tokyo, Japan

ISBN 978-981-13-1683-8 ISBN 978-981-13-1684-5 (eBook)
https://doi.org/10.1007/978-981-13-1684-5

Library of Congress Control Number: 2018948708

This Springer imprint is published by the registered company Springer Nature Singapore Pte Ltd.
The registered company address is: 152 Beach Road, #21-01/04 Gateway East, Singapore 189721, Singapore

Preface

A factory producing goods has been a basic unit of economic society since the eighteenth century. Locations of the factories form the spatial skeleton of modern economic activity in geographical area. Economic agents, especially, the regional governments are required to deliberate sand strategical perspective of locations of factories for creating sound society. As this requirement is widely accepted among many regions and countries, the factories' location attracts attention from the various disciplines. And the analysis of location factors that influence the locations of the factories keeps an important position in economics. This book develops the location analysis centering on the factory's location selections and its impact on the regional economy.

Importance of the factories' locations in regional economies is successfully confirmed by referring regional economic development by three kinds of the industries. There are three types of representative methods for the regional economic development: they are agricultural development, tourism development, and manufacturing industrial development. Advantages of the agricultural development are obvious. Agriculture is operated using the natural condition of the region, and local people have long experience in agricultural management suitable to the region. And farmlands, irrigation, etc. are relatively well maintained by the local farmers. Since various agricultural products are necessities for daily lives and there are always certain amounts of the demands, the management of agricultural activity is relatively stable. From these reasons, a region is relatively easy to develop local economy by using the agricultural industry. On the other hand, there are serious weaknesses that agricultural development is susceptible to influence the changes in the natural condition such as weather. In addition to this, it has the following economic nature: Since the income elasticity of demand for products is low, agricultural production does not increase corresponding to an increase in the incomes; and the agricultural industry provides a region with only a small amount of employments and it supplies local people with a few diversities in occupation in local society.

Advantages and problems of the tourism in the regional development are summarized as follows. The characteristics of the tourism industry are partially similar to those of the agricultural industry. The resort field of the tourism industry uses the natural environment in local area. And the field relying on the historical places makes use of the existing well-known resources in the area. Regions which have some advantages in natural and historical contexts easily carry out the tourism development with relatively small initial investments. In addition to these, the tourism development is evaluated from the fact that the tourism industry could play an important role in a creation of innovation: a technological innovation in the globalization economy becomes a decisively important factor for economic development, and some high-skilled workers who take charge of the advanced technology are interested in local culture and technologies. If the region draws their attention, and by this reason the technology exchange with other parts of the world progresses, the possibility of technological innovation could be created in the region. As a result, the tourism may play a role in enhancing regional industrial composition in the region.

While, the tourism development has the same weakness as the agricultural one. The tourism development is susceptible to influence of the changes in the natural conditions such as weather fluctuation in own country and other countries. Seasonal fluctuation also affects employment in this industry. And the tourism development does not create employment on a large scale and does not provide the large diversities in occupation in regions.

Finally, the manufacturing industrial development does not have serious weakness of the above two development methods. And the manufacturing industrial development has its own advantages different from the above two industries. Its advantages are better represented by the machine-assembled industry such as the automotive sector. The machine-assembled industry is related to many other industrial sectors. For this reason, the location of the machine-assembled industry attracts various sorts of the related sectors and they attract a great deal of workers and provide diverse occupations in a region. The location site of them becomes an accumulation place of diverse individualities and talents. Consequently, the manufacturing industrial development does have a great opportunity to provide large amounts of employments and great diversities in occupation in region. The region where diverse personality and talent gather is vibrant and highly likely to be an imaginative area. The realization of such a region is the primary purpose of the regional development, and the manufacturing industrial development is judged as the advantageous method for realizing such regions.

The manufacturing industrial development has also problems that should be resolved as well as the other development methods. Production infrastructure and workers' lifeline are indispensable to operate the factories smoothly. Therefore, the region is required to spend huge payments which are invested in equipment for the production activities. And in a case of attracting the factories from outside the region, various subsidies and income tax exemptions may be necessary. The implementation of these attraction policies is a considerable financial burden for the region. In addition, since regions attract the factories that conform to the industrial composition for which the region aims, it must carefully select the factories to attract over time.

Although the challenges mentioned above are in the manufacturing industrial development, the long-term achievement achieved by the manufacturing industrial development is more than offsetting them. It is said, therefore, that many regions in the world have been oriented toward regional vitalization by attracting industrial factories.

Based on the above facts, this book starts to analyze the location factors which influence the factory's location. The first part of Part I selects three kinds of the traditional location factors from many factors that affect fundamentally factories' locations, the transportation cost, and the agglomeration economies. Their locational works are analyzed in the different frameworks: The transportation cost is a decisive location factor before the industrial revolution and basically decides locations of the many kinds of factories. Due to the development of transportation infrastructure, its relative influence is gradually reduced, but it is still a central position among the location factors. Therefore, we consider systematically the transportation costs from an economic geographical point of view ("K. Schliephake"). Then, during the period from the Industrial Revolution to the 1970s, the agglomeration economies strengthen its influential power on location determination, and it becomes a strong location factor to align shoulder with the transportation cost. Meanwhile, the content of the agglomeration economy is changed from the simple use of the external economy related with a large production infrastructure to the utilization of the external economies generated from the enormous production relationships within and between the agglomeration sites. Against this background, it is examined how agglomeration economy plays a role in regional economy ("D. Nakamura"). After elucidating locational effect of these traditional factors, we will examine the industrial parks attracted the factories' locations by integrating the workings of the above location factors. The industrial park's location and its production composition clearly express how three kinds of the traction powers of transportation costs, labor costs, and agglomeration economy are integrated and how they influence the factory's location. Since industrial park can integrate the traction powers of these three location factors, it is considered as a powerful means of attracting the factories and has been applied in many countries since the 1960s. Since the establishment of the industrial park requires a huge initial investment, the regional government becomes a powerful developer of the industrial parks. And they use industrial parks as a strategic tool to revitalize regional economies: Regional governments can integrate the multiple factories in a specific intended area through an industrial park. In this part, the location of the industrial park and its production composition are theoretically analyzed from the viewpoint of location theory ("T. Ishikawa").

In the next analysis of Part 1, two new location factors emerged in the globalization economy are selected: one factor is the government policy. In the development stage where the globalization economy progresses, the government's location policy plays an important role in inducing factories from the foreign countries to regions in home country. Normally, a factory is oriented to the reduction of its production cost, thus, the place at which the production cost is minimized becomes one of the strong location candidate sites. Thus, until globalized era, the places having advantage in transportation cost, labor cost, and agglomeration economies attract many factories. However, recently, the cases have been reported in which the regional governments proposed to provide the firms with large amounts of demand for their goods and they succeeded in attracting the factories. Such a case seems to be theoretically possible, but it has not been considered much in the traditional location theory. The analysis here takes an example of the factories that move from Taiwan to the inland China by the location policy and it inquires the process of the location movement of the factories ("Y. Sun"). Similar to the government's location policy, the corporate tax rate of the country may affect the firm's determination of its factory location. Locational influences of the tax systems of the country are examined: The cost cutting competition between the manufacturing firms due to the globalization economy makes the firms' production processes fragmented and the fragmented processes disperse internationally to realize lower cost. For this reason, the firm's production organization becomes international and the location site of factory is affected by the institutional differences between the countries: Artificial institutions and strategical policies that are devised by various countries begin to greatly affect the locations of the factories and the facilities of the management. The analysis deals with the overdraft expense system and adjustment method of international double taxation, etc. are selected as the location factors and their location effects are examined ("J. Itoh").

Part II of the book moves its main focus to the city and the city systems. Cities are the places where many production and consumption activities are variously connected and realized in different forms. Since these two kinds of the economic activities are conducted by people living in urban areas, the city is a place that represents the human economic activities in general. It could be said that if the cities do not exist, the factories do not achieve their works and the industrial management cannot operate in the modern world. Part II considers the relationship between the factories and the city and city system as follows. The factories locate in the industrial area in which the factories enjoy the localization economy generated in the area. Industrial area does not exist isolated manner apart from a city, but the area locates in the city area to use the urbanization economy provided in the city. And the city also does not exist in isolation, but it exists as a member of a city system and enjoys the comprehensive urban economies provided by the city system. And then the city system enjoys the network benefits from the connections between the city systems. Factories, industrial areas, cities, and city systems are interdependent from each other in the modern world. These mutual dependencies between them affect the regional economy in terms of the factory's products and the city's function composition.

From the viewpoint of a firm that strategically manages its factories, it is important to grasp the characteristics of the cities and the city systems in searching factory's location. Firms analyze what kind of benefits the city and city system provide to the factory. While, understanding characteristics of the cities and the city systems in the region is also important for the government planning to attract production activities to the intended place. Without understanding of them, the governments cannot plan to attract appropriate the factories into the region.

Considering the above background, Part II develops the analysis of the city system as follows. Many empirical studies on the distribution of the cities' populations indicate that there are certain regularities in the distribution. The rank size rule is known as a theory explaining the regularity of the distribution of the cities' populations. Hence, the relationship between the rank size rule and the city system is analyzed theoretically ("H. Kozu"). And then, the focus of the analysis is shifted to the question of how the position of a city changes in the rank size rule when the city's population varies ("T. Ishikawa"). Last analysis of Part II inquires the relationships between the city system and the region's performances. The logic behind the analysis here is as follows. The factories enjoy external economies from cities through the industrial areas, and then, the cities are affected by receiving various influences from the city system. Hence, the economic performances achieved in a region may be reflected in the structure of city system in the region. Based on this logic, the relationships between the city systems and the regional performances are examined using Chinese data. The results derived from the examination show the positive relationships, thus, they may be used as useful data for making the government's strategical location policy ("N. Wang"). In the era of the globalization economy, the structure and characteristics of the city systems are judged to be an important location factor to the firm's location selections and the government's location policy.

Part III of this book deals with the production activities in the regions and the countries on the framework of the empirical economic analysis. Many countries are trying to enhance their industries and to proceed their economic development for the long time. And as means of achieving these goals, the governments often build industrial estates. In these days, the individual industrial parks are established to achieve the specific objective clearly: The governments construct the industrial parks to achieve the formation of economic basements for regional development, to construct new city, to advance the industrial composition, and promotion of technology transfer. In accordance with these purposes, the name of the industrial park has been expressed as managed workshops, enterprise zones, business and innovation center, and technology park. Part III proceeds the analysis as follows: Industrial parks and company zones have been strategically devised for supporting economic growth and forming the foundation of regional development. Thus, it considers what kind of expectation the industrial park and enterprise zone are being expected by the primary economic agents such as the manufacturing firms and the governments, and it evaluates the possibility of the role that industrial parks can play in regional development in industrialized countries using Sweden as case ("L. Westin"). And then, the analysis selects Philippine and studies Philippine's case as to what role the strategically planned industrial park has played, and it clarifies how much achievement has been achieved in Philippine ("A. Dumayas").

Finally, the scope of the analysis in Part III is moved from the production realm to the related areas, and two things are selected. That is, the economic impacts of the trade system surrounding the production activities are analyzed in the

ASEAN countries ("H. Taguchi" and "E. Nishi"). Then, it considers the problem of poverty and inequality caused by production activities in China, which is advancing economic development at an extremely fast rate. ("N. Wang"). And the analysis focuses on India, and it examines the economic disparities in this country ("M. Hayashi", "K. Kalirajan"). These considerations provide important insights to the economic agents trying to maximize the effectiveness of the industries expected to produce liveliness and creativity in the regions. The locations of the factories should socioeconomically contribute to both the firms and the areas where the factories are located. The analyses of this book are expected to contribute to building such a reciprocal relationship between firms and regions.[1]

Hachioji, Japan Toshiharu Ishikawa

[1]The many academic results presented in his book have been achieved through the support of the Japanese Ministry of Education, Supported Program for the Strategic Research Foundation at private University, 2013–2017, and the Japan Society for promotion of Science (Grant-in-Aid for Scientific Research(C) 17K03712).

Contents

Part I
Locational Movement of Firms' Activities—Function of Locational Factors

Chapter 1
Transport Costs in Space—Geographical Models and Contradictions

Konrad Schliephake

Abstract Economists work with theories and models to depict the correlation between supply and demand. This all happens in a world where the provision of goods and services necessitates efforts and costs. In cooperation with economists—or on their own—economic geographers and spatial scientists add the element of space in their visions and models. They know that distances have to be covered in order to bring any good and most services to the consumer. Classical researches, namely H. von Thuenen, A. Weber, A. Loesch, and more recent scientists like E. Ullman, R. Abler, J. Adams and P. Gould and P. Dicken thus developed a vision of interactions in space, where transportation costs played a notable role. They helped to define optimal locations for producers (and consumers) in a homogenous or variably equipped economic landscape. A current look at such models proposed in the last 150 years gives the impression that classical and neoclassical spatial models have lost their relevance. Shrinking transportation costs and even a "collapse of time and space" have ironed out spatial differences and the protective effects of previous high transportation costs. Is this the end of all distributive and delimitating models which were based on distance and transport efforts, as voiced by some of today's analysts? A solution comes from the findings of modern marketing approaches. Our Fig. 1.1 combines the marginal costs concept, based on the economies of scale, with the reality of segmented markets. Protected or trusted items fetch a better price, and this generally happens in the relative proximity to the producer. In contrast, when considering the economies of scale the supplier will be able to cope with lower revenues per unit in more distant markets. Transportation costs still do exist, but they are hidden behind current market strategies. With a coming perspective of increasing transportation costs again, resulting from rising energy prices, the relevance of transport- and trade-off models may appear again in the real world of producers and consumers.

Keywords Spatial models · Transportation costs · Bid rent theory · Marginal costs · Segmented markets · Economic geography

---

K. Schliephake (✉)
Department of Geography, University of Würzburg, Würzburg, Germany
e-mail: k.schliephake@uni-wuerzburg.de

T. Ishikawa (ed.), *Locational Analysis of Firms' Activities from a Strategic Perspective*, https://doi.org/10.1007/978-981-13-1684-5_1

Fig. 1.1 The global decrease in transportation costs 1920 (=100) to 1990 (index of real prices)

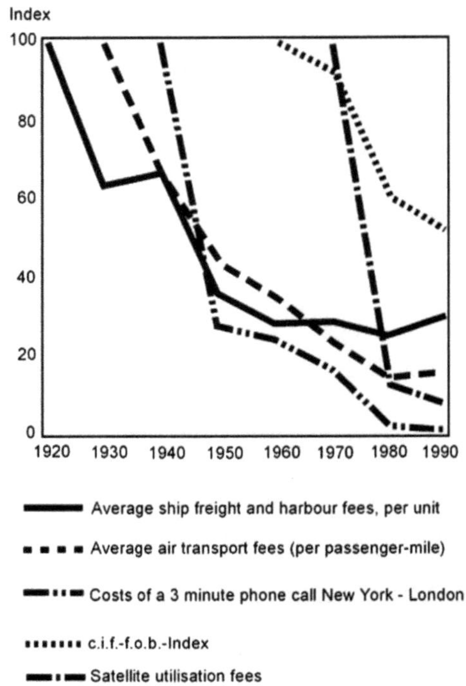

After World Development…1995 (Design: K. Schliephake)

1.1 Introduction—Theories and Realities

Economists as well as economic geographers try to explain the economic life in our world, based on an offer and demand scheme, in various models. Their theories and the models derived from them are generally consistent in themselves. When comparing them with day-to-day reality, observers—and scientists—are more and more frustrated, as their theories do not match realities in the way scientists prefer. This is the case, inter alia, with models linking the elements of production, transport, and consumption in a spatial vision. They have been developed and further elaborated since the Northern German agriculturalist Heinrich von Thünen proposed, in 1826, his concept of a territory with one city (i.e., main consumer) in the middle of a homogenous agricultural landscape. There, transportation costs of the main nutritional items (vegetables, intensive agriculture, pasture with milk products and meat, extensive grazing, etc.) towards the city decide upon the location and the intensity of production in function of an optimal “land rent”. From this heuristic approach, an important school of thinking and research has developed, which links to personalities like Weber (1909a, b), Lösch (1954), Ullman (1956), Lloyd and Dicken (1990), and current researchers. Handbooks of (spatial) economics and of economic geography still teach the models (see, for instance, Minerva and Ottaviano 2009;

Beckmann 2009; Capello 2009; Rodrigue et al. 2017), but with a cautious warning for innocent students that "this model is completely unrealistic in todays' world" (Kasperova 2009). Krugman (for instance 1991) questioned their relevance without giving a decisive answer.

The continuous decline in transportation costs (see Chap. 2), promoted by technical progress, cheap fossil energy and free exchange of news and knowledge through the internet, is one of the reasons for doubt. Another element—closely linked to the first—is the new approach of producers towards their potential markets, which we explain in Chap. 6. In conclusion, it has to be admitted that shrinking costs (and time) as well as the Internet do reshape economic geography, but they will not destroy the classic interdependence between distance, costs, and the allocation of economic (and notably productive) activities in space (according to World Development… 2016, p. 59).

1.2 Cost Developments in Transport

The world is shrinking and the economy is becoming global. Classical models including high transportation costs saw a protection of local producers from their competitors anywhere in the world, even if the latter had comparative cost advantages (see Chap. 3). Today it seems that the classical resp. neoclassical transportation theory which allocated the spheres of production and of consumption in accordance with costs in space comes to an end. Empirical findings contradict the "iron rules" of classical economic modeling.

The first and most visible element to be considered is the relative decrease in (freight) transportation costs. According to calculations published by the World Development Report (1995, see Fig. 1.1), the index of average transportation costs by ship for selected international relations (including port handling fees) dropped from 100 in 1920 to approx. 25 in 1995, and the trend continues. The reasons for this development are manifold: technical progress, heavy public investments in rail and road infrastructure and, most of all instrumental in this change, lowering prices for fossil energy. For instance, in relation to purchasing power, in Germany gasoline was three times more expensive in the 1960s than at the beginning of the millennium (see Schliephake 2001). In the countries of the European Union, the transport sector today is the biggest consumer of energy with a share of nearly 32%. Its demand is growing, since 1990, by 1.3% p.a., to be compared with total growth by all sector of the European economy of 0.3% (according to World Energy Outlook 2017, p. 648). The concern about this development should be voiced, although it is not exactly part of our paper.

Shrinking costs stem from multiple measures and self-reinforcing effects, such as technological progress and cheaper fuel. With an increased offer in transport infrastructure and equipment at ever lower prices demand followed, and both profited from the economies of scale (see Fig. 1.10).

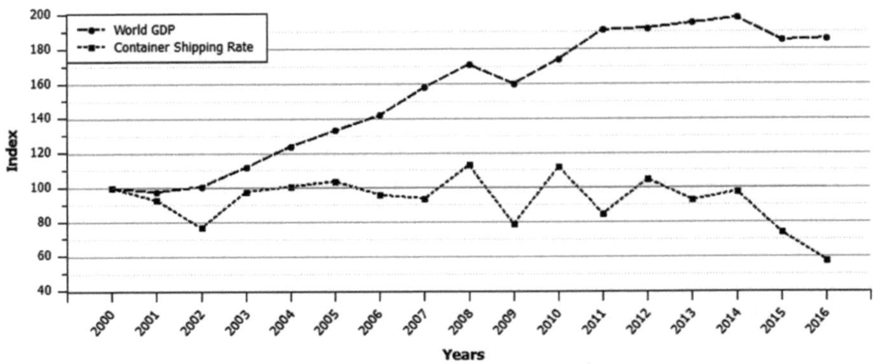

Source: Calculations and estimates by K. Schliephake after World Bank (GDP), Rodrigue et al. 2017 (for container shipping rates up to 2014), China Containerized Freight Index (2013 to 2016), figures for July of each year.

Fig. 1.2 Index of world gross domestic product per capita in current US-S 2000 (=100) to 2016 and of container shipping rates 2000 (=100) to 2016

More recent data underline this trend. According to World Trade Statistical Review (2017, p. 37), from 2012 to 2016, the average receipts of transportation companies from passengers and cargo has decreased by 5–15% p.a., although the number of passengers has increased continuously. Our Fig. 1.2 further illustrates this. World GDP per capita—as the simplest measure of welfare (but including inflation) nearly doubled from 2000 to 2016, whereas container-shipping rates were volatile with a negative trend.

Improved infrastructure as well as technical progress also led to enormous savings in traveling time and thus again to a reduction in costs (as for freight and persons, transport time has to be monetarized). Janelle (1991) called this "convergence of time and space", which we illustrate in Fig. 1.3.

Looking at the sphere of communication (i.e., the transport of information) it seems that the world is even moving towards a collapse of space and time. Information speeds around the globe in real time and, generally, distance no longer affects the cost structure of its transmission. In the main, access to the internet only requires a lump sum payment.

Although the decrease in costs is less important within freight transport where movement of goods in space will always need a certain effort, its impact on the world trade is enormous. From 1978 to 2000 trade increased by 7.6% p.a. Since then, growth by value slowed to 5.6% from 2000 to 2016, due to lower prices for raw materials and notably fossil energy. Even if we consider a worldwide inflation rate of approx. 2.5% p.a. this implies that world trade today is around three times as important as 20 years ago and its growth rate is double that of the world economy. With all these elements in mind, we now have to ask about their correlation with space and its patterns.

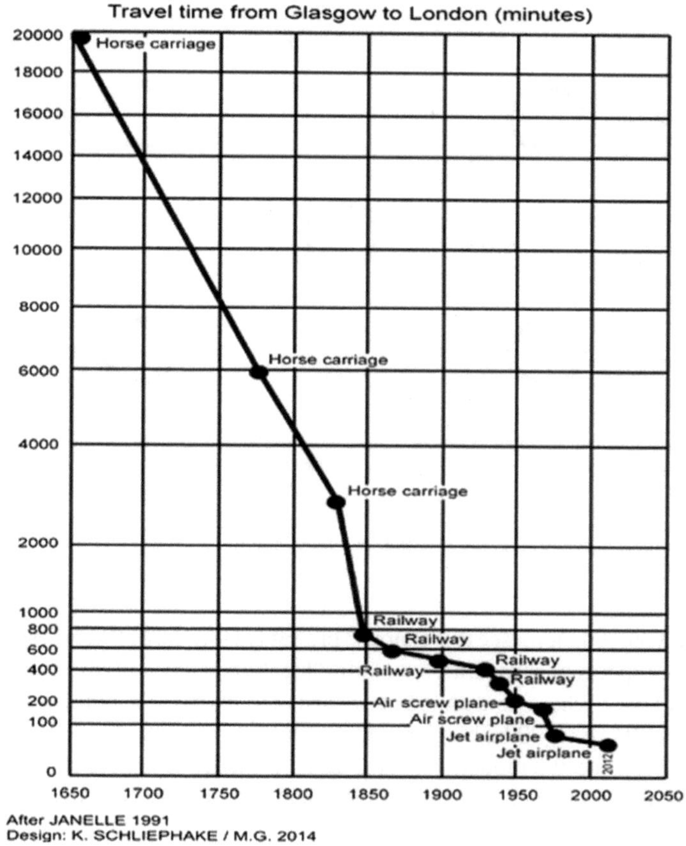

Fig. 1.3 The convergence of time and space in personal transport—Glasgow to London from 1650 to 2012

1.3 The Neoclassical Approach to Transport in Space

The historical basis of modern transportation geography was the evaluation of costs and benefits of locations and interactions in space. This looks quite simple at first glance. Figure 1.4 gives evidence of some basic correlations. In a homogenous space (yes, this must be), five cities with a similar population number have to be supplied with a simple product, which can be produced anywhere (let it be yogurt). Under ceteris paribus conditions, transportation costs are decisive for the choice of optimal location. Potential producers in cities A, B, C, and D each have to cover a distance of ax7, whereas a producer in E only covers ax4. The producer will choose E-City as an optimal location, which has a definite advance over any competitor. This explains, in part, the worldwide concentration process first summarized by Myrdal (1957).

The heuristic model of Fig. 1.4 gives a first evidence, but lacks further explanation of the continuous processes in space.

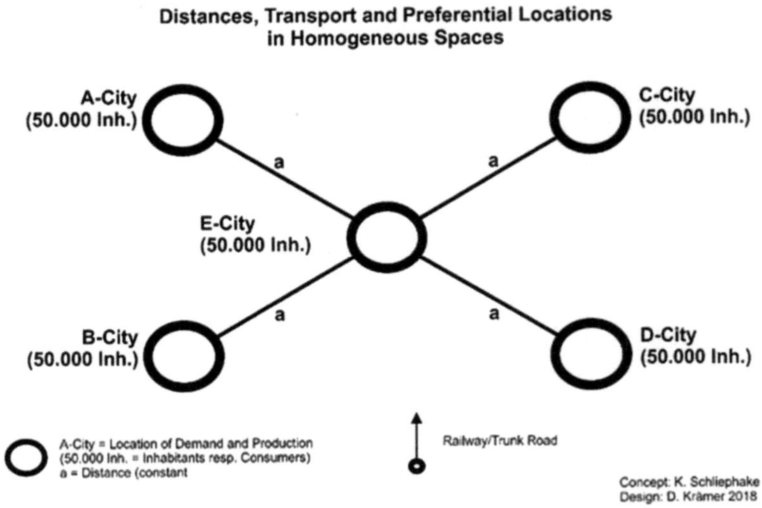

Fig. 1.4 Distance, transport and preferential locations in homogeneous spaces

After H. von Thuenen, (see this chapter) probably Hotelling (1929) first introduced the dynamic aspects of competition with his "location game" of two ice cream sellers in a market space where consumers are distributed evenly. From these approaches, scientists like Weber (1909a, b), Christaller (1966), Lösch (1954, 1962), and Ullman (1956) have constructed models of distribution in space, which are best summarized by Abler et al. (1971) and in their mathematical contents by Beckmann (2009) and Ishikawa (2007, 2013).

Looking at the factor costs of production, for the graphs presented here, we take the costs of labor, land and capital/entrepreneurship as stable (which they are not, in reality). The basic equation, calculated per unit of a product, goes as follows:

$$C_{\mathrm{aLabour}} + C_{\mathrm{bspace\ r}} + C_{\mathrm{ccapital}} + C_{\mathrm{dtransport}} \leq \text{benefits or income from supply resp. sales}$$

where
C = costs per unit;
a = quantity and quality of labor force;
b = necessary space and natural resources;
c = direct (investments) and indirect (machinery, technology) capital costs;
d = infrastructure, means of transport, loss of time and quality.

Starting from there, markets in homogenous space for given products from a number of locations can be delimited by isodapanes or isopleths (lines of similar value around a given center). The results have been called "Loeschian landscapes" (see Wood and Roberts 2011, p. 31). In Fig. 1.5 such a "landscape" is constructed as a vertical (a) and horizontal (b) plan.

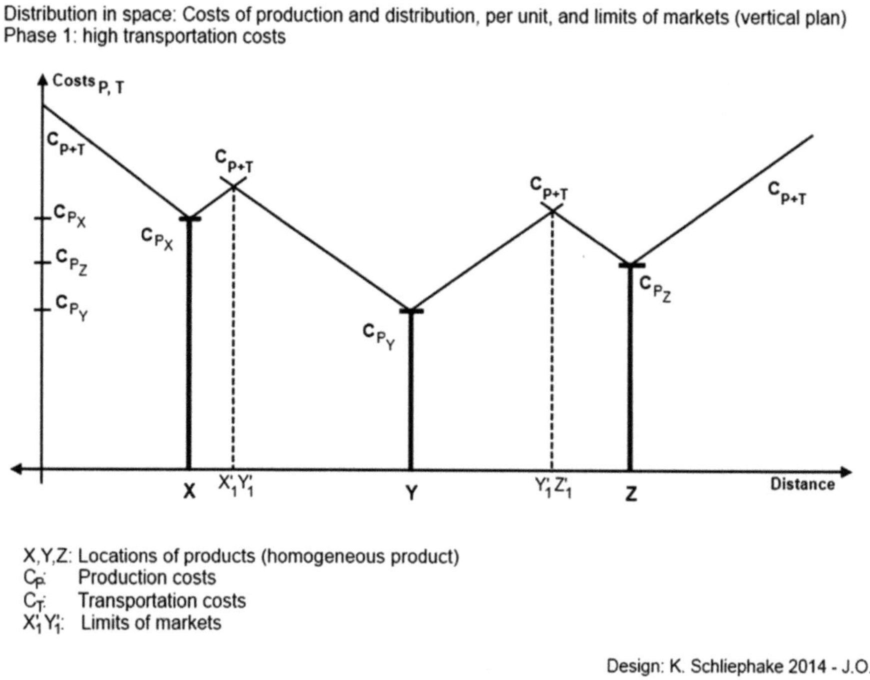

Fig. 1.5 Production and supply in space with high transportation costs—vertical plan

Figure 1.5 shows variations of costs per unit for three producers at X, Y, and Z. According to their geographical setting, they work with different factor costs. The price of land/natural resources and labor generally varies in space (but also in time, which is poorly represented in the model). To the differing production costs, we add transportation costs solely in relation to distance. This works on the assumption that producers act in a homogeneous market with an even distribution of consumers and that there is a linear growth of transportation costs in sole dependence on distance. However, production costs are thought to vary from one location to another due to possible comparative cost advantages (variations in costs of inputs, economies of scale, etc.). On the horizontal plane in Fig. 1.6, using the same values, isopleths circle around the three locations X, Y, and Z. They lead to an increase in price (CP + CT) of the product with growing distance. Where the lines of the same value meet, the limits of the individual markets are drawn. Within the model, every producer has a well-defined distribution area free from competition.

However, as we learned from Figs. 1.1 and 1.2, this is not an eternal law, and in Fig. 1.7, we learn about the effects of the decrease in transportation costs. These will improve the position of the cheaper producer Y. Producer Z still survives with a much-restricted share of market. Finally, Y will intrude into the markets of both competitors, driving them—finally—to leave the markets altogether in relinquishing their activities (by contrast, higher transportation prices would instead protect the weaker producers).

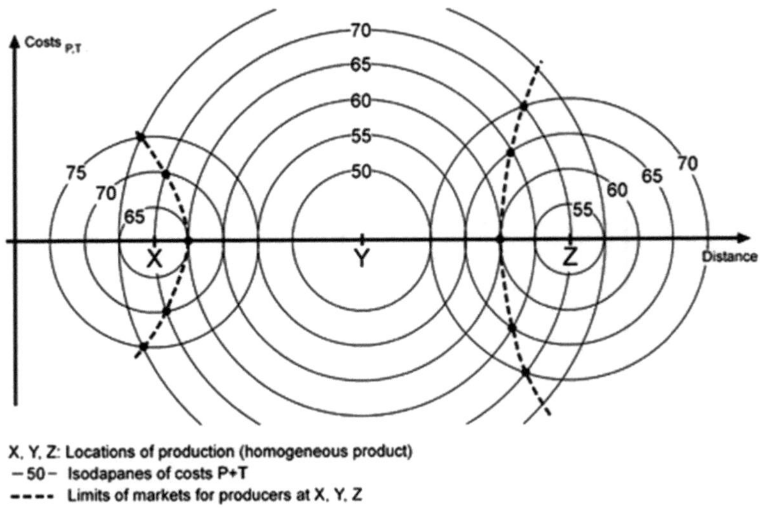

Design: K. Schliephake

Fig. 1.6 Production and supply in space with high transportation costs—horizontal plan

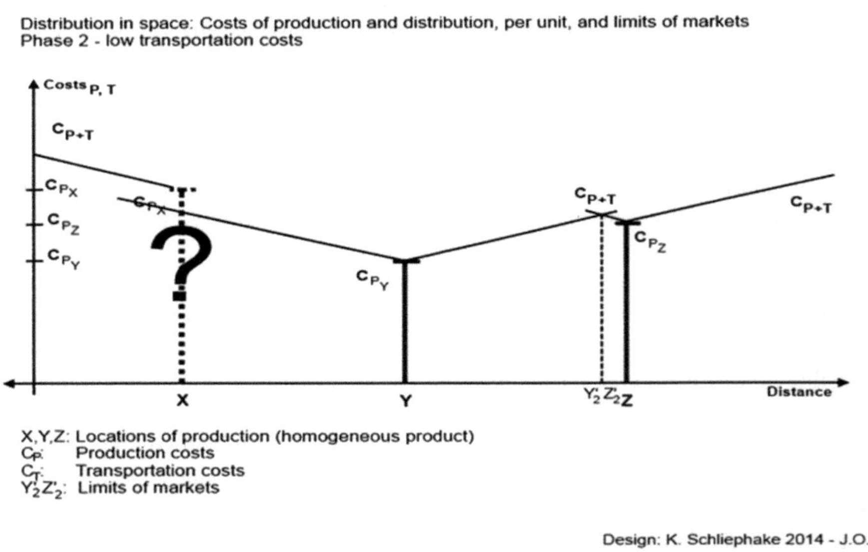

Fig. 1.7 Production and supply in space with low transportation costs—vertical plan

Figure 1.8 draws the essence from the previous Figs. 1.5, 1.6 and 1.7 with the sole dynamic element of transportation costs. They are given for the three periods of

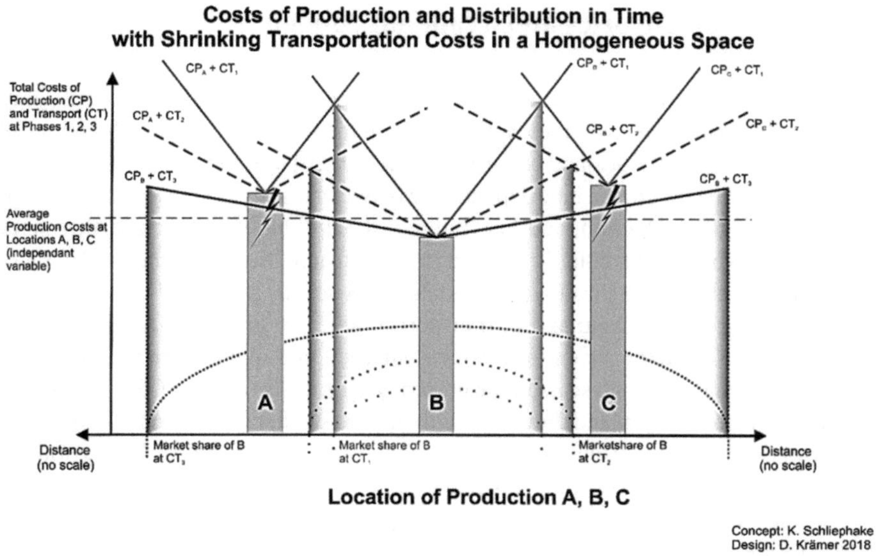

Fig. 1.8 Costs of production and distribution in space (one unit of homogeneous products in three locations)

- high transportation costs (phase 1), maybe 1850
- middle range transportation costs (phase 2), maybe 1950
- low transportation costs (phase 3), maybe today.

Producers at locations *A* and *C* see their markets shrink until *B* serves the entire space. *A* and *C* have no chance and will disappear except if they manage to lower their production costs (for instance by lowering wages or after discovering important natural resources—or by introducing revolutionary, cost-saving technologies).

Our assumptions in Figs. 1.5, 1.6, 1.7 and 1.8 are typical for models under ceteris paribus conditions, and the theory does not always match the reality.

In fact,

- market areas are not homogeneous and demand notably depends on unequal distribution of population as well as differences in consumer behavior;
- freight rates are not in linear dependence on distance but show a tapering tendency with decrease per unit and growing distance;
- production costs are constantly changing due to technological progress and variations in factor costs.

These amendments to the classical models, however, do not prove them wrong. The truth within their message has remained obvious since the time of early economists: the further the distance from the factory the more expensive the unit of a given product (or service) should be. Chapter 5 presents the reality.

1.4 Bid Rent Theories and Trade-off Models

The graphs presented in Chap. 3 are consistent, but they contain only transport costs as dynamic elements. However, they help to explain the search for optimal locations of various economic activities and accordingly their distribution in space. Von Thünen (1966) gave a first hint to the interdependence between transport and typical locations for (agricultural) production, and his "bid rent theory" has developed further since (see Alonso 1964). It can notably be used to explain activities and locational choices around urban centers in "trade-off" models proposed by O'Farrell and Markham (1975), linking costs of land and of transport. Figure 1.9 gives evidence around an urban center UC, maybe a Central Business District, or a major town in a relatively homogenous landscape (no scale in the graph). There, costs of space CS ("land rent") to buy or rent are highest, and they drop with increasing distance from the center (see empirical evidence and discussion in Schliephake and Schenk 2005). Transportation costs CT show the inverse trend for activities in relation to the center UC, where they are lowest. Individual land users seeking their optimal location can combine both cost elements as CS + CT. If they need less space (young singles) or receive high income/land rent from their central location, as it is the case with prestigious "High Street"—Commerce, they will select a place as near as possible to the center. Choice of habitat will depend on income, size and life cycle of household as well as individual preferences. Activities like warehousing and industrial production move further outside, where, gradually, agriculture uses the remaining free spaces with decreasing intensity. The model is not static: any change in transportation and rent costs will change the conditions for the users of land: With decreasing transportation costs, activities like housing and space-consuming commerce will move further away from the center. This, however, may lead to a lowering of rents for landed property in the urban center, possibly inciting several activities to come back—as we learn from evidence in middle-sized towns in Europe and USA.

There are—as always—restrictions to the model proposed in Fig. 1.9. Geographical space is, of course, not homogenous. Numerous Central Places (in the sense of Christaller 1966), each with an own Urban Center; compete in space with overlapping spheres of influence (as depicted by Ullman 1956). In addition, individual decisions are often depending on noneconomic factors like the attraction of natural environment (for housing), embeddedness in creative clusters and historical or cultural ties. However, this does not falsify the trade-off model.

1.5 Victory of the Segmented Markets—End of Neo-Classics?

Figures 1.5, 1.6, 1.7, 1.8, and 1.9 show the theory—but the reality may be very different: German cars are cheaper in Spain than around the factory, steel from South Korea is dumped in the Arab Gulf area, butter from the European Union is best bought in South Africa, and poultry from Brazil abounds on the markets of Iraq.

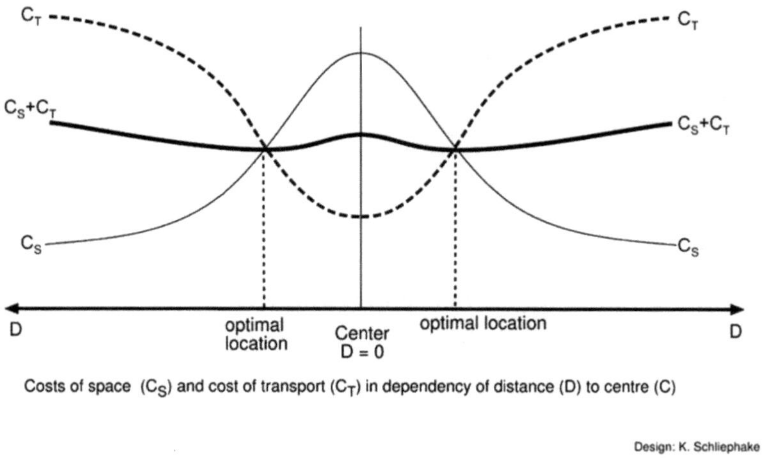

Fig. 1.9 The trade-off model—costs of land and transport around an urban center

Such empirical evidence from all over the world supports the opinion that the neoclassical approach to transportation in space, as summarized for instance by Lloyd and Dicken (1990), is obsolete. Today, optimal sites for the production of modern goods and services are often said to depend on embeddedness and the will of the entrepreneur to integrate himself into creative environments. At that stage, locational choices considering transportation costs would no longer play a role and this would mark the end of the neoclassical era (as voiced by Granovetter and Swedberg 1992). The discussion on this topic is wide open and we feel that the protagonists on both sides have their strong arguments:

- the theoretical approach seems logical under all conditions;
- the empirical findings cannot be shifted away and are totally in contradiction to the model presented in Figs. 1.5, 1.6, 1.7, 1.8 and 1.9.

Since the 1970s surveys with industrialists in Germany, when asked about the most important elements required for the optimal location of their plant, put the elements of infrastructure, and transport at the lower end of their rankings.

Were they right or not? In fact, the road network is ubiquitous, and road haulage is responsible for 73% of all inland freight movements in the European Union (EU-25). Transportation costs now only form a small part of overall production costs and marketing, estimated to range from around 5% to a maximum of 10%. This trend continues towards a decreasing share of transportation in the total (see Fig. 1.2), notably at a time of stagnating energy costs.

The dynamics of the market counterbalance all projects from the state and from benevolent transportation planners: It is not the railway as the most energy-efficient element of transportation which improves its position on the markets in spite of proposed new technologies (see Bozicnik and Schliephake 2005), but road transport only is gaining from the increases. The same findings apply to personal movements with a growing gap between public concepts and personal behavior. Individuals know and fear the greenhouse effect (see World Development Report 2009), but it is the energy-wasting air transportation that shows the largest growth notably after deregulation and a massive price decay—what a contradiction to all White Books and Papers on Transport (White Paper… 2011 and current data).

1.6 Putting Ends Together—Marginal Costs and Segmented Markets

In a volatile world of fragmented markets, exists an unknown number of producers (supply) and varying consumers with a continuous change in behavior (demand): It seems that economy in space became too complex to be explained by simple graphs and models. Do scientists therefore have to restrain themselves to "best practice" and trial-and-error approaches?

The combination of two sets of models, one pertaining to the classic methodologies and one from modern marketing concepts, will help to outline an explanative approach, which reconciles both modelists and empirical analysts.

This must start with the model of a given industrial production process where production costs per unit decrease with growing use of capacity. The marginal cost concept, where the "last unit" is always the cheapest, is an everyday reality. For instance, petrochemical factories, which operate even at 110% of their nominal annual capacity, today dominate worldwide markets. They can drop their product at lowest prices (see SABIC Annual Reports with data from Saudi Arabia). According to Fig. 1.10, the fixed costs per unit C_{fix} (resulting from investments in land, machinery and various overheads) are rapidly decreasing, and even the variable costs C_{var} (raw materials, part of manpower) should, in reality, gradually lower with greater use of capacity and larger turnover (according to the law of economies of scale). Therefore, the maximum use of capacity is an important goal for producers of industrial goods (and some providers of capital-intensive services, e.g., telecommunications).

How can industrialists find their markets in a world full of competitors and where transportation costs nevertheless play a—relative—role?

The concept of segmented markets as presented by microeconomists (see Wöhe et al. 2016) helps to continue with the analysis. Marketing strategists know that the sectoral and spatial markets for a given product are not homogeneous but consist of a—possibly unlimited—number of segments. In each segment, the product can fetch a certain price in dependence of the location of competitors, the image/market penetration of the product (or brand), and the purchasing power or the behavior of the consumers respectively.

Figure 1.11 presents a limited number of market segments with varying levels of possible revenue. Market segment no. 1 may be "around the chimney". There, consumers know and estimate the product/brand, it fetches the best price. In the fol-

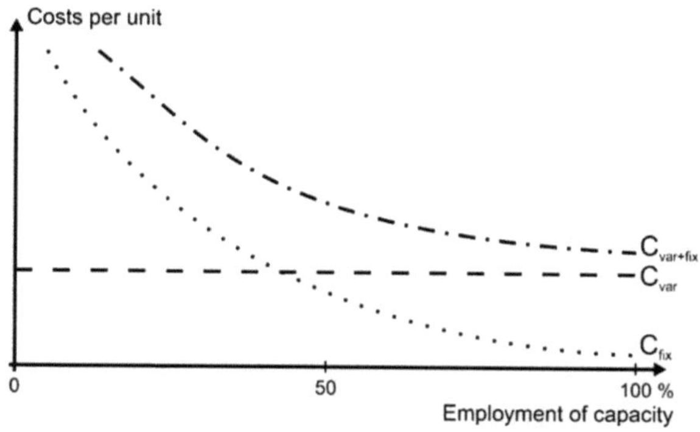

Concept: K. Schliephake

Fig. 1.10 Production costs per unit with relation to employment of industrial capacity

lowing segments, competition will be stronger and/or the purchasing power lower. However, in order to maximize its output the industrialist will nevertheless place his product there as long as the marginal revenue fits into the model of decreasing marginal costs (Fig. 1.10). Looking at the arrangement of the individual market segments from an empirical point of view, we quickly realize that today this generally follows a geographical pattern: With increasing distance from the place of production, competition is more intensive and the possible revenue will drop accordingly. Therefore, the vertical axis of Fig. 1.11 cannot only be defined as giving the share of employment of capacity. It also acts as a distance axis—leading away from the original location 0, without a precise scale.

Figure 1.11 includes the transportation costs but these no longer play the decisive role in the model. Although they still present variables depending on distances, their importance and notably their perception is greatly reduced. They are “hidden” in the cost calculation for each of the market segments, but they lost relevance for the selection of spaces of distribution and, therefore, the spatial definition of markets (as shown in Figs. 1.5, 1.6, 1.7 and 1.8). On the contrary, distant markets can be supplied at lower marginal costs (to the producer) and these will still guarantee the necessary profits for the producer. Transportation costs have disappeared from the surface and are wiped out from the memory of consumers and outside analysts. However, market analysts looking for outlets of their products consider them when caring about economies of scale in the long run and decreasing marginal costs in everyday business (Fig. 1.10).

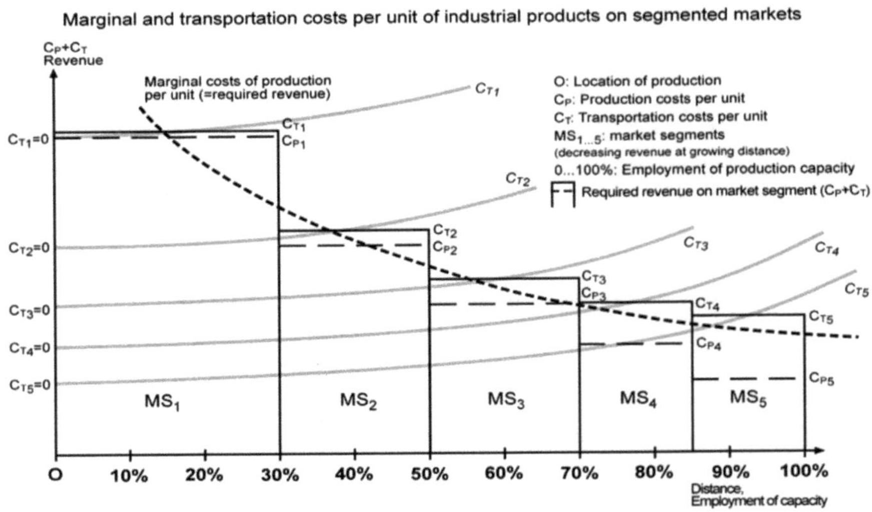

Design: K. Schliephake

Fig. 1.11 Marginal and transportation costs per unit of industrial products on segmented markets with increasing distance

1.7 Conclusions

Is the neoclassical approach to transportation geography with its stringent modeling of costs in space obsolete? Some authors have promoted this opinion which is supported by empirical findings. The truth lies elsewhere. Today we have to combine the findings of three sets of concepts:

- classical distribution models based on increasing transport costs with distance;
- marginal costs models where production costs per unit decrease with the rising use of a given capacity (under the assumption of relatively high fixed costs in the production process), supported by economies of scale;
- concepts of segmented markets whose order generally follows a geographical pattern.

In that context, the neoclassical approach must not be discarded. Transportation costs are hidden resp. counterbalanced by the decrease in marginal cost. They have lost their former decisive role of defining optimal locations and delimitation of markets for a given product.

In the future, things may change again as the combined model proposed in Fig. 1.11 only works for individual producers bringing their goods to nontransparent markets under conditions of low transportation costs. If all possible producers act in the same way and only strive to minimize their marginal costs, as depicted in Fig. 1.10, no consolidated "market around the chimney" will remain. The possible revenues will again be more or less similar for all market segments. For companies producing capital-intensive goods and services, three alternative strategies are possible to overcome this dilemma, notably by

1. creation of "strategic alliances" to avoid a cannibalization of the respective markets;
2. buying out their competitors and trying to create monopolies or oligopolies, respectively;
3. returning to the neoclassical model with its recognition of true costs in production and distribution.

Transportation geography should start by analyzing basic economic facts, and the ideas proposed here may be helpful in that respect. Economists and regional scientists should do not discard neoclassical concepts but combine them with current and very visible developments in the world of marketing and of transportation.[1]

References

Abler, R., J. Adams, and P. Gould. 1971. *Spatial organization—The geographer's view of the world*. Englewood Cliffs, NJ.

Alonso, W. 1964. *Location and land use. Towards a general theory of land rent*. Cambridge, MA: HUP.

Beckmann, M.J. 2009. The pure theory of spatial markets. In *New directions in regional economic development*, ed. C. Karlsson et al., 34–46. Heidelberg.

Bozicnik, S., and K. Schliephake. 2005. Freight transport innovations of European railways. *PROMET Traffic – Traffico* (Zagreb) 17(1): 33–41.

Capello, Roberta. 2009. Space, growth and development. In *Handbook of regional growth and development theories*, ed. R. Capello, P. Nijkamp et al., 31 ff. Cheltenham.

Christaller, W. 1966. *Central places in southern Germany*. Englewood Cliffs, NJ (first published in German in 1933).

Granovetter, M., and R. Swedberg (eds.). 1992. *The sociology of economic life*. Oxford: OUP.

Hotelling, Harold. 1929. Stability in competition. *Economic Journal* 39: 41–57.

Ishikawa, T. 2007. An analysis of the relationship between manufacturer's profit and spatial economic structure in the retail market. In *Time and space in economy*, ed. T. Asada and T. Ishikawa, 283–296. Tokyo: Springer.

Ishikawa, T. 2013. Effects of spatial retail structure on the manufacturing firm's location. In *Mobility in space and time* (= *Würzburger Geographische Manuskripte*, vol. 80), ed. K. Schliephake et al., 1–12. Würzburg.

Janelle, D. 1991. Global interaction and its consequences. In *Collapsing space and time*, ed. S. Brunn and T. Leinbach, 49–81. London.

Kasperova, Valentina. 2009. *Christallers central place theory*. University of Wageningen. https://www.slideshare.net/ecumene/christallers-central-place-theory?next_slideshow=3.

Kramberger, T., et al. (eds.). 2016. *Sustainable logistics and strategic transportation planning* (=*Advances in logistics, operations and management science*). Hershey PA: IGI Global Eds.

Krugman, Paul. 1991. Increasing returns and economic geography. *Journal of Political Economy* 99 (3): 483–499.

[1]Several ideas and graphs were taken from Schliephake and Schenk (2005) and discussed with Kramberger et al. (2016).

Lloyd, P., and P. Dicken. 1990. *Location in space. A theoretical approach to economic geography*. London, New York.

Lösch, A. 1954. *The economics of location*. New Haven.

Lösch, A. 1962. *Die räumliche Ordnung der Wirtschaft*. Stuttgart (first published in 1940).

Minerva, G.A., and G.I.P. Ottaviano. 2009. Endogenous growth theories: Agglomeration benefits and transportation costs. In *Handbook of regional growth and development theories*, 86–97 Cheltenham: Edward Elgar.

Myrdal, Gunnar. 1957. *Economic theory and underdeveloped regions*. London.

O'Farrell, P.N., and J. Markham. 1975. Commuting costs and residential location. *Tijdschrift voor Econ. en Sociale Geographie* 66: 66–74.

Rodrigue, Jean Paul, et al. 2017. *The geography of transport systems*. New York: Routledge.

Sabic—Saudi Basic Industries Corporation. Annual Report, Riyadh.

Schliephake, K. 2001. Passenger transport in Germany—Transport systems in competition. *PROMET Traffic – Traffico* 13(2–3): 187–198 (Zagreb, Portoroz & Trieste).

Schliephake, K., and T. Schenk. 2005. Verkehr und Mobilität. In *Allgemeine Anthropogeographie* (=*Perthes Geographie Kolleg*), ed. W. Schenk and K. Schliephake, 531–571. Gotha & Stuttgart.

Ullman, E.L. 1956. The role of transportation and basis for interaction. In *Man's role in changing the face of the earth*, ed. W.L. Summers, 862–880. Chicago.

Von Thünen, J.H. 1966. *The isolated state*. Cambridge MA (Original version was published in 1826).

Weber, A. 1909a. *Ueber den Standort der Industrien*. Tuebingen.

Weber, A. 1909b. *Theory of the location of industry*. Chicago.

White Paper on Transport. 2011. *Road map to a single European transport area*. Luxembourg: European Union.

Wöhe, G., et al. 2016. *Einführung in die Allgemeine Betriebswirtschaftslehre*. Muenchen.

Wood, Andrew, and S. Roberts. 2011. *Economic geography—Places, networks and flows*. New York: Routledge.

World Energy Outlook (annually), Paris (IEA/OECD).

World Development Report. 1995, 2009, 2016. Washington DC.

World Trade Statistical Review. 2017. (annual). Washington DC.

Chapter 2
A Role of Agglomeration Economies for a Self-Sufficient Regional Economy

Daisuke Nakamura

Abstract This chapter examines a self-sufficient or self-sustaining regional economy, which focuses on a role played by agglomeration economies. Agglomeration economies have been primarily studied on the framework of industrial activity. In order to conduct a detailed examination, it may also be important to consider regional agglomeration economies. These economies not only enhance local utility level of households but also are beneficial for local firms and industries. The study also explores how agglomeration economies keep on working in a small-scale region.

Keywords Agglomeration economies · Regional development · Industrial location · Household economics · Regional welfare

JEL Classification D62 · I31 · P25 · R13

2.1 Introduction

The primary objective of this chapter is to reveal that a self-sufficient or self-sustaining regional economy is partially achieved by agglomeration economies. Agglomeration economies have mainly been studied on the framework of industrial activity such as localisation economies and activity complex economies as well as urbanisation economies (see Marshall 1892; Weber 1909[1928]; Hoover 1937; Isard 1956; Evans 1972; Parr 2002, 2015). In addition, the notion of regional agglomeration economies may have important roles which not only enhance local utility level of households but also be beneficial for local firms and industries.

Regional agglomeration economies are slightly but conceptually different from existing notions of agglomeration economies. In external terms, localisation economies were initially addressed by Marshall (1892) which Weber (1909[1928])

D. Nakamura (✉)
International College of Arts and Sciences, Fukuoka Women's University, 1-1-1 Kasumigaoka, Higashi-ku, Fukuoka 813-8529, Japan
e-mail: dnakamura@fwu.ac.jp

T. Ishikawa (ed.), *Locational Analysis of Firms' Activities from a Strategic Perspective*, https://doi.org/10.1007/978-981-13-1684-5_2

followed on the framework of location theory. Localisation economies are spatially constrained external economies of scale, which include labour cost savings, joint action for input extraction, specialised services, and other advantages to engage production of the product. More benefits on localisation economies should refer to Nakamura (2015).

Hoover (1937) added the idea of urbanisation economies. Urbanisation economies are not necessarily relating to other firms and those advantages are well-organised infrastructure, better administrative accessibility, a variety of labour supply, and highly advanced transportation and communication system (see Parr 2002). Evans (1972) also revealed these disadvantages of congestion. As investigated by Glaeser et al. (2001), urbanisation economies also include various benefits for households, and these advantages enhance centripetal forces of migration and local economic activity. Parr (2002) further expanded by introducing activity complex economies as spatially constrained external economies of complexity which can be found at Chicago automobile assembly plant complex in the United States, for instance.

Finally, regional agglomeration economies have yet been argued in the relevant field of study. Advantages are similar to urbanisation economies but regional agglomeration economies may be recognised at rural areas where local population and economic activity are not enough to satisfy urbanisation economies. Parr (2015) indicated the notion of 'regional externalities' and this might be the same principle. Regional agglomeration economies in this chapter also include the following arguments.

First, these economies are beneficial not only for local industries but also local households. This point perhaps has a relation to the term 'specialised function goods' which exemplified 'a particular range of consumer goods and services, and resort and tourism facilities, as well as certain types of healthcare and education services' by Parr (2017). Second, there are no diseconomies as seen in urbanisation type which has congestion, pollution, and high price of land.

Table 2.1 shows how each element of spatially constrained external economies affects local economic agents on an individual level. In the table, 'Work' stands for an opportunity to engage in a job for local residents, 'Life' implies that agglomeration economies contribute to improve the quality of life on local residents, and 'Rural' indicates that whether these economies are applicable to small regions.

In this way, regional agglomeration economies may cover whole elements if a proper arrangement is organised within a region. One of primary reasons why regional agglomeration economies are important is that many countries now face severe inter-

Table 2.1 Agglomeration economies and local economic activity on an individual level

	Work	Life	Rural
Localisation economies	X		X
Urbanisation economies	X	X	
Activity complex economies	X		X
Regional agglomeration economies	X	X	X

national economic competition, and advanced spatial organisation is mandatory for utilising the domestic economic activity. This is possibly the background of the recent remarkable increase of urbanisation in many countries.

At the same time, rural areas need to be sustainable unless the total population solely accommodates at large metropolitan areas. As long as the national population disperses across the economic plane, the consideration for a self-sufficient or self-sustaining regional system in rural areas is essential to investigate. In particular, this is inevitable in countries in which the total population constantly decline and ageing issues are primary concern across the nation. As argued by Nakamura (2018), a stable rural economic growth requires centripetal forces to that area. Here, centripetal forces work with factors as attractiveness of a region for firms and households. For firms, these can be revenue increasing or cost-saving factors. For households, those may be related to factors on amenity or quality of life.

An attempt is made in this chapter to organise such systematic arrangement by employing the notion of regional agglomeration economies. From the following section, we present a mechanism of regional agglomeration economies as well as existing spatially constrained external economies. Section 2.2 introduces a fundamental framework of location model, which is followed by a discussion of regional agglomeration and welfare in Sect. 2.3. An application of a wider areal coordination is also examined observing a trade-off between accessibility and coordinating benefit in Sect. 2.4. Finally, Sect. 2.5 explores further avenues of research that discusses possibilities of expansion of this study.

2.2 Location Model

This section introduces a simple location model in order to reveal the impact of changes in regional agglomeration economies on the utility level of local households and the profit level of local firms. In the model, there are local households, local firms, and the local government in a rural area named region r. The local government's objective is to maximise the welfare level of this region, W_r, which is determined by the utility level of the representative local household, U_r, and by the profit level of the representative local firm, π_r, as represented in Eq. (2.1) under a given budget constraint of the local government, $G_r\left(=\overline{G_r}\right)$ (note that $G_r > 0$, and $\overline{G_r} > 0$) in Eq. (2.2).

$$\max \ W_r = (U_r, \pi_r) \tag{2.1}$$

$$\text{s.t.} \quad G_r = \overline{G_r} \tag{2.2}$$

It is assumed that the utility level of the representative local household, U_r, is maximised by consuming a composite good, x_r ($x_r > 0$), and receiving a composite externality, y_r ($y_r > 0$), as expressed in Eq. (2.3) under a given budget constraint, B_r ($B_r > 0$) in Eq. (2.4). Here, the composite externality is available by means of well-organised arrangement of regional agglomeration economies. As stated in Eq. (2.4), it is noted that the composite good involves f.o.b. pricing system. For instance, if the good, x_r, is locally unavailable, the amount of transportation costs, $t_r^x\left(t_r^x > 0\right)$, becomes larger. If the composite good, x_r, is locally available, transportation costs takes a smaller value. While the consumption of composite externality has no price, access cost is assumed to bear by the individual which is the same system as transportation costs, and is expressed as $t_r^y\left(t_r^y > 0\right)$.

$$\max\ U_r = U_r(x_r, y_r) \tag{2.3}$$

$$\text{s.t.}\quad B_r = \overline{B_r}(w_r) = \left(p_r + t_r^x\right)x_r + t_r^y y_r \tag{2.4}$$

Regarding the composite externality, examples can be benefits such as providing advanced system of local job search service, offering time-flexible working environment, secured accessibility to shopping and clinic within a walking distance, supplying safety pavement, and other factors which are not possible to coordinate by an individual level. The composite externality can be a negative value but this study solely considers a positive externality, since the analysis focuses on uncongested rural areas.

Also, it is assumed that the profit level of the representative local firm in region r, π_r, is maximised by producing a final good q $(q > 0)$ employing labour, L, and capital, K. The firm bears costs for unit wage, w_r $(w_r > 0)$, for L in region r, and unit price k_r $(k_r > 0)$ for capital in region r. The product is sold at price p_q $\left(p_q > 0\right)$. These are expressed in Eq. (2.5) under given production function with the element of externality σ_r $(0 \leq \sigma_r < 1)$ as stated in Eq. (2.6). Here, the parameter σ_r approaches 1 as regional agglomeration economies effectively work.

$$\max\ \pi_r = p_v q_r - ((1-\alpha_r)w_r L + (1-\beta_r)k_r K) \tag{2.5}$$

$$\text{s.t.}\quad q_r = \frac{1}{(1-\sigma_r)} f(L, K) \tag{2.6}$$

It is noted that additional symbols α_r $(0 \leq \alpha_r < 1)$ and β_r $(0 \leq \beta_r < 1)$ in Eq. (2.5) respectively represent unit rates of cost-saving opportunity by locating this region: $\frac{\partial \pi}{\partial \alpha_r} > 0$ and $\frac{\partial \pi}{\partial \beta_r} > 0$.

In this way, it is apparent that regional agglomeration economies may improve the level of utility on local households, as well as improve the profit level of local firms through parameters σ_r, α_r, and/or β_r. Together with other attributes of agglomeration economies, each parameter may achieve at more advantageous level by localisation economies and activity complex economies if the region already has already taken advantage of those economies.

Since these parameters are dominated by $\overline{G_r}$ in Eq. (2.2), it is now also necessary to discuss the relationship between regional agglomeration economies and regional welfare which is studied in the following section applying the model framework in this section.

2.3 Regional Agglomeration and Welfare

Hitherto, it has revealed that regional agglomeration economies are closely related to the level of regional welfare. This section analyses the mechanism of the impact of changes in regional agglomeration economies on the welfare level of region. Figure 2.1 illustrates representative household's indifference curves under given budget constraints. Here, the horizontal axis plots the amount of composite good, x_r, and the vertical axis is the amount of positive externality, y_r, such as an availability of better amenity which is exclusively available at that region. When the positive externality is more available within the region, this individual's budget constraint line becomes more relaxed and much higher utility level, U_r', is achieved.

While the budget constraint line normally involves price of commodities, the composite externality does not have any pricing system. Alternatively, we can argue that more availability of composite externality nearby the individual's location reduces the level of access cost, t_r^y, in Eq. (2.4), and the individual's budget constraint line is eventually relaxed as can be clearly observed with Eq. (2.7) which solves Eq. (2.4) by the vertical axis, y_r, in Fig. 2.1.

$$y_r = \frac{B_r}{t_r^y} - \left(p_r + t_r^x\right)\frac{x_r}{t_r^y} \tag{2.7}$$

This specific case shows that the optimal point moves from E to E'. More precisely, the movement or the expansion path guarantees that both composite good and composite externality are implicitly defined as 'normal goods'. That is, the location proximity to the composite externality always increase the quantity demanded of the composite externality: $y_r < y_r'$. However, this is not always applicable to the composite good, x_r; namely, the case which the substitution effect on the composite good, x_r, by a decrease of t_r^y is much larger than its income effect.

For local firms, Fig. 2.2 shows the impact of changes in the availability of regional agglomeration economies on a representative local firm through revenue and cost

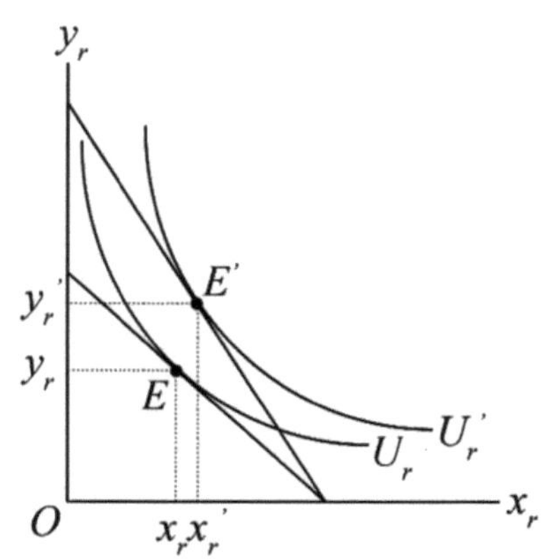

Fig. 2.1 Household's constrained utility maximisation problem

functions. In the figure, the horizontal axis plots the quantity of output, q_r, and the vertical axis depicts the level of cost or price of output, C and p_r. The initial combination is the total cost curve, C, and the total revenue curve, R, which maximises the profit of the firm by π_r at the output level q_r. The availability of regional agglomeration economies may improve the profit level in the following two types of process.

First, a cost-saving opportunity can be expected, and the total cost, C, as well as the average and marginal cost, MC, in Fig. 2.3 decline. Second, an improvement of processing stage may supply a more product-differentiated product. This rises price level, p_r, that is illustrated by a steeper total revenue curve, R', in Fig. 2.2, and much higher level of marginal revenue line, MR', in Fig. 2.3. When both effects are taken into account, this firm would face a better profit maximising level at π_r' under the total revenue curve, R', the total cost curve C', the marginal revenue, $MR' \left(= p_r'\right)$, the marginal cost, MC', and the corresponding output level, q_r'.

With these figures, it has clarified that the improvement of regional welfare, which is brought about by regional agglomeration economies, is measurable within the limited condition on the theoretical framework. Next section examines the way of charge for offering regional agglomeration economies which are exclusively available within the region to local economic agents those who take advantage of these economies.

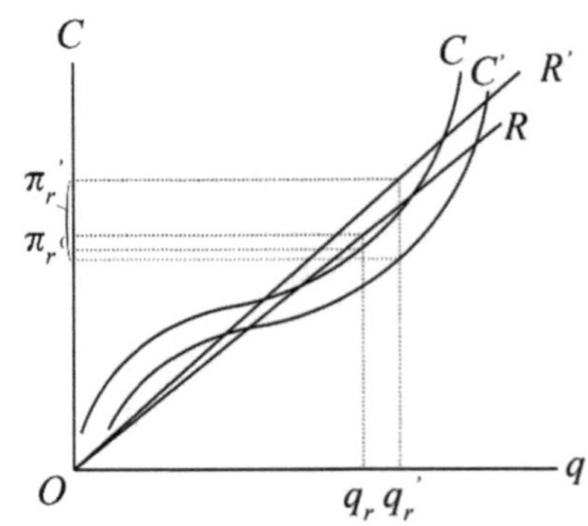

Fig. 2.2 Constrained profit maximisation problem

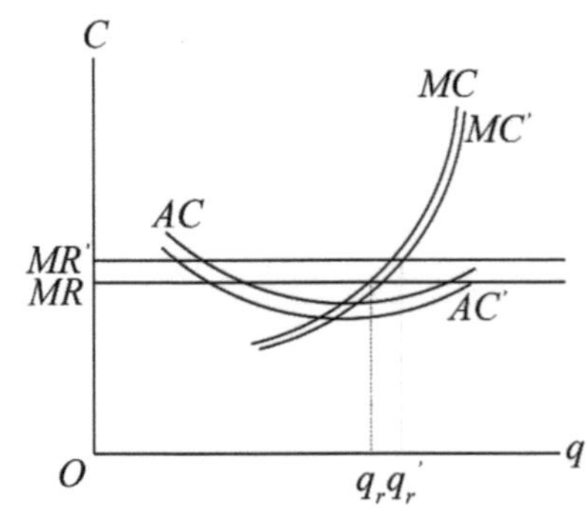

Fig. 2.3 Average and marginal cost curves, and marginal revenue lines

2.4 Regional Policy

In the previous section, it has revealed that both local households and local firms can receive benefits of regional agglomeration economies which bring a better achievement of welfare as a regional level. This section argues how such economies are continuously supplied within the region. Also, an idea of wider regional coordination is demonstrated to overcome insufficient economies of scale and scope when a self-sufficient or self-sustaining mechanism does not properly work in the long run.

It may be no problem for supplying local services which are beneficial for both on local households and on local firms as long as there are little costs to provide. Otherwise, these need to be operated under a sufficient budget condition. For instance, services may be provided by publicly owned agents. In general, the financial source of publicly owned services can be a council tax or a municipal tax. However, if these services are solely available at a specific area, the source should involve other origins. For instance, in the argument of public economics, club goods can charge from preregistered members. The level of charge would be equivalent to the income effect for households and to cost-saving amount or revenue increased amount for firms as long as the benefit is solely dominated by local economic agents. In other words, it is noted that club goods require the condition of excludability of use on services.

When the condition of excludability is difficult to maintain, one of alternative options is to organise a wider regional coordination. This is also effective at a situation which the economies of scale and of scope do not work within the level of a single region. The wider regional coordination may require agreement to have affiliations. This is more important when some regions are physically distant from others. A methodological framework on a negotiation process has already been given by Isard (1956) as an application of the critical isodapanes in the location triangle model of Weber (1909[1928]). If the wider regional coordination develops better physical interregional connectivity, transportation costs for obtaining composite good, t_r^x, and composite externality, t_r^y, in Eq. (2.4) can decline, and the utility level of local households is expected to improve. Regarding the relationship between the enhancement of wider regional coordination and physical interregional access, the reader should refer to Nakamura (2016).

In this study, the trade-off can be additional advantages of regional agglomeration economies and interregional transportation costs. If more benefit of these economies and further reduction of the interregional transportation costs are available, the wider regional coordination would be feasible. More benefit on regional agglomeration economies can be partly observed by an increase of y_r in Eq. (2.3) for households. There, the increase of y_r improves the utility level, U_r, through a reduction of budget constraint, B_r, in Eq. (2.4) that allows this individual to reduce the volume of composite good, x_r. If composite good, x_r, is reexpressed as an expanded form, $\{x_r^1, \ldots, x_r^n\}$, the reduction can increase the variety of consumption which brings much higher utility level under the assumption of 'a love of variety' in Dixit and

Stiglitz (1977). This is also applicable to pay more transportation costs to obtain importing item.

The final argument is given to the budget constraint of the local government, $\overline{G_r}$. If benefits on local households and firms are able to convert into monetary terms, the actual amount can be charged. If the level of charge does not suffice the required cost level, the payment system needs to expand regularly fee (i.e., monthly charge) to the registered economic agents. For non-registered economic agents, a visitor's tariff can be charged which is equivalent to the sum of council tax or municipal tax plus membership charges. If the revenue marks a high level, more rapid arrangement of regional agglomeration economies is feasible. It should be noted that the charge may have two parts; one is actual operating cost and another is the payment of interest rate if the initial launch of these economies involves external debt.

2.5 Further Avenues

There are several possibilities to expand the scope of this analysis. First, local firms can be classified as export-base industry or non-export industry. Local industry may have both types and the important point is to specify the ratio between two types. Second, the council or municipal tax may be a part of whole local governmental budget, and the mixture of national tax should be argued when a self-sustaining or self-sustaining regional economy is analysed. Third, interest rates would influence this analysis if the initial setup of regional agglomeration economise involves debt at the first period and repayment in the future as was examined in the previous section. At the same time, the rate of regional economic growth is necessary to consider. This is the same idea as the sustainable public finance on the level of national economy.

For a detailed argument, income effect and substitution effect by regional agglomeration economies can be extended to measure according to the local household's preference on quality of life in addition to the local firm's extent of economic development stage in Rostow's sense (see Rostow 1956). Parr (2001) investigated the stage of economic growth in a regional term, and demonstrated that regions grow through the process of industrial changes from the primary to the secondary, the secondary to the tertiary. Regional agglomeration economies may have various services, and it would be important to specify which services are necessary to each region which can be affected by the stage of regional economic development.

While this study observes the impact of changes in regional agglomeration economies, more concrete system may be useful to discuss. As addressed by Senn and Fratesi (2009), regional development needs to consider a regional strength which has two parts; namely, external strength and internal strength. The external strength can be connected with interregional economic competition which is enhanced by regional export by expanding basic industries. By contrast, the internal strength would be partially linked with community development that contributes to engage more flexible and solid local economic activity through cooperative behaviour.

The idea is applicable to localisation economies but regional agglomeration economies do not enclose the affiliation of specific firm or industry in that region.

Finally, the system of location model in Sect. 2.2 has a possibility to examine as a general equilibrium model. In that case, the examination needs to set the ratio between local labour supply and interregional commuting labour supply, which could be specified by the ratio between basic industry and nonbasic industry of that region as well as interregional physical accessibility and connectivity. Also, produced goods are partly consumed by local households and by consumers in other areas. When local consumption is included in the composite good, the analysis can investigate more complex but can address a closed model.

2.6 Concluding Comments

This chapter has examined the concept of regional agglomeration economies in order to discuss self-sufficient or self-sustaining regional economy. The analysis presented that regional agglomeration economies affect both on local households and on local firms. As discussed in previous sections, the argument is particularly important for regions where they are located in rural areas and there are constant declines in local population and economic activity. In such regions, it would be necessary to organise a wider regional coordination if sufficient economies of scale and scope are unavailable. While the conceptual framework of regional agglomeration economies has certain similarity with urbanisation economies, the study demonstrated that regional agglomeration economies work at rural areas together with the wider regional coordination and/or localisation economies and activity complex economies.

Acknowledgements This work has partially been supported by Japan Society for the Promotion of Science (JSPS) KAKENHI, Grant Number 16K03643.

References

Dixit, A.K., and J.E. Stiglitz. 1977. Monopolistic competition and optimum product diversity. *American Economic Review* 67: 297–308.

Evans, A.W. 1972. The pure theory of city size in an industrial economy. *Urban Studies* 9: 49–77.

Glaeser, E.L., J. Kolko, and A. Saiz. 2001. Consumer city. *Journal of Economic Geography* 1: 27–50.

Hoover, E.M. 1937. *Location theory and the shoe and leather industries*. Cambridge Massachusetts: Harvard University Press.

Isard, W. 1956. *Location and space-economy*. Cambridge Massachusetts: M.I.T. Press.

Marshall, A. 1892. *Economics of industry*, 3rd ed. London: Macmillan and Co., Limited.

Nakamura, D. 2015. Firm location and agglomeration economies. In *Firm's location selections and regional policy in the global economy*, ed. T. Ishikawa. Heidelberg: Springer.

Nakamura, D. 2016. Alternative spatial structure for sustainable rural economy: A note on socially optimal firm location. *International Regional Science Review* 41: 86–102.

Nakamura, D. 2018. Location economics analysis on attractiveness of a region. *Studies in Regional Science* (in printing).
Parr, J.B. 2001. On the regional dimensions of Rostow's theory of growth. *Review of Urban and Regional Development Studies* 13: 2–19.
Parr, J.B. 2002. Missing elements in the analysis of agglomeration economies. *International Regional Science Review* 25: 151–168.
Parr, J.B. 2015. The city and the region as contrasts in spatial organization. *Annals of Regional Science* 54: 797–817.
Parr, J.B. 2017. Central place theory: An evaluation. *Review of Urban and Regional Development Studies* 29: 151–164.
Rostow, W.W. 1956. The take-off into self-sustained growth. *Economic Journal* 66: 25–48.
Senn, L., and U. Fratesi. 2009. What policy for interconnected territories? Conclusions and openings. In *Growth and innovation of competitive regions*, ed. U. Fratesi and L. Senn. Berlin Heidelberg: Springer-Verlag.
Weber, A. 1909[1928]. *Über den Standort der Industrien*. Mohr: Tübingen, English version: Weber A (1928) *Alfred Weber's Theory of the Location of Industries* (trans: Friedrich CJ). Chicago: University of Chicago Press.

Chapter 3
Theoretical Analysis on Location and Production Composition of Industrial Park

Toshiharu Ishikawa

Abstract The main purposes of this chapter are to analyze the following four issues about industrial park. First, this chapter derives the concept of location prospective area in which industrial park is likely to be established. Using this location prospective area, it identifies the relationship between the location of industrial park and the business types of the tenant factories in the industrial park. Second, the chapter examines the effects of the external economies generated in industrial park on the profits and the numbers of the factories in the industrial park. Third, it analyzes the influences of urbanization economies on industrial park. The influences of the urbanization economies on the production composition of industrial park are clarified. Lastly, the focus of the analysis moves to the role of the government as a developer in establishing an industrial park. It elucidates the theoretical reason that the government should exercise its power to alter the production composition in the park, and that the government's policy has more complicated effects on the tenant factories of the park than expected.

Keywords Industrial park · External economies · Location
Location prospective area

3.1 Introduction

The economic globalization gives rise to a harsher price competition among the manufacturing firms, and it leads to a cost-cutting competition in the manufacturing industry on a global scale. To cope with the economic globalization, many manufacturing firms fragment their production processes into small blocs. Many fragmented small production processes are scattered across the nations' borders to the places that

T. Ishikawa (✉)
Faculty of Economics, Chuo University, Hachioji, Tokyo, Japan
e-mail: ishiy@tamacc.chuo-u.ac.jp

T. Ishikawa (ed.), *Locational Analysis of Firms' Activities from a Strategic Perspective*, https://doi.org/10.1007/978-981-13-1684-5_3

bring lower production costs to the manufacturing firms. The places that attract the fragmented processes from the foreign countries usually have production conditions suitable to the production processes. And these places are equipped with adequate infrastructure enough for the firms to smoothly operate their factories and to stably make connections with the organizations concerned. In this context, industrial parks are highly reevaluated by the manufacturing firms and the governments of the emerging countries: Since industrial park is built in consideration of characteristics and quality of the factories being induced to the park, industrial park surely provides the tenant factories with appropriate external economies in the park. Thus, when manufacturing firm determines a new factory's location, it naturally considers industrial parks as an important location factor in searching site in foreign countries. While, because the government can develop an industrial park to agglomerate factories at a place and to induce the factories to an intended site, the government often uses an industrial park as one of vital tools to vitalize regional economy. In addition, an industrial park equips various sorts of offices and business functions through IT and ICT technologies for the firms and the departments of the government to proceed their works speedily. Industrial park is highly emphasized to attract the factories in several ways to vitalize regional economies.

This chapter first elucidates location prospective area in which industrial park is likely to be established. And using this location prospective area, it identifies the location of industrial park and business types of the factories that are copresence in an industrial park. Second, it examines the locational effects of the external economies generated in industrial park on the factories. Third, the influence of urbanization economies, which are generated outside industrial park, on industrial park are dealt with, and the effects of urbanization economies on the production composition of industrial park are clarified. Lastly, the chapter examines the role of the government in establishing an industrial park. It is shown that the production composition in industrial park is not unique but there are alternatives in a certain range; this fact gives an allowance room for the government to exercise its power to alter the production composition in the park. Along the flow of this analysis, it is clarified that although the government's investment to improve production environment surrounding industrial park increases the total profits generated industrial park, it does not always make the profit of individual factories higher because of the change of the production composition in the industrial park.

3.2 Derivation of Location and Production Composition of Industrial Park

3.2.1 Assumptions and Framework of Analysis

According to the traditional location theory, assumptions are introduced and the framework of the analysis is constructed as follows.[1] A firm produces final products through two production processes, the first process and the second one. The first process is conducted by the factory 1 which is in the home country. This factory produces intermediate goods (mq). The second process is assigned to the factory 2 which locates in the foreign country. This factory 2 composes the final product by using the intermediate goods transported from the factory 1. And the factory 2 uses one unit of the intermediate good to produce one unit of the final product. When the intermediate goods are transported from the factory 1 to the factory 2, the concept of the transfer price (mp) is used by the firm.[2] The factory 2 sells the finished goods to the marketplace in the foreign country. There is no tariff system between the home and the foreign country. The factory 2 is in the position of the monopoly in the market. The factory 2 can determine the supply quantity (Q) of the final goods at the market to maximize *the factory 2's profit*. On the other hand, the factory 1 decides the transfer price of the intermediate good to maximize *the firm's profit*. The corporation tax rates of the home and the foreign country are given by t and t^*, respectively.

3.2.2 Derivation of the Profit Function of the Factory 1

The profit of the factory 1 (Y_1) is given by Eq. (3.1)

$$Y_1 = (1 - t)[\text{mp} * \text{mq} - C(\text{mq}) - F_1] \tag{3.1}$$

where C (mq) is the cost function of the factory 1 and F_1 is fixed cost. The cost function C (mq) is derived on the following assumptions. The factory 1 uses two different kinds of materials m_1, m_2 to produce the intermediate goods. And the factory 1 needs a kind of lubricating oil m_3 to operate machines. The materials m_1, m_2, and the oil m_3 are produced at points M_1, M_2, and M_3 which are identified by coordinates (x_1, y_1), (x_2, y_2), and (x_3, y_3), respectively. These materials are transported

[1] The basic framework is constructed according to the works of Weber (1909), Puu (1998) and Ishikawa (2016). The mechanism that a firm's production system organized by internationally is clearly explained by Shi and Yang (1995).

[2] The transfer price is explained by Hirshleifer (1956).

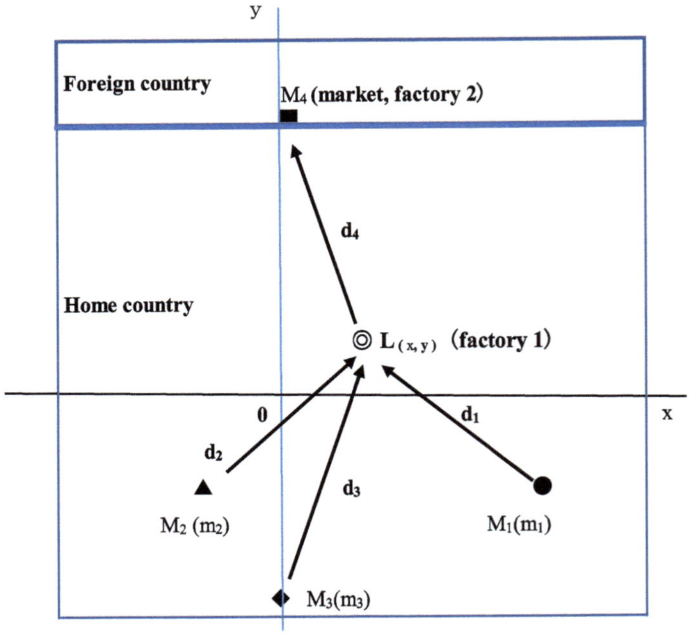

Fig. 3.1 Location figure

to the factory 1 located at point L which is indicated by (x, y). Figure 3.1 describes the geographical relationships between the factory 1, the factory 2, the market, and points of the three materials. Freight rates of the materials m_1 and m_2 are denoted by t_m, and the freight rate of the oil m_3 is given by t_e. The marketplace at which the factory 2 locates is indicated by point M_4, (x_4, y_4). The freight rate of the intermediate goods is t_g. Mill prices of these materials and oil are assumed to be given for the simplicity, and these prices are denoted by p_1, p_2, and p_3.

The territory of the home country is shown by the large rectangular area and that of the foreign country is upper small rectangle area. The market is indicated by the black square mark. The border between the two countries is shown by the horizontal bold line in Fig. 3.1.

The production function of the factory 1 is given by Eq. (3.2),

$$\mathrm{mq} = A m_1^{\alpha} m_2^{\beta} \tag{3.2}$$

where A indicates the production efficiency of the factory 1, α and β are parameters and they are defined as $A > 0$, $0 < (\alpha + \beta) < 1$. And the distances between the material places, M_i $(i = 1, 2, 3)$ and the factory 1 are represented by d_1, d_2, and d_3, respectively

$$d_1 = ((x - x_1)^2 + (y - y_1)^2)^{0.5} \tag{3.3a}$$

$$d_2 = ((x - x_2)^2 + (y - y_2)^2)^{0.5} \tag{3.3b}$$

$$d_3 = (x^2 + (y - y_3)^2)^{0.5} \tag{3.3c}$$

The distance between the factory 1 and the factory 2 is given by d_4,

$$d_4 = (x^2 + (y - y_4)^2)^{0.5} \tag{3.3d}$$

The delivered prices Pi ($i = 1, 2, 3$) of the two materials and the lubricating oil at the location site of the factory 1 are shown by Eqs. (3.4a, 3.4b, 3.4c), respectively:

$$P_1 = p_1 + t_m d_1 \tag{3.4a}$$

$$P_2 = p_2 + t_m d_2 \tag{3.4b}$$

$$P_3 = p_3 + t_e d_3 \tag{3.4c}$$

And the transportation of the intermediate goods is borne by the factory 1. Thus, the price of the intermediate goods at location of the factory 2, DP, which is needed to calculate the revenue of *the factory 1*, is represented by Eq. (3.5),

$$\mathrm{DP} = \mathrm{mp} - t_g d_4 \tag{3.5}$$

Making use of the law of equi-marginal productivity, that is, the ratio between the productivities of the two raw materials should be equal to the ratio between their delivered prices, quantities of them are derived as Eqs. (3.6a) and (3.6b): (For simplicity, α and β are assumed $\alpha = \beta = 0.4$):

$$m_1 = A^{-1.25}\mathrm{mq}^{1.25}((p_2 + t_m d_2)/(p_1 + t_m d_1))^{0.5} \tag{3.6a}$$

$$m_2 = A^{-1.25}\mathrm{mq}^{1.25}((p_1 + t_m d_1)/(p_2 + t_m d_2))^{0.5} \tag{3.6b}$$

The quantity of the oil m_3 is given by a linear function of amount of the final goods as Eq. (3.6c),

$$m_3 = \mathrm{mq} \tag{3.6c}$$

From above equations, the cost function C (mq) is obtained as Eq. (3.7),

$$C(\mathrm{mq}) = 2A^{-1.25}\mathrm{mq}^{1.25}(p_1 + t_m d_1)^{0.5}(p_2 + t_m d_2)^{0.5} + \mathrm{mq}(p_3 + t_e d_3) + F_1 \tag{3.7}$$

The profit function of the factory 1 can be rewritten as Eq. (3.8),

$$\begin{aligned} Y_1 = (1 - t)\big[&\mathrm{mq}\big((\mathrm{mp} - t_g d_4) - (p_3 + t_e d_3)\big) \\ &-2\mathrm{mq}^{1.25}A^{-1.25}(p_1 + t_m d_1)^{0.5}(p_2 + t_m d_2)^{0.5} - F_1\big] \end{aligned} \tag{3.8}$$

3.2.3 Profit Functions of the Factory 2 and the Manufacturing Firm

Let us derive the profit of the factory 2. The profit is derived under the following assumptions: The market demand function is represented by Eq. (3.9),

$$p = a - vQ \tag{3.9}$$

where p is the market price of the final goods, a is the maximum reservation price, and v is a parameter. For simplicity, a and v are assumed 600 and 1, respectively. If the cost of composing the intermediate goods to the finished goods is represented by $C(Q)$ and the fixed cost of the factory 2 is represented by F_2, the profit of the factory 2 (Y_2) is represented by Eq. (3.10),

$$Y_2 = \left(1 - t^*\right)\left[pQ - \mathrm{mp} * \mathrm{mq} - C(Q) - F_2\right] \tag{3.10}$$

Suppose that the composing cost $C(Q)$ is given by Eq. (3.11),

$$C(Q) = \gamma Q(\delta + Q)^2 / \varepsilon \tag{3.11}$$

where parameters γ, δ, and ε are assumed as 1.5, 2, and 200 for the simplicity of the calculation, respectively.

Since the factory 2 uses one unit of the intermediate goods to produce one final goods, the mq can be replaced by Q. The profit function is rewritten by Eq. (3.12),

$$Y_2 = \left(1 - t^*\right)\left[(p - \mathrm{mp})Q - 1.5Q(2 + Q)^2/200 - F_2\right] \tag{3.12}$$

Since the market price of the final good, p, is a function of the sales quantity Q as shown by Eq. (3.9), the optimal quantity supplied at the market to maximize the profit of the factory 2 can be derived by using Eq. (3.12). The optimal supply quantity is given by Eq. (3.13),

$$Q = 0.22(-206 + (582{,}409 - 900\mathrm{mp})^{0.5}) \tag{3.13}$$

As the supply quantity Q is a function of the transfer price of the intermediate goods, the profit of the factory 2 is also represented as a function of the transfer price as Eq. (3.14),

$$\begin{aligned} Y_2 = \left(1 - t^*\right)\Big[&\left(600 - \left(0.22\left(-206 + (582{,}409 - 900\mathrm{mp})^{0.5}\right)\right) - \mathrm{mp}\right) \\ &\left(0.22\left(-206 + (582{,}409 - 900\mathrm{mp})^{0.5}\right) - F_2\right)\Big]. \end{aligned} \tag{3.14}$$

Summing up the profits of the two factories, the firm's profit (Y) can be obtained as Eq. (3.15). The firm's profit is a function of the transfer price (mp) and the location (x, y) of the factory 1.

$$
\begin{aligned}
Y =\ & (1-t)\Big[\Big(0.22\big(-206+(582{,}409-900\mathrm{mp})^{0.5}\big)\Big)(\mathrm{mp}-t_g d_4)-(p_3+t_e d_3) \\
& -2\Big(0.22\big(-206+(582{,}409-900\mathrm{mp})^{0.5}\big)\Big)^{1.25}A^{-1.25}(p_1+t_m d_1)^{0.5}(p_2+t_m d_2)^{0.5}-F_1\Big] \\
& +(1-t^*)\Big[\Big(600-\Big(0.22\big(-206+(582{,}409-900\mathrm{mp})^{0.5}\big)\Big)-\mathrm{mp}\Big) \\
& \Big(0.22\big(-206+(582{,}409-900\mathrm{mp})^{0.5}\big)\Big)-F_2\Big].
\end{aligned} \tag{3.15}
$$

3.2.4 *Derivation of Location Prospective Area*

3.2.4.1 Usefulness of Chaotic Phenomenon

Let us derive the optimal location (X, Y) of the factory 1 and the optimal transfer price of the intermediate goods by using Eq. (3.15). To derive the transfer price and location of the factory 1, the gradient dynamics is used (Puu 1998; Ishikawa 2009). This method is useful because even if the solution cannot be specified, the area in which the solution is included is indicated by a chaotic phenomenon. The essence of the gradient dynamics is that first, an initial value set is given to x_n, y_n, and mp_n in the following Eqs. (3.16a, 3.16b, 3.16c) as a temporal solution, and obtain the second tentative values of x_{n+1}, y_{n+1}, and mp_{n+1} by calculations indicated by the three Eqs. (3.16a, 3.16b, 3.16c). The same calculation is iterated until a given tentative solution can be approximately judged as the solution: If the values of (x_{n+1}, y_{n+1}, mp_{n+1}) in Eqs. (3.16a, 3.16b, 3.16c) become approximately the same as those of (x_n, y_n, mp_n), the values can be admitted as the solution.

$$x_{n+1} = x_n + j * \partial Y/\partial x, \tag{3.16a}$$

$$y_{n+1} = y_n + j * \partial Y/\partial y, \tag{3.16b}$$

$$\mathrm{mp}_{n+1} = \mathrm{mp}_n + j * \partial Y/\partial \mathrm{mp}, \tag{3.16c}$$

where j is the width of a step and n shows the number of the calculation. And $\partial Y/\partial x$, $\partial Y/\partial y$, and $\partial Y/\partial \mathrm{mp}$ are given by Eqs. (3.17a, 3.17b, 3.17c), where the production efficiency A is assumed as 1 and the corporation tax rates of the two countries are assumed as $t = t^* = 0.82$.

$$
\begin{aligned}
\partial Y/\partial x =\ & 0.18\big[-tgx(299.4-0.5\mathrm{mp})/d_4+(299.4-0.5\mathrm{mp})\big(-t_g(x/d_4)-t_e(x/d_3)\big) \\
& -1^{-1.25}(299.4-0.5\mathrm{mp})^{1.25}t_m\Big[\Big\{(p_2+t_m d_2)^{0.5}/(p_1+t_m d_1)^{0.5}\Big\}(x-x_1)/d_1 \\
& +\Big\{(p_1+t_m d_1)^{0.5}/(p_2+t_m d_2)^{0.5}\Big\}(x+x_2)/d_2\Big]\Big]=0
\end{aligned} \tag{3.17a}
$$

$$
\begin{aligned}
\partial Y/\partial y =\ & 0.18\big[-tg(y-1)(299.4-0.5\mathrm{mp})/d_4+(299.4-0.5\mathrm{mp})\,(-t_g((y-y_4)/d_4)-t_e((y-y_3)/d_3) \\
& -1^{-1.25}(299.4-0.5\mathrm{mp})^{1.25}t_m\Big[\Big\{(p_2+t_m d_2)^{0.5}/(p_1+t_m d_1)^{0.5}\Big\}(y+y_1)/d_1 \\
& +\Big\{(p_1+t_m d_1)^{0.5}/(p_2+t_m d_2)^{0.5}\Big\}(y+y_2)/d_2\Big]\Big]=0
\end{aligned} \tag{3.17b}
$$

$$
\begin{aligned}
\partial Y/\partial \mathrm{mp} =\ & 0.18[-(0.5*\mathrm{mp}-299.4)+0.22\big(299.4-2*0.5\mathrm{mp}+0.5t_g d_4+0.5(p_3+t_e d_3)\big) \\
& +2.5*1^{-1.25}(p_2+t_m d_2)^{0.5}(p_1+t_m d_1)^{0.5}(299.4-0.5\mathrm{mp})^{0.25}]=0.
\end{aligned} \tag{3.17c}
$$

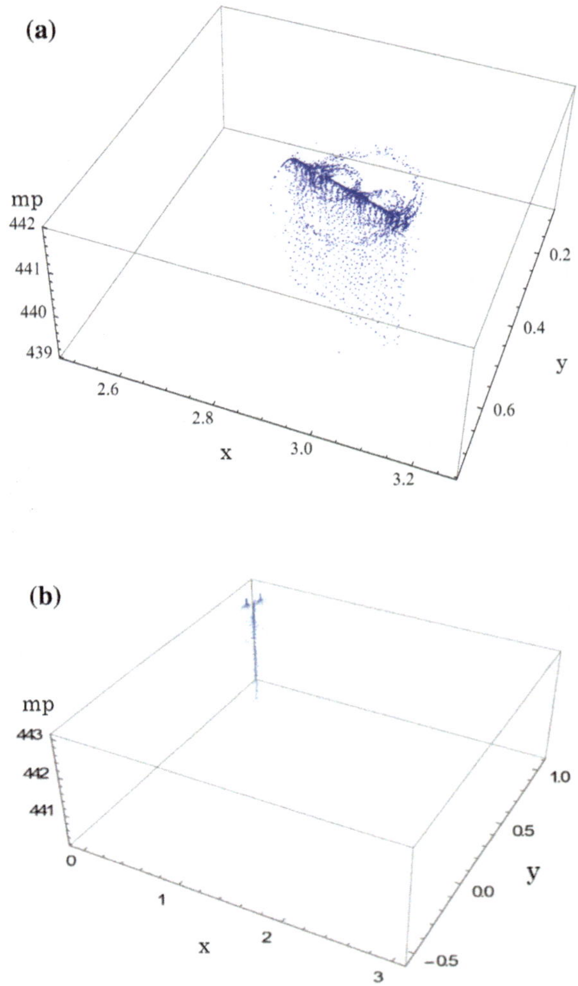

Fig. 3.2 **a** Location prospective area of factory in low freight rate. **b** Location prospective area of factory in high freight rate

Let us derive optimal location of the factory 1 and the transfer price by assigning numerical values to parameters as follows: ($x_1 = 3$, $y_1 = -0.5$), ($x_2 = -3^{0.5}$, $y_2 = -0.5$), ($x_3 = 0$, $y_3 = -1.5$), ($x_4 = 0$, $y_4 = 1$), $p_1 = 0.25$, $p_2 = 2$, $p_3 = 0.2$, $t_m = 0.11$, $t_e = 0.01$, $t_g = 0.225$, $F_1 = 5000$, $F_2 = 2500$. The calculation results derived from the gradient dynamics are shown in Fig. 3.2a. This figure indicates that the optimal transfer price is approximately 442 and the optimal location site is hidden by a chaotic phenomenon.[3]

[3]The phenomenon shown in Fig. 3.2 is a *chaos* or a *chaotic* phenomenon which is generated from the Cauchy convergence in the solution derivation process. The study to identify this phenomenon is not conducted in this paper because this problem does not make any obstacle to logical development. This interest issue is going to be discussed elsewhere.

Table 3.1 Location, transfer price, and profit of factory in different freight rates

Freight rate	Location	Transfer price	Amount	Profit of firm	Profit of factory 1
$t_g = 0.225$	Around $\boldsymbol{M_1}$	442	49.19	3482	2968
$t_g = 0.85$	Around $\boldsymbol{M_4}$	443	48.97	3450	2948

Although the accurate location of the factory 1 is not identified by the appearance of the chaotic phenomenon, the chaotic phenomenon provides an important information that the optimal location site is within the area where a chaotic phenomenon appears because phenomenon appears surrounding the optimal solution. If the firm locates the factory 1 within the chaotic area, the firm's profit is not varied so much.[4] When the firm locates the factory 1 at point M_1, the profit is derived as 3482. The firm can obtain the almost same profit when the factory 1 locates at any point within this area.

In the above situation, if the location of the factory 1 is fixed at point M_1, profits of the factory 1 and the firm and production amount can be derived; they are shown at the upper row in Table 3.1. And if the freight rate of the intermediate goods is higher as 0.85, as shown in Fig. 3.2b, the Location Prospective Area appears around the marketplace. When the location of the factory 1 is fixed next to the marketplace, profit and transfer price of the factory 1 and profit and production amount of the firm are derived, and they are indicated in the lower row in Table 3.1.

3.2.4.2 Interpretation of Location Prospective Area

The chaotic phenomenon can be interpreted as follow: If a firm decides the location of the factory 1 and the transfer price of the intermediate goods in the sphere of the chaotic phenomenon, the firm's profits are almost same because the optimal solution is contained in this sphere. It can be, therefore, considered that the spatial range of the phenomenon indicates a Location Prospective Area (hereafter LPA) for a possible factory's location. By setting an LPA in large geographical space by using the chaotic phenomenon the firm can squeeze the searching area into a small range; they can reduce the searching costs. Chaotic phenomenon may provide a firm with useful information in the case a firm does not have adequate information about regions in a large geographical area. Furthermore, the Location Prospective Area provides a firm with an opportunity to pay attention to the various location factors: When a firm decides the factory's location within the LPA, a firm can consider the factory's location in a broader perspective: A firm incorporates many factors such as education, culture, and welfare into its decision-making. Considering locational effects of these factors, a firm can find out the location of its factory that would be the best site within the LPA for the firm's activity.

[4]The difference between the two profits may be estimated less than 1% to the obtained profit.

3.2.5 Construction of Industrial Park and Business Types of Factories in Industrial Park

It is noticed from the above analysis of factory's location that industrial park's location is not confined to a specific site, but it is determined by referring the LPAs of the factories. And the factories which possess the resemble characteristics in terms of the factory's products are likely to coexist at the same industrial park. Hence, when a developer of industrial park establishes industrial park in a region, the developer induces the factories of which LPAs make an overlapping area, and the developer constructs the park within an overlapping area. If the factories' LPAs are not overlapped, these factories are not likely to coexist in the same industrial park. Figure 3.3a, b describe these situations.

Two chaotic phenomena in Fig. 3.3a are shown based on the analysis in the previous section. In this figure, the two factories' LPAs do not make an overlapping area, these factories may not locate in the same industrial park (the freight rate of the intermediate goods of the factory of which LPA appears near market is 0.825). While Fig. 3.3b shows that the two chaotic phenomena of the two factories are overlapped near point M_1 (the parameter A of the factory with the small LPA is 0.5). These factories are induced into the same industrial park near M_1. These facts imply that the location and the business types of the tenant factories in industrial park are interconnected.

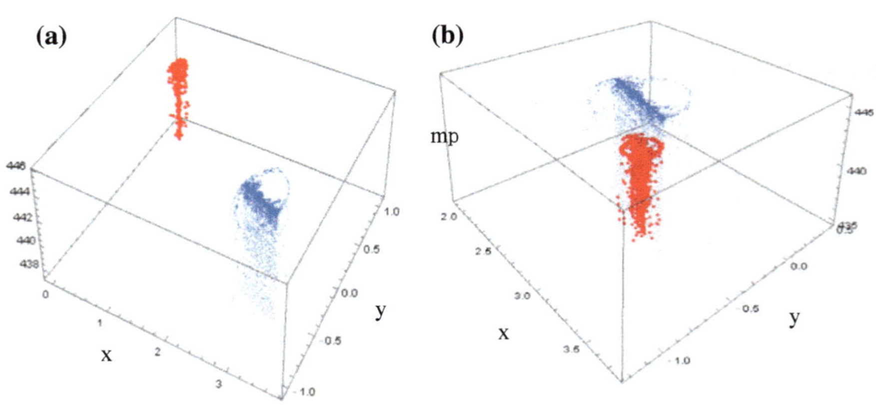

Fig. 3.3 **a** Two LPAs departing each other. **b** Two overlapping LPAs

3.3 Relationships Between External Economies and Production Composition of Industrial Park

3.3.1 *Combination of Business Types of Factories in Industrial Park*

To examine effects on industrial park of the difference of business types of the tenant factories, suppose three kinds of the factories which belong to the different business types, a, b, and c. Although they are in the same spatial and production situation shown in Sect. 3.2, they are different in terms of production of the intermediate goods: the factory 1_a which belongs to business type a is assumed that the production efficiency A_a is 1 and the freight rate of the intermediate goods t_{ga} is 0.225; and the factory 1_b of business type b is that $A_b = 1$ and $t_{gb} = 0.7728$; and the factory 1_c of business type c is that $A_c = 1.05$ and $t_{gc} = 0.825$.

Let us derive chaotic phenomena of the two factories, 1_a and 1_b. Figure 3.4 shows two chaotic phenomena of the two factories. Since LPA of the factory 1_b is long from point M_1 to the marketplace, the LPAs make overlapping area near point M_1. And then, chaotic phenomena of the two factories, 1_b and 1_c, are shown in Fig. 3.5. In this case, LPAs of the two factories, 1_b and 1_c, are overlapped near the marketplace. It is said, therefore, that the industrial park established near point M_1 is composed by the factories, 1_a and 1_b, while, the industrial park established near marketplace is composed by the factories, 1_b and 1_c. Since the factory 1_b has a long LPA, the firm has a possibility to locate its factory $1b$ at either industrial parks.

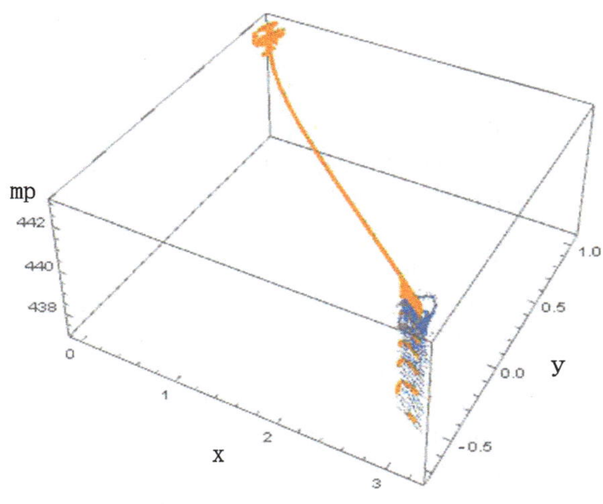

Fig. 3.4 Overlapping of LPAs of two factories near point M_1

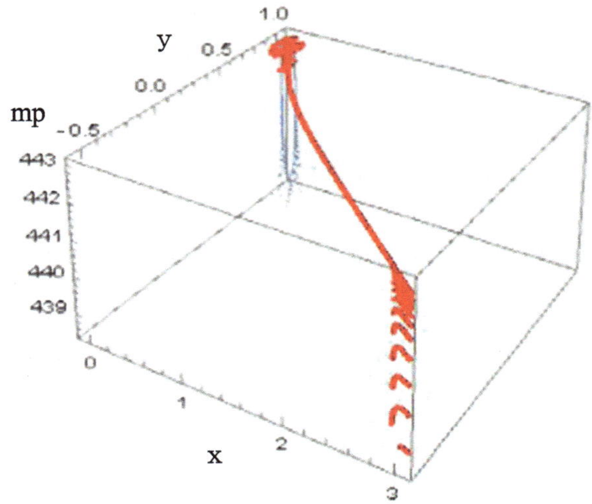

Fig. 3.5 Overlapping of LPAs of two factories near the marketplace

3.3.2 Decrease in Production Costs of Factories by Enjoying External Economies

The number of the factories located in an industrial park is not confined to two. Industrial park contains several factories. Thus, let us examine the number of the factories in industrial park by introducing external economies generated in the park into the analysis. And to this examination, seven assumptions are added in the framework of the analysis:

(1) The business types of the factories are classified to the three types, *a*, *b*, and *c*; and based on the result derived in the previous section, if industrial park is constructed near point M_1, the combination of business types is confined into the combination of *a* and *b*: And if industrial park is established near the marketplace M_4, the combination is *b* and *c*.
(2) The number of the factories (N_i, $i = a, b, c$) of each business type in industrial park is determined by the developer of each industrial park to maximize the profit of each tenant factory.
(3) Each factory employs workers (L_i, $i = a, b, c$) to manage the factory's operation in the park. The number of workers of the factory is determined by the factory to maximize the factory's profit.
(4) Industrial park provides two different kinds of external economies: One of external economies (EEv) reduces the factory's variable cost, and the extent to which the economies reduce the cost is a function of the sum of the numbers of workers employed in the industrial park. Equation (3.18) shows the function of EEv.

$$\mathrm{EEVI} = -h(0.05(\mathrm{TL}_I)^2 + j(0.05(\mathrm{TL}_I)) - k \quad (3.18)$$

$$I = M_1, M_{4,}$$
$$\mathrm{TL}_{MI} = N_a * L_a + N_b * L_b,\ \mathrm{TL}_{M4} = N_b * L_b + N_c * L_c$$

where TL_I ($I = M_1, M_4$) is the number of workers in each park, and h, j, and k are parameters. Labor cost of each factory is a function of the number of workers who are employed in *each business type*; labor cost (wL) of the factory of each business type is indicated by Eq. (3.19),

$$wL_i = g(N_i L_i)^{\Phi} \tag{3.19}$$

$$i = a, b, c$$

where $N_i L_i$ is the number of the workers employed by all factories of business type i ($i = a$, b, and c), g and Φ are parameters.

(5) Other externality economies ($\mathrm{EE_F}$) reduce the fixed cost of the factory, and the extent to which the external economies reduce the fixed cost is a function of the total quantity (TQ) produced in the park. Equation (3.20) shows the function of the external economies of ($\mathrm{EE_F}$),

$$\mathrm{EE}_{\mathrm{F}I} = -\alpha(\mathrm{TQ}_I)^2 + \beta(\mathrm{TQ}_I) - D \tag{3.20}$$

$$I = M_1, M_4$$
$$\mathrm{TQ}_{MI} = N_a * \mathrm{mq}_a + N_b * \mathrm{mq}_b,\ \mathrm{TQ}_{M4} = N_b * \mathrm{mq}_b + N_c * \mathrm{mq}_c$$

where α, β, and D are parameters. When industrial park is constructed near point M_1, TQ is shown by TQ_{MI}, while, if the park is constructed near the marketplace, TQ is given by TQ_{M4}. In this section, it is supposed that the fixed cost contains not only the costs which are directly related with production of goods but also the overhead costs of training of workers, guest accommodation, catering, and so on.

(6) Lot size for every factory in industrial park is the same. The land cost (CL) borne by every factory is given. The cost is assumed to be zero for simplicity of the analysis.

(7) Production amount and transfer price of each factory have been determined in the same way used in the previous section. Therefore, minimizing the production costs is compatible with maximizing profit of the firm.

3.3.3 Derivation of the Numbers of Factories and Workers in Industrial Park

Using the analysis in the previous section, profit of individual factories is obtained by Eq. (3.21),

$$\begin{aligned} Y_{1i} =& (1-t)\big[\mathrm{mq}_i\big((\mathrm{mp}_i - t_g d_4) - (p_3 + t_e d_3)\big) \\ & -\Big(2\mathrm{mq}_i^{1.25}(A_i)^{-1.25}(p_1 + t_m d_1)^{0.5}(p_2 + t_m d_2)^{0.5}\Big)/\mathrm{EE_v} - F_1/\mathrm{EE_F} - g(\mathrm{Ni} * \mathrm{Li})^{\Phi} - \mathrm{CL}\big] \end{aligned} \quad (3.21)$$

$$i = a, b, c$$

Let us suppose that using the results in the previous section, production amount and transfer price of the factory 1_a are that $\mathrm{mq}_a = 49.19$, $\mathrm{mp}_a = 442$, and those of the factory 1_c are $\mathrm{mq}_c = 49.09$, $\mathrm{mp}_c = 442.5$. And when the factory 1_b locates in the park established near point M_1, production amount and transfer price are $\mathrm{mq}_b = 49.09$, $\mathrm{mp}_b = 442.5$; while, when the factory 1_b locates in the park near marketplace, they are $\mathrm{mq}_b = 48.97$, $\mathrm{mp}_b = 443$. Based on the supposition, let us analyze the production composition of each industrial park.

Developer of industrial park decides the number of factories of each business type to maximize profit of individual factories. The developer which establishes an industrial park near point M_1 determines the numbers of the factories, 1_a and 1_b. And each kind of firm decides the number of workers to maximize its profit. Thus, the number of each factory and the number of workers of each factory in the park near point M_1 are derived by solving equation system (22_i, $i = a, b, c, d$) with respect to N_a, N_b, L_a, and L_b,

$$\partial Y_{1a}/\partial N_a = 0 \quad (3.22a)$$

$$\partial Y_{1b}/\partial N_b = 0 \quad (3.22b)$$

$$\partial Y_{1a}/\partial L_a = 0 \quad (3.22c)$$

$$\partial Y_{1b}/\partial L_b = 0 \quad (3.22d)$$

In the same way, the numbers of the factories, 1_b and 1_c and the numbers of workers of the factories in the industrial park near market are obtained.

Assuming that the parameters that indicate the external economies generated in the industrial parks are given as shown in Table 3.2, let us derive the numbers of two kinds of the factories and the number of the workers of the two kinds of the factories in the park near point M_1.

Table 3.2 Parameters' values that define external economies and labor cost

h	j	k	α	β	D	g	Φ
0.01	4	0.2	0.0008	0.71	52.57	0.6	0.15

Solving equation system (22_i, $i = a, b, c, d$) with respect to N_a, N_b, L_a, and L_b gives the production composition of the industrial park near point M_1. The composition is indicated in Table 3.3a. Similarly, the production composition of the park near the marketplace is indicated in Table 3.3b. The comparison of the production compositions in the industrial parks that are shown in Table 3.3a, b indicates that even if the parks are the same size and quality, the production composition and the factories' profits generated in the parks are different. Their changes result from the difference of production characteristics of the factories which coexist in the industrial park.

It is interesting to compare the profits of the factory 1_b which are indifference in the factory's location between point M_1 and the marketplace in the case that there are no the external economies. Since the factories $1b$ can obtain the higher profit by locating in the industrial park near the market place than the park near point M_1, they determine to locate in the park near the marketplace.

The profit difference of the factory 1_b is yielded by the difference of external economies in the parks, and the difference is created by the combination of the business types of the tenant factories: In the case that there are no external economies, if the factory 1_b locates at point M_1, the profit of the factory 1_b is 2947.9, when the factory locates at the marketplace, the profit is 2948.1. The profit difference is only 0.2 which can be negligible. In the case that the external economies are created in the parks, if the factory 1_b locates in the industrial park at point M_1, its profit is increased by 928. While the factory 1_b locates in the park near the marketplace, its profit is increased by 946. These profit increases are generated by enjoying the external economies in the parks. And the factory's profit difference of 12 in between the two industrial parks is yielded by the difference of the combination of the business

Table 3.3 **a** The production composition and profits of the industrial park near point $M1$. **b** The production composition and profits of the industrial park near market place

	Number of factories	Number of workers	Production amount	Profit of factory 1
(a)				
Factory 1_a	–	85.23	49.26	3896
Factory $\mathbf{1_b}$	–	***121.37***	***49.09***	***3876***
Business type $1a$	5.29	450.4	261	20,605
Business type 1b	3.74	***454.3***	***183.6***	***14,496***
Industrial park	9.02	904.7	443.7	*35,101*
(b)				
Factory $\mathbf{1_b}$	–	***119.52***	***48.97***	***3894***
Factory 1_c	–	95.2	49.09	3897
Business type 1b	***3.79***	***504.7***	***185.6***	***14,758***
Business type 1c	5.30	452.9	260	20,654
Industrial park	9.05	957.7	443.8	*35,412*

types of the factories. It can be said that external economies change location and production composition in the industrial park.

3.4 Effects of Urbanization Economies on Production Composition in Industrial Park

3.4.1 Incorporation of Urbanization Economies into the Analysis of Industrial Park

One of the merits of industrial park is to provide the tenants with external economies appropriate to them. These economies are usually generated by the production infrastructure equipped with the park and localization economies created by the tenant factories. There are external economies which industrial parks hardly provide to the tenants: It is difficult for industrial park to serve the factories with so-called urbanization economies that are usually provided by the cities. Urbanization economies are generated by various kinds of public and private facilities and functions in the cities with a certain population size. Some industrial parks tend to be established within urban areas of large and medium cities. Especially, when the factories need to use various sorts of labors and some cumbersome management supports, the industrial park is likely to be established near large city to enjoy efficiently labors and facilities provided by large city. Figure 3.6 illustrates the relations between the internal and external economies. These economies reduce the various kinds of production costs by interlocking each other inside and outside an industrial park in a city.

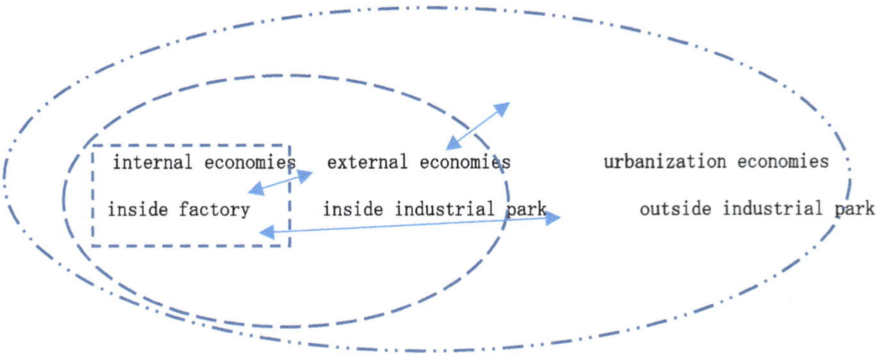

Fig. 3.6 Relations between internal and external economies

3.4.2 Assumptions of the Analysis of External Economies

Let us analyze relationships between urban economies which are generated in a city and the production composition in industrial park. Some assumptions are changed from the previous analysis: Industrial park is established only at point M_1. Thus, the combination of the business types of the factories is confined to type a and b in the industrial park. And by referring to the previous analysis, the production amount and the transfer price of the factory 1_a are given that $\text{mq}_a = 49.19$, $\text{mp}_a = 442$: While the production efficiency A_b of the factory 1_b is changed to be 0.5, the production amount and the transfer price of the factory 1_b are changed as such $\text{mq}_b = 48.28$, $\text{mp}_b = 445.8$.

City's size is classified into three classes, large, medium, and small: Large city provides high urbanization economies, but industrial park in this city is small due to high land price. While, the urban economies of small city are not so high as those of the large city, and the park is large in the small city. And medium city has intermediate features in between those of the large and the small city.

3.4.3 Effects of Urbanization Economies on Production Composition in Industrial Park

The external economies EEv and EE_F in the industrial park are changed according to the city size. The efficiencies of these two external economies in each sized city are indicated by the parameters' values shown in Table 3.4.

Based on the parameters' values shown in Table 3.4, the two kinds of the external economies are illustrated in Figs. 3.7a, b and 3.8a, b. Figure 3.7a shows the relationships between the external economies (EEv) and the number of workers (L) in the two industrial parks in the large city and the medium city. The large city provides higher externalities, which is shown by dotted line, than those of the medium city, but the economies become lower than those of the medium city in a range of large number of workers. Figure 3.7b shows the relationships between the external economies (EE_F) and the production amount (TQ) in the two industrial parks at the large city and the medium city. The relationships are like the case of EEv. The large city provides higher externalities, which is shown by dotted line, than those of the

Table 3.4 Parameters' values that indicated external economies and labor cost in industrial park

City size	h	j	k	α	β	D	g	Φ
Large	0.0277	2.094	0.1	0.00156	1.46	105.14	1	0.2
Medium	0.02	2	10	0.0007	0.73	54.57	0.75	0.15
Small	0.0135	1.443	8.57	0.00033	0.3842	27.67	0.6	0.4

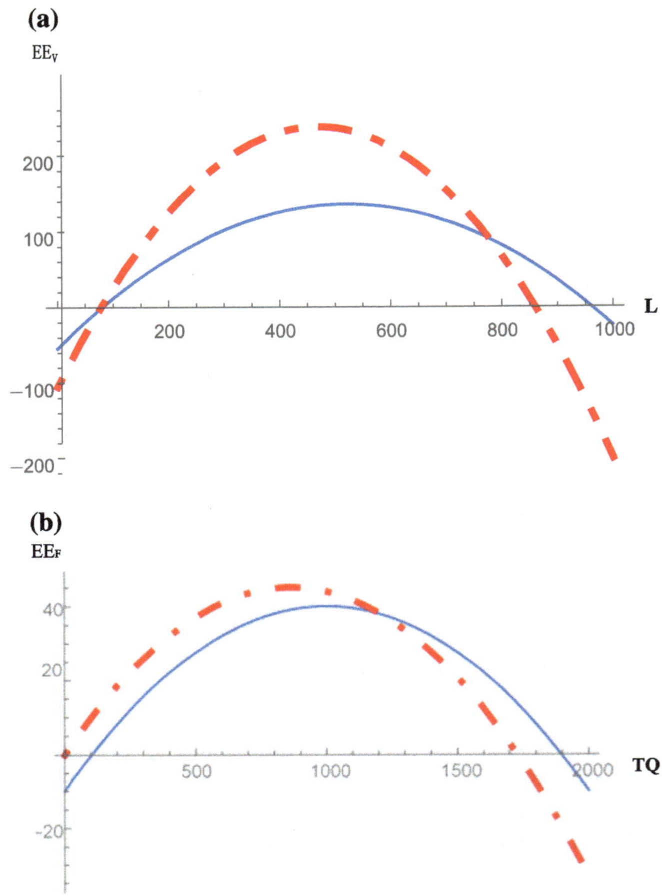

Fig. 3.7 **a** The relationships between external economies and the number of workers in large and medium city. *Note* Dotted line indicates the relation between EEv and number of workers in large city. **b** The relationships between external economies and the production amount in large and medium city. *Note* Dotted line indicates the relation between EE_F and production amount in large city

medium city, but the economies (EE_F) become zero at the less production amount than that of the medium city.

Figure 3.8a shows the relationships between the external economies (EEv) and the number of the workers (*L*) in two industrial parks at the medium city and the small city. The small city provides lower externalities, which is shown by dotted line, than those of the medium city, but the economies become higher than those of the medium city in a range of large number of the workers.

Figure 3.8b shows the relationships between the external economies (EE_F) and the production amount (TQ) in two parks at the medium and the small city. The relationships are like the case of EEv. The small city provides lower the externalities,

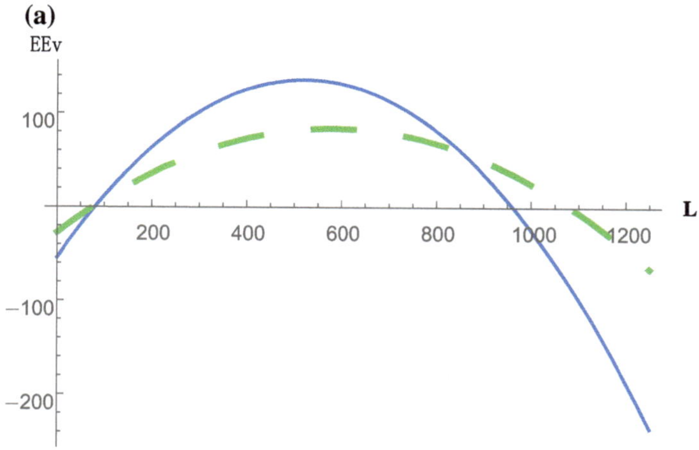

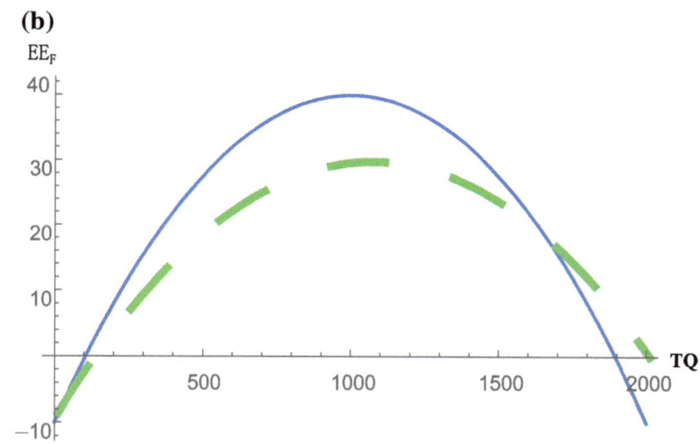

Fig. 3.8 **a** The relationship between external economies and the number of workers in medium and small city. *Note* Dotted line indicates the relation between EEv and number of workers in small city. **b** The relationship between external economies and the production amount in medium and small city. *Note* Dotted line indicates the relation between EE_F and production amount in small city

which is shown by dotted line, than those of the medium city, but the economies become zero at the larger production amount than that of the medium city.

Lastly, Fig. 3.9 shows the relationships between the number of the workers (N_iL_i, $i = a, b$) in each business type and labor cost (wL) to the three different sized cities.

The relationship between labor cost and the number of workers is indicated by the parameters g and Φ in Table 3.4. The relationship in the small city is explained by the following logic: The labor cost of the small city is the lowest when the number of workers is small, but as the workers increase in the industrial park, it becomes higher than those of the large and medium city. Because the transportation infrastructure surrounding the small city is supposed not to be adequate, the commuting area of

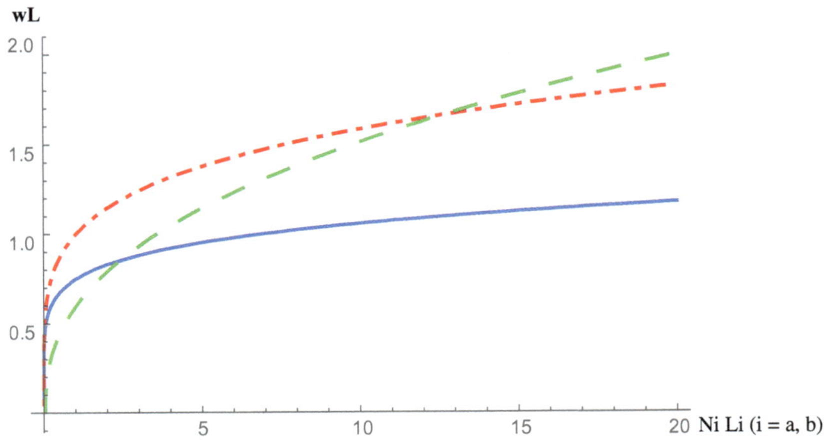

Fig. 3.9 Relationship between labor cost and the number of workers of each business type for different city sizes

Table 3.5 Production construction and profit of the industrial parks in the different sized cities

Size	Number of factory 1*a*	Number of factory 1*b*	Workers of factories 1*a*	Workers of factories 1*b*	Profit of factory 1*a*	Profit of factory 1*b*	Total profit of factories in park
Large	6.71	2.89	492	170	3899	3844	37,034
Medium	7.23	3.44	259	699	**3904**	**3841**	41,158
Small	8.38	3.47	146	595	3928	3870	46,038

the workers to the park is so small that the supply capacity of the workers is limited, thus, labor cost becomes higher rapidly as the number of workers increases.

Now, let us derive the production compositions and profits of individual factories and industrial park for the three different sized cities. Table 3.5 shows the results derived from the calculations of equitation system (3.22a, 3.22b, 3.22c, 3.22d) in the previous sections.

As shown in Table 3.5, profits of the individual factories are maximized when they locate in the industrial park in the small city. It is the individual private firms that have the largest power to determine location and production composition of industrial park. Hence, the possibility of industrial park constructing at the small city is the highest. And the government as a developer which pays attention to the number of the employments in the park considers locating industrial park at the medium city since the number of workers is the largest. While the large city is likely not to be selected from the viewpoints of profit level and employment numbers. Considering the profits of the factories and the numbers of workers in the parks, the small and the medium city may be favored as a site of industrial park. But, it should be noted that the number of workers of the business type *a* in the large city is much larger than those of the medium and small city. This fact characterizes the employment composition of the large city and it might give an economic suggestion if the industrial park is built in a large city.

3.5 Role of the Government in Establishing Industrial Park

3.5.1 Derivation of Alternatives of Production Composition in Industrial Park

To inquire role of the government in establishing industrial park, this subsection deals with alternatives of production composition in the park that makes the profits of the factories the same level: If industrial park locates in the medium size city, as shown in the middle row of the Table 3.5, profits of the factory 1*a* and the factory 1*b* are 3904 and 3841, respectively. And if the parameters indicating external economies and the parameter *g* in industrial park are changed to those indicated by Table 3.2, the profits of the factory 1*a* and the factory 1*b* in this *alternative* park become to 3904 and 3840. These profits levels in the *alternative* park are the almost same as those obtained in the *original* park. But total profits of the park, the number of the factories and the production composition, which are shown in Table 3.6, are different from the original park.

It is interesting to know that even if the external economies and labor cost of industrial park are different, the profits of the factory 1*a* and 1*b* remain the almost same level, but the numbers of the factories and workers in industrial park are clearly different. Figure 3.10 indicates the combinations of the numbers of the factories and the numbers of workers that make the profits of the factories the same level: The square marks combined by the real lines are the combinations of the numbers of the factories and the workers in existing industrial park which is indicated in the middle row of Table 3.4; while the square marks combined by the dotted lines are combinations of the number of the factories and the number of the workers in the alternative industrial park which is indicated in Table 3.2. It can be suggested, therefore, that by coordinating the two kinds of external economies generated in the park and changing parameter of *g*, many different industrial parks can create the same profit level of the factories. That is, there is a certain combination range that makes the profits of the factories the same level and there are many alternatives

Table 3.6 Alternative production construction and profits of the industrial park in medium city

Size	Number of factory 1*a*	Number of factory 1*b*	Workers of factories 1*a*	Workers of factories 1*b*	Profit of factory 1*a*	Profit of factory 1*b*	Total profit of factories in park
Medium	6.14	2.94	678	255	**3904**	**3840**	35,262

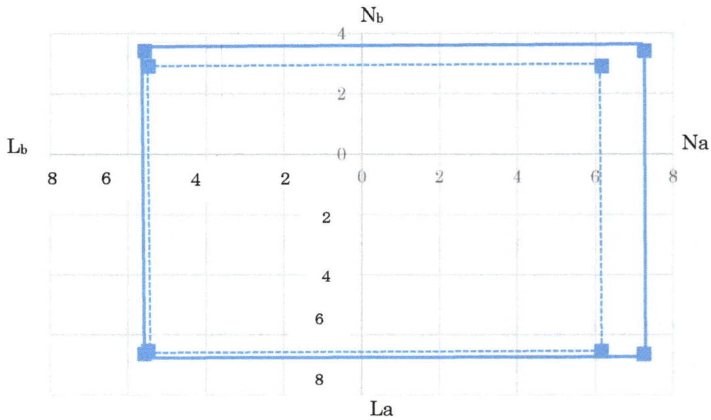

Fig. 3.10 The alternative of production composition in industrial park

in the certain combination range. This certain range that covers these production compositions may be named as the Composition Prospective Range (CPR).

3.5.2 A Role of the Government in Establishing Industrial Park

Since a factory determines its location and the number of workers, it is the profit level of the individual factories that decides the production composition in industrial park as well as the park's location. However, if the factory's profit level is the same between different industrial parks, the location and the production composition of an industrial park are eventually selected by a developer of industrial park. Considering this fact, when the government is a developer of an industrial park, the role of the government in vitalizing regional economy is very important.

If regional economy of the medium size city in question is lowering and the government intends to revitalize the economy, the industrial park with high external economies will be selected by the government; while, if the regional economy is in high level, and the supply of workers is relatively tight, the industrial park with low external economies tends get selected. Considering the condition of regional economy, the government's selection of industrial park is possible as far as the production compositions are contained within the Composition Prospective Range.

It is essential for the government to understand that the production composition of industrial park is not unique, but there are alternatives of the composition within the Composition Prospective Range: The government should deliberate the production composition in industrial park to contribute regional economy as much as possible, considering the situation of the regional economy and examining the intentions of the regional economic agents.

3.5.3 *Effects on Industrial Park of the Government's Policy to Improve Infrastructure*

This subsection analyzes the effects on industrial park of the government's investment to improve the transport infrastructure surrounding the park, using the results of the analysis conducted in Sect. 3.4.

In the analysis of Sect. 3.4, it is assumed that when an industrial park is established at the small city, the labor cost is raised rapidly as the number of workers in the park increases. This is because that the transport infrastructure is not adequate within urban area of the small city and the commuting area of workers is narrow. Based on this logic, the parameter Φ is set to be high of 0.4. It is considered, however, that if the government invests to improve the infrastructure, the rise of labor cost is curbed, and labor costs become lower than before the investment is made.

Assuming that the parameter Φ is lowered to 0.3 at the industrial park in a small city and the two kinds of external economies in the park are indicated by the third row in Table 3.4, this subsection analyzes the effects on the industrial park established in the small city of the government investment to improvement of the infrastructure. When the parameter Φ is lowered to 0.3, the production composition and profits of the factories are derived by the same way used in the Sect. 3.3 and they are shown in Table 3.7.

It is interesting to know that (1) the production composition is changed, but the total number of the factories, 11.85, is not changed: (2) the profit of the factory 1_a is slightly decreased by 2 which can be negligible, the profit of the factory 1_b is maintained to the same level. Total profits of the industrial park are increased by 252: It could be said based on this results that the government's investment to improve the infrastructure increases the total profits of the industrial park, but it does not make individual factories' profits increase due to the changing the production composition in the park.[5] It is important for the factories and the government to realize the effects of the locational policy because the government's policy which seems to be seconded by every economic agent does not always increase every factory's profit by the change of the production composition in the industrial park.

Table 3.7 Production construction and profits of the industrial park in better infrastructure

Size	Number of factory $1a$	Number of factory $1b$	Workers of factories $1a$	Workers of factories $1b$	Profit of factory $1a$	Profit of factory $1b$	Total profit of factories in park
Small	8.85	2.99	712	213	**3926**	**3870**	**46,290**

[5]It is shown by carrying out many calculations that when the reduction of the parameter Φ exceeds a certain value, the profits of the factories start to increase. This is because the effect of the reduction is not offset by the changes in the production composition in the industrial park.

3.6 Concluding Remarks

In the period of the globalized economy, the production processes of the manufacturing firms are fragmented into small blocs, and some of them are scattered over the world. And many governments try to induce these fragmented processes into their territory to vitalize regional economy. In this context, industrial parks are attractive to both the manufacturing firms and the governments because industrial park provides the factories with appropriate external economies and appropriate production infrastructure, and it attracts many factories to an intended site in a region.

The primary results derived from the analysis in this chapter are summarized as follows: The location of industrial park is not limited to a specific site, but it could be settled at any sites within an overlapping area of the Location Prospective Areas of the factories. External economies generated in industrial park exert influences on the individual firms' profits, the combination of the business types of the tenant factories, and the production composition of the industrial park. In addition, urbanization economies provided by the cities with different sizes affect industrial park in different ways. It is suggested from the analysis of effects of urbanization economies that the small cities tend to be favored by the manufacturing firms as the location site of the industrial park, while the medium cities have a chance to be selected by the governments. Lastly, the production composition in an industrial park should not uniquely determined but there are the alternatives in a certain range. Therefore, the government has an opportunity to alter the production composition in the park to improve the regional economy as much as possible. In addition, it is also shown in the analysis that there is a case that the government's investment aiming to reduce the labor cost in industrial park does not always increase every firm's profit. These facts imply that the government as a developer of industrial park should deliberate the influences of establishing the industrial park, including the side and indirect economic influences on the regional economic agents.

References

Hirshleifer, J. 1956. On the economics of transfer pricing. *Journal of Business* July: 172–184.

Ishikawa, T. 2016. *Dynamic location phases of economic activity in the globalized world*. Singapore: Springer.

Ishikawa, T. 2009. Determination of a factory's location in a large geographical area by using chaotic phenomena and retailers location networks. *Timisoara Journal of Economics* 2: 141–150.

Puu, T. 1998. Gradient dynamics in Weberian location theory. *Knowledge and networks in a dynamic economy*, ed. Beckmann et.al. Springer.

Shi, H., and X. Yang. 1995. A new theory of industrialization. *Journal of Comparative Economics* 20: 171–189.

Weber, A. 1909. *Über den Standort der Industrien*. Tubingen: J.C.B. Mohr.

Chapter 4
Locational Movement of PC Manufacturing Firms in East Asia

Yanwei Sun

Abstract It is difficult for inland region to attack foreign investment because of the poor infrastructure and location condition. Chongqing, the inland region of China, succeeds in attacking Taiwanese PC companies and became the notebook PC production base of China in a short time. Taiwanese PC company is the main notebook PC producer in the world because of the competitiveness of cost and shipping speed. To maintain the competitiveness of cost and shipping speed, Taiwanese notebook PC companies relocated to the coastal area of China (Yangtze river delta) in 2000 from Taiwan and then relocated to inland region of China (Chongqing) in 2010. The purpose of this chapter is to consider the changing location of Taiwanese PC companies in China and its factors. The difference of twice relocation is that the latter case is led by demand provided by Chongqing government. That is Chongqing government earned order from PC brand company instead of Taiwanese notebook PC companies and provided the order to them. Besides that, Chongqing government developed transport infrastructure and became a new transport hub between China and Europe. In this way, because of the provided demand and potential of export convenience, Taiwanese notebook companies accumulated to the inland region China, Chongqing.

Keywords PC production network · Taiwanese PC company · Relocation
China · Inland region

4.1 Introduction

With the progress of the globalization and digitization in 1990s, large-scale production of PC (personal computers) was required on a global scale. In the expansion of PC production network, Taiwanese PC companies received orders from American PC companies as the manufacturing enterprise because of their competitive advantage of price and speed. In 2010, Taiwanese PC companies produced 90% of

Y. Sun (✉)
Institute of Economic Research, Chuo University, Hachioji, Tokyo, Japan
e-mail: piliweiwei@yahoo.co.jp

T. Ishikawa (ed.), *Locational Analysis of Firms' Activities from a Strategic Perspective*, https://doi.org/10.1007/978-981-13-1684-5_4

the world's notebook PC. In other words, Taiwanese PC company is the producer of notebook PC in the world.

Taiwanese PC companies produced desktop PC and related parts in Pearl River Delta (Guangdong Province) in China in 1990s. Since 2000, the production base of notebook PC was moved to Yangtze Delta (Shanghai and neighboring regions) after Taiwanese government removed the ban on the production of notebook PC in China. Thereafter, Yangtze Delta became the production base of notebook PC in the world. In 2008, production of notebook PC in Yangtze Delta accounted for more than 70% of global production.

However, Taiwanese PC companies tend to move production base to inland areas of China. In 2009, American computer brand company Hewlett-Packard and major Taiwanese computer manufacturers, Foxconn, Quanta, and Inventec located in Chongqing and Chengdu, the inland regions in China, moved their bases one after another. Chongqing and Chengdu developed rapidly as a notebook PC production base and tablet production base. In this way, Chongqing and Chengdu became the third computer production base after Pearl River Delta and Yangtze Delta. By the end of 2014, top six PC ODMs (all Taiwanese companies) and 875 parts companies moved to Chongqing. In the same year, the production of notebook PC in Chongqing accounted for more than one-third of global production. In addition, notebook PC manufacturing industry had a positive productivity effect on other industries in Chongqing (Sun and Taniguchi 2015).

In this way, Taiwanese PC company, the producers of PC in the world, had two relocations from Taiwan to the coast of China and inland China. What factors caused two relocations to happen? Especially why the second relocation in the inland city Chongqing?

In previous research, cases of relocation to Pearl River Delta and Yangtze River Delta had been discussed. Zhu (2003) and Wang et al.(2003) compared the investment environment, Seki (2005) did field study, and Kika (2006) discussed from the viewpoint of the international production network. According to their studies, factors of relocation to Pearl River Delta and Yangtze River Delta are cheap labor, locational convenience of export, and attractiveness of Chinese domestic market. However, there are still few studies on location in the inland city Chongqing of Taiwanese computer companies. If we can find out the factor of it, it will be an important implication to not only for company strategy but also for the development of the industry of the backward region.

In this chapter, first, we consider the movement of Taiwanese PC companies from Taiwan to the coastal area of China. In this section, we study the background in global PC industry and Taiwanese PC industry structure, then compare the two times relocation. Second, we consider relocation from Yangtze River Delta to inland city Chongqing and Chengdu. In this section, we study the case of major Taiwanese ODMs and approach the location factors of Chongqing in demand side and supply side.

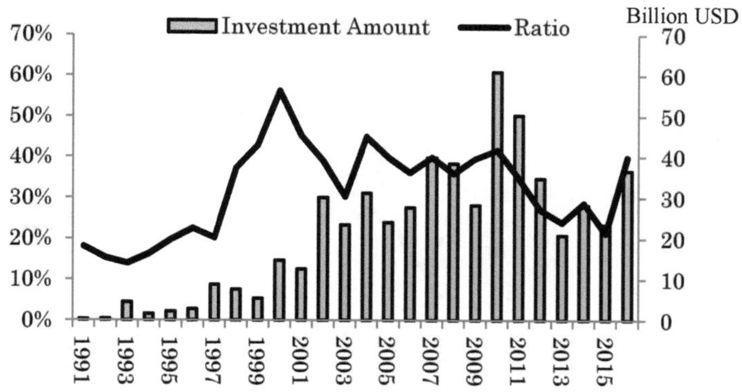

Fig. 4.1 Investment amount of PC and electronic Industry of Taiwan in China, the percentage of PC and electronic Industry in Taiwanese total investment in China. *Source* Investment Commission, Ministry of Economic Affairs, Taiwan FDI Statistics Summary Analysis

4.2 Relocation from Taiwan to China's Coastal Area

4.2.1 Overview of Taiwanese PC Companies Relocate from Taiwan to China

The reason Taiwan began to invest in China was the sharp rise in the exchange rate between Taiwan dollar and US dollar. After the World War II, Taiwan government took "three non-policies:" no contact, no negotiation, and no compromise and banned investment and trade in China.[1] In the end of 1987, Taiwan government lifted the ban of visit to relatives in China and at the same time wage rose rapidly in Taiwan. As these changes, the indirect investment via third country or region to China was accepted by Taiwan government. However, regulations on investment amount and investment field were still strict, so the number of Taiwanese companies investing in China increased in secret.

Let us have an overview of PC and electronic industry investment of Taiwan in China (Fig. 4.1). PC and electronic industry is a major investment industry of Taiwanese investment in China, and the ratio raised rapidly from latter of the 1990s. In 1997, it was 20.2% and in 2000, it raised to 56.2%, subsequently it remained in 30–40% until 2012. Investment amount of PC and electronic in China expanded rapidly from around 2002, however, there was slower growth because of the influence of Lehman shock, and the investment amount in 2010 reached the highest record (660.9 billion dollars) which is about twice that in 2002 and four times of that in 1997. In this way, PC and electronics industry is the major investment of Taiwan in China and the rapid growth around 2000 showed a strong lead in Taiwanese investment in China.

[1] Kawakami (2012) p. 147.

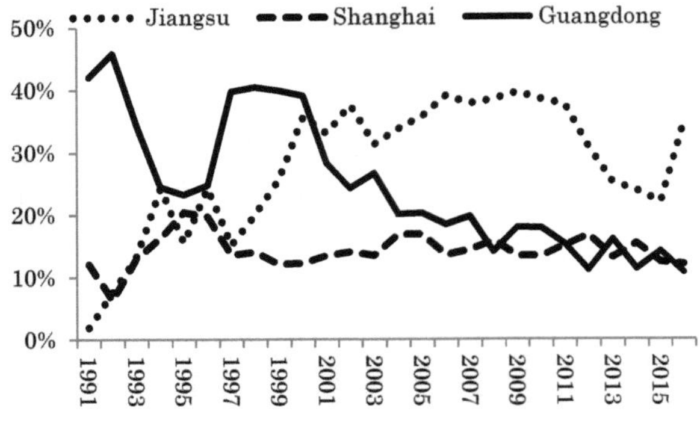

Fig. 4.2 The three main regions for Taiwanese investment in China. *Source* Investment Commission, Ministry of Economic Affairs, Taiwan FDI Statistics Summary Analysis

On the other hand, Taiwanese investment amount almost concentrated in eastern coastal area in China, especially Guangdong of Pearl River Delta and Jiangsu Province and Shanghai which belongs to Yangtze River Delta. According to Fig. 4.2, the proportion of Guangdong accounted for about 40% of the total in the 1990s, however, it began decreasing since 2000 and reached 10.7% in 2016. The proportion of Jiangsu Province increased suddenly from 1997, exceeded Guangdong's proportion in 2000. Jiangsu Province became the most concentrated region for Taiwanese investment from 2002. Moreover, Shanghai's proportion was 20% in 1995 and remained above 10% until now, hence Shanghai is an important investment area from the beginning for Taiwan. From Fig. 4.2, we can see that Taiwanese investment concentrated in Pearl River Delta (Guangdong) before 2000 and transferred to Yangtze River Delta's Jiangsu after 2000. Especially, Jiangsu is the most concentrated area of Taiwanese investment. In this way, investment of Taiwanese PC and electronic industry began to shift from Pearl River Delta to Yangtze River Delta in the late 1990s.

In 1990s, Guangdong was the desktop PC and parts production base of Taiwanese PC companies hence concentrated most of the Taiwanese investment in China. Since 2000 Taiwanese notebook PC companies relocated from Taiwan to Yangtze River Delta (especially Jiangsu), Jiangsu became the region Taiwanese investment most concentrated.

As shown in Fig. 4.3, notebook PC production in Taiwan expanded rapidly since the mid-1990s, and began to decrease from 2002. On the other hand, in China, PC production increased rapidly from 2002, especially the production expansion of notebook PC. It means the movement of Taiwanese PC companies from Taiwan to China contributed to the production expansion of PC in China.

In 2010, almost all Taiwan notebook PC production moved to China's Yangtze River Delta. In addition, more than 70% of world notebook PCs are produced in Yangtze River Delta.

However, although Yangtze River Delta is the major investment area of Taiwan notebook PCs, and Taiwanese ODMs of notebook PCs began to relocate rapidly to Chongqing and Chengdu, the inland regions in China. As shown in Fig. 4.2, the proportion of Jiangsu has declined since 2010 and this means the relocation of Taiwanese companies from Jiangsu. In 2009, the proportion of Chongqing and

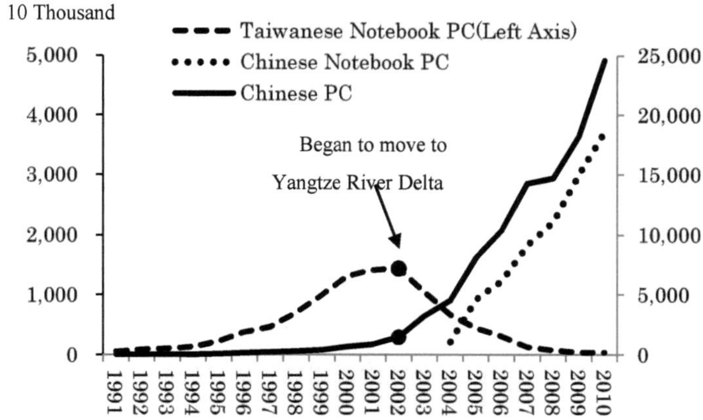

Fig. 4.3 Changes in the volume of PCs produced in Taiwan and China. *Source* Department of Statistics, Taiwan Ministry of Economic Affairs, China Statistical Yearbook, Intelligence Research Group

Sichuan (Chengdu)[2] among Taiwanese investment was 0.94 and 0.73%, ranking 12th and 16th in 31 regions of China. Nevertheless, in 2010, the proportion of Chongqing was 3.74% (6th) and in 201,1 the proportion of Sichuan was 6.45% (4th). Moreover, in 2010 and 2011, Chongqing and Sichuan (Chengdu) became the most concentrated region of Taiwanese investment in China western region.

Furthermore, let us consider the relocation of Taiwanese ODMs to the western region from the change in regional production of notebook PCs in China. According to regional notebook PC production in 2010, Jiangsu was 83.8 million, Jiangsu was 84.2 million, Chongqing was 1.8 million and Sichuan (Chengdu) was 0.16 million. In 2014, Jiangsu was 61.3 million, Shanghai was 44.7 million, Chongqing was 63.4 million, and Sichuan (Chengdu) was 74.3 million.[3] Actually, production amount of notebook PC in Chongqing and Chengdu exceeded that of Yangtze River Delta from 2014. That means Chongqing and Chengdu became the third PC production base in China.

4.2.2 *Background of Taiwanese PC Enterprise from Taiwan to China*

In this section, we consider the background of Taiwanese companies relocated to China from PC industry structure.

---

[2]Chengdu is provincial capital of Sichuan, and it is the only investment area in Sichuan.

[3]The date is the total amount of notebook PC and tablet PC. PC produced in Chengdu is almost tablet PCs.

Fig. 4.4 Changes in the volume of PCs produced in Taiwan and China. *Source* Wistron Annual Report

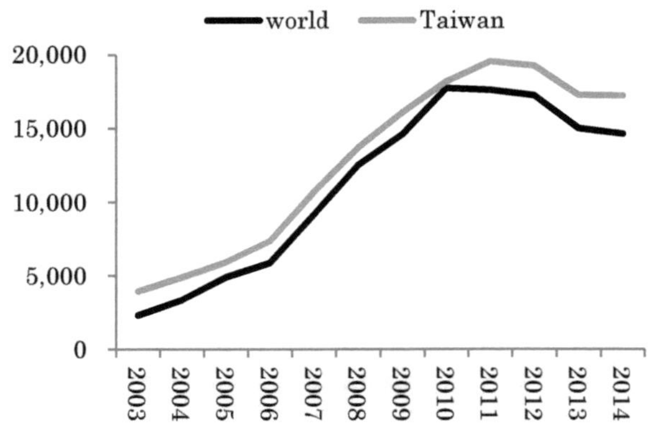

4.2.2.1 The Role of Taiwan PC Enterprise in PC Industry

Since the mid-1990s, the focus on competition in PC production shifted from technology to price and development speed of new product, and PC companies increased the outsourcing of production. Under these circumstances, Taiwanese PC companies seized the opportunity and developed PC ODM industry (Asamoto 2011). As a result, Taiwanese PC companies produce more than 90% of worldwide notebook PCs as original design manufacturers (ODMs) in PC production network (see Fig. 4.4).

Let us see the relationship between PC brand companies and ODMs. According to Table 4.1, Taiwanese ODMs produced notebook PC shipment volume of the top 7 brand companies. Moreover, Taiwanese Acer and ASUS joined the top 7 of PC brand companies. Thus, the position of Taiwanese companies of PC industry is not only a manufacturer but also as a brand company.

Whereas Taiwanese ODMs play an important role in PC global production network, their added value is still small compared to brand companies. Since in PC production most of the added value belong to core parts and sales, there is only a small percentage left to Taiwanese ODMs. Furthermore, Taiwanese ODMs are the large-scale production with large factories and employing a large number worker, hence the cost is relatively high. In this way, for Taiwanese ODMs, cost reduction is always the problem to overcome.

In addition, under the price competition in PC industry in the 1990s, the request of the brand companies became strictly in the quality, speed, cost and production capacity of ODMs. Hence, component procurement capability and logistics capacity became more important for Taiwanese ODMs. Therefore, the component procurement system was formed between Taiwanese major ODMs and component suppliers. Additionally, Taiwanese ODMs tended to locate in central areas of transportation for the convenience of exporting to improve the logistics speed. In this way, the position of Taiwanese ODMs in PC production network not only promoted the relationship between Taiwanese ODMs and component companies but also affected the location in China.

Table 4.1 Shipment of Notebook PC brand companies and ODMs in 2010

Rank	1 Quan	2 Com	3 Wis	4 Inven	5 Pega	6 Fox	7 Fex	Other
1. HP	2,400	300	300	300		300	430	
2. Acer	500	1,800	850		200			
3. Dell	400	1,100	1,000		200	300		
4. Toshiba	460	800		1,155				
5. Lenovo	600	700	700	150				
6. ASUS					845	400		
7. Apple	550				300	200		
Other	300	210						1,000
Total	5,210	4,910	2,850	1,605	1,545	1,200	430	1,000

Source Shuimuqinghua Research Center, Global and China notebook PC: Report 2010–2011
Note 1 Full name of ODMs are 1. Quanta, 2. Compal, 3. Wistron, 4. Inventec, 5. Pegatron, 6. Foxconn, 7. Fextionics
Note 2 Except Fextionics all the ODMs in Table are Taiwanese ODMs and Fextionics withdrew from ODM business in 2011

4.2.2.2 Vertical and Horizontal Production Structure

In this section, we consider the reason of Taiwanese PC companies' competitive advantage in cost and speed from industry structure.

From 1985 to 1995, the growth of the information electronics industry in Taiwan was due to PC parts and peripheral equipment manufacturing rather than PC manufacturing. The fact that PC parts and peripherals occupied a large global share at an early stage was due to the entry of Taiwanese SMEs. In particular, since the late 1980s, newcomers of PC parts and peripherals manufacturing enterprises increased rapidly compared to PC manufacturing. According to the Industrial Statistics Survey Report of 1998, the total number of enterprises in the information electronics industry is 10,950, of which 10,460 (95.5%) are SMEs less than 200 person and the number of microenterprises less than 20 person is 6127 (56%).[4] Thus, in the PC industry in Taiwan, the proportion of SMEs is extremely high and held an important position.

In the 1980s, SMEs and big companies had a competitive relationship with each other. However, in the 1990s, they were complementary because they divided into suppliers or subcontractors of intermediate products and producers of final products (Kawakami 1998).

In the 1980s, SMEs worked to reduce cost and shorten lead times, in order to obtain stable orders for the intense competition of order among SMEs. Due to this, in Taiwan PC industry SMEs were born in harsh environments and had advantages

[4] Yang (2000) p. 120.

of cost and speed. In addition, information on quantities, quality, delivery, etc. of orders were shared among SMEs, hence the close division of labor network and high flexibility to deal with various orders were the characteristics of Taiwanese SEMs. With such characteristics, SMEs made it possible to supply parts cheaply and quickly to big companies. Under such a system of vertical division and horizontal division of industry structure, Taiwanese OEMs received large orders from brand companies and this led to the development of the ODM industry afterwards.

For example, the procurement of parts of Quanta is formed as vertical structure by primary supplier, secondary supplier, and micro-fabrication maker and most secondary supplier and micro-fabrication maker are SEMs. It is necessary to keep close the cooperative relationships with parts suppliers of Quanta for supplying high quality, low price, and large quantity of products.

Additionally, information between ODMs and parts suppliers is shared in an open intercompany network. For example, Acer and Quanta shared some parts suppliers.[5]

Thus, vertical and horizontal divisions of labor are formed in Taiwanese PC industry. Under such a division of labor structure, the close network of SEMs supports large enterprises of final products as parts suppliers.

4.2.3 Relocation of Taiwanese PC Enterprise to Pearl River Delta and Yangtze River Delta

4.2.3.1 Relocation to the Pearl River Delta

Pearl River Delta is part of Guangdong Province, including Hong Kong, Macau and facing Taiwan across the straights. Because the advantageous location condition and cheap labor, Pearl River Delta was one of the regions that policy of reform and opening-up was implemented earliest in China. Since the 1980s, Pearl River Delta developed on the export economy in the processing trade by foreign investment. Since then, the products processed upgraded from low-value products to electronic machines, parts assembly, therefore Pearl River Delta became the agglomeration of manufacturing industries in electronic machinery and related parts. In this way, Pearl River Delta came to be know as the "world's electronic machinery factory". In the early 2000s, about half of peripheral equipment were produced in Guangdong.[6]

As mentioned in Sect. 4.2.2.1, since the 1990s, the requirements from brand companies became more stringent in cost, speed, production capacity, and quality. Due to this, to maintain cost competitiveness, Taiwanese companies which produced PC component and peripheral equipment began to relocate to Pearl River Delta for the cheap labor and preferential policies for special economic zones. Since 1994, with the lifting the ban of desktop PC and peripheral equipment to China, Taiwanese desktop PC industrial cluster was formed quickly in Pearl River Delta. As the PC

[5] See Yang (2001).

[6] Zhuang (2004) p. 204.

demand in China was still small in 1990s, Pearl River Delta became the production bases aiming at export of Taiwanese PC companies. In particular, Dongguan was the area many Taiwanese PC companies accumulated in.

Dongguan of Pearl River Delta

Dongguan was the underdevelopment region in Guangdong Province, hence land price and labor cost were relatively lower than Shenzhen and other regions in Pearl River Delta. Furthermore, Dongguan had the geographical advantage of less than 100 km to the port of Hong Kong which was another important factor that attacked Taiwanese companies.

Until mid-1990s, Taiwanese companies located in Dongguan produced low added value such as keyboard, mouse, cable, switch, etc. under the investment restrictions by Taiwan. In 1994, as the investment of desktop PCs and high value added was lifted, desktop computer assembly industry developed in Dongguan. By 2005, there were 14,000 Taiwanese companies located in Guangdong, more than a half concentrated in Dongguan and PC-related production companies in Dongguan were approximately 3000.[7]

Small enterprises were more than big enterprises of Taiwanese companies concentrated in Dongguan. Since upstream and downstream companies moved to Dongguan together, division of intra-industry was formed. Therefore, due to the group movement of Taiwanese companies, PC production processes such as the supply of PC-related raw material, parts production, and assembly were formed in Dongguan at the beginning. In 2002, 95% of the parts required for desktop PC production could be procured in Dongguan in one hour by car.[8] The export value of Dongguan in 2010 was 69.6 billion dollars (13% of that of Guangdong) and 71% was electronic goods. In this way, Taiwanese PC companies in Dongguan, mainly small and medium enterprises, export PC-related products in the world and Dongguan became to be known as the world PC production base.

In summary, the reason Taiwanese PC companies relocated to Pearl River Delta is considered to be due to the cheap labor force and geographical convenience of exporting that is close to Hong Kong.

4.2.3.2 Relocation to the Yangtze River Delta

Yangtze River Delta is an eastern coastal area of China, including Shanghai, southern Jiangsu Province, and northern Zhejiang Province. Jiangsu Province had been a development area that many state-owned enterprises were located because of advantageous geographical conditions and infrastructure and resources. Shanghai one of four municipalities of China, a part of Jiangsu, is the most developed region in China because of not only rich in incredible talent but also taking the initiative of national preferential policies. In 1990, Shanghai Pudong New Area and many other industrial

[7]Kika (2006) p. 171.

[8]Zhu (2003) p. 19.

development Zone were established. While Pudong New Zone was advanced as a financial center in China, Chinese government attracted foreign investment to the industrial park in Shanghai.

Under the low-price competition of PC market began in the 1990s, Taiwanese ODMs faced the price competition. Moreover, as the price of notebook PCs reduced, brand companies required Taiwanese PC companies to relocate the production process in China for cost reduction and mass production.[9] Since 2001, Taiwan government accepted the investment of notebook PCs, LCD (Liquid Crystal Display) and semiconductor in China. Hence, since 2002 Taiwanese PC companies relocated, the production process of notebook PCs form Taiwan to Yangtze River Delta. Especially, many Taiwanese PC companies concentrated in Suzhou of Yangtze River Delta.

Suzhou of Yangtze River Delta

Suzhou was a favorable location for Taiwanese PC companies because of the geographical condition being less than 100 km to Shanghai and the cheap labor compared to Shanghai. We can see that the initial condition of Suzhou is similar to that of Dongguan with cheap labor and nearby the core area which has port for export. However, the difference was that in Suzhou, Taiwanese PC companies are mainly big companies producing high-tech products such as notebook PCs and semiconductors.

Moreover, until 2001, the group relocation of Taiwanese PC companies and component suppliers also relocated to Suzhou for considering the procurement of parts that were inefficient in China in the initial stage.[10] In 1993, BenQ, a subsidiary of Taiwanese PC companies Acer, relocated in Suzhou accompanied with 14 related parts suppliers for the production of monitor. In 1995, Compal relocated the monitoring factory in Suzhou accompanied with 30 parts suppliers. Afterward, many Taiwanese PC-related parts suppliers relocated to Suzhou from Pearl River Delta. Therefore, notebook PCs industry was formed rapidly in Suzhou after the investment of notebook PCs to China was lifted in 2002.

In this way, many major PC companies and parts suppliers relocated in Suzhou, by 2012, the top 10 notebook PC ODMs in Taiwan, top 20 listed companies, and 5 of top 10 IC chip companies had located in Suzhou and IT companies exceeded 3000. In addition, Suzhou's export value was 153.1 billion dollars (half of the export value in Jiangsu) and 82.1% of which was electronic goods.

4.2.3.3 Comparison of Relocating to Both Regions Common Features

In relocation of Taiwanese PC companies in the Pearl River Delta and Yangtze River Delta, ODMs tended to relocate in China in collaboration with parts suppliers. In a word, Taiwanese PC companies located to China with the upstream and downstream

---

[9]For example, Dell requested Taiwanese ODMs to relocate to China for mass production as part of low-price strategy.

[10]Seki (2005) p.100.

enterprises. As a result, in China, Taiwanese PC industry integration was formed in the short period and the localization rate of PC parts was high.

However, why Taiwanese PC companies chose the group movement to China? There are three reasons considered which are as follows.

The first is the relationship between Taiwanese Companies and brand companies in the international production network of notebook PC. As already discussed, Taiwanese ODMs became the PC manufacturer because of competitive edge at cost and speed. To maintain the cost and speed competitive edge, ODMs had to locate nearby parts suppliers, thus ODMs relocated in China accompanied with part suppliers to maintain their position in the international production network.

The second is a close network between in Taiwanese PC industry. As mentioned in Sect. 4.2.2.2, vertical and horizontal network structure was formed in Taiwanese PC industry, due to this, there are many parts suppliers who tended to follow ODMs to China.

The third is the economic relations between China and Taiwan. From 1990 to 2001, direct investment was not allowed between China and Taiwan and trade had to be carried out via a third country such as Hong Kong. Due to this, if only ODMs relocated to China, parts procurement must only be imported via the third country and this caused inefficiency of production.

In this sense, group movement of Taiwanese PC companies was a reasonable action that took effect to maximize profit and minimize costs of companies. In other words, it also can be said that Taiwanese PC companies tended to relocate to China in a reasonable action under the restraint of PC market and institutions between China and Taiwan.

Difference

First, the background of the group relocation is different. Background of relocating to Pearl River Delta was because of the strict regulation between China and Taiwan, and the cost was reduced by group relocation. On the other hand, the background of relocating to Yangtze River Delta was to respond to brand companies' request and create a more flexible production system.

Next, the initial conditions of both regions are different. To maintain the production cost and the shipment speed, highly functional economic development zone is important to Taiwanese PC companies. Compared to Pearl River Delta, Yangtze River Delta was the government-led industrial cluster and the national level economic development zone was established in the 1990s in Suzhou. In 1994, Suzhou Industrial Park Comprehensive Customs Zone had integrated the three functions of China's first anhydrous bonded port, bonded area, bonded logistics center, and export processing zone.[11] In contrast, provincial level industrial park finally established in Dongguan. Therefore, provision of economic development zone with high export convenience by the government was attractive to Taiwanese PC companies which emphasis on speed.

[11] JETRO (2011) p. 255.

On the human resources side, there are many advanced human resources in Yangtze River Delta. Desktop PCs are modular products, while assembly of notebook PCs is more difficult for many parts that are not standardized. Moreover, notebook PCs need both development and manufacture in order to make motherboards in-house and make the shape compact. Therefore, human resources of development are necessary for the production of notebook PC. In addition, researchers are required for the manufacture and development of high-tech parts such as semiconductors. Due to this, the concentration of advanced human resources in Yangtze River Delta, the most development region in China, is another appeal for Taiwanese PC companies.

Furthermore, there is also an element on the demand side. On the market side, not only the export market but also demand for PC in China was expected to increase. Taiwanese PC companies had the merit of being able to respond to the expansion of domestic market by locating desktop PCs manufacturing in Pearl River Delta in south China while expanding the base of notebook PCs in Yangtze River Delta in the north.

In this way, as a request to tighten shipping speed and cost by 2000, Taiwanese PC companies relocated in Yangtze River Delta for maintaining competitive advantage, accessing domestic market and the expansion of production base in China.

4.3 Relocation from Coastal Area to Inland in China

4.3.1 Relocation of the Major Taiwanese ODMs in China

4.3.1.1 Location of the Four Major Taiwanese ODMs

First, we consider the location situation of Taiwanese ODMs in China. According to Table 4.2, PC manufacturing department of ODMs is mainly concentrated in the western region. Since 2010, many ODMs moved PC production processing and R&D department from Yangtze River Delta to the western region. However, core parts suppliers also concentrated on Yangtze River Delta and other peripheral parts suppliers widely deployed in China.

Table 4.2 also shows us the division of labor between regions of major Taiwanese ODMs. In other words, western regions, Chongqing and Chengdu, are PC production bases, and Shanghai and Suzhou, in coastal area, are PC sales bases, R&D, and manufacturing base for new products and service of Taiwanese ODMs. Thereby, Taiwanese ODMs not only located PC manufacturing to Chongqing and Chengdu but also developed new product and service other than PC. As the reasonable behaviors of Taiwanese PC companies, it is thought that major ODMs are conducting regional division of labor by maximizing the superiority of each region and maximizing profits. Why did Taiwanese PC ODMs had the change in location and their business fields? We shall present an overview of the situation of the Taiwanese ODMs from 2000 to 2010.

Table 4.2 Relocation of major Taiwanese ODMs in China

Regions	City	Quanta	Compal	Wistron	Pegatron
North	Beijing	Service (Communication)		Sales (Electronic communication product)	Mfg./Sales (Electronic products)
Yangtze River Delta	Shanghai	Service (Communication)		Sales (PC)	R&D/Sales (Electronic communication product)
	Kunshan (Class city of Suzhou)		CS/Sales (PC)	R&D (Electronic products)	Mfg. (Server/Drive/Satel equipment
	Suzhou	Mfg./Sales (Electronic products)			Sales (Printed board)
	Nanjing		R&D (Hard Software)		R&D/Mfg. (Digital products)
South	Zhang shan			R&D/Sales (Monitor/parts)	
West	Chongqing	Mfg./Sales (PC)	Mfg./R&D (PC)	Mfg. (PC)	Mfg./R&D (PC/parts communication product)
	Chengdu		Mfg./R&D (PC/Tablet)	Mfg. (PC)	

Source Annual Report of Taiwanese ODMs
Note Mfg. is manufacturing, CS is customer service

4.3.1.2 Background of Four Major Taiwanese ODM Companies Relocating to Chongqing

First, we shall take a look at the role of the major Taiwanese ODMs in the production of notebook PC in the world. Major Taiwanese ODMs are Quanta, Compal, Pegatron, Wistron, Inventec, and Foxconn. In 2010, the year began relocating to west, shipment volume of Taiwanese ODMs accounted for 97.4% of the worldwide shipments, the proportion of each major ODM company was 27.8% for Quanta, 26.2% for Compal, 15.2% for Wistron, 8.6% for Inventec, 8.2% for Pegatron, and 6.4% for Foxconn. The total of 6 major Taiwanese ODMs was more than 90% of Taiwan and more than 80% of world's share in 2010. Therefore, the trend of these ODMs is representative of the trend of Taiwanese PC companies. Due to the restriction of data of Inventec

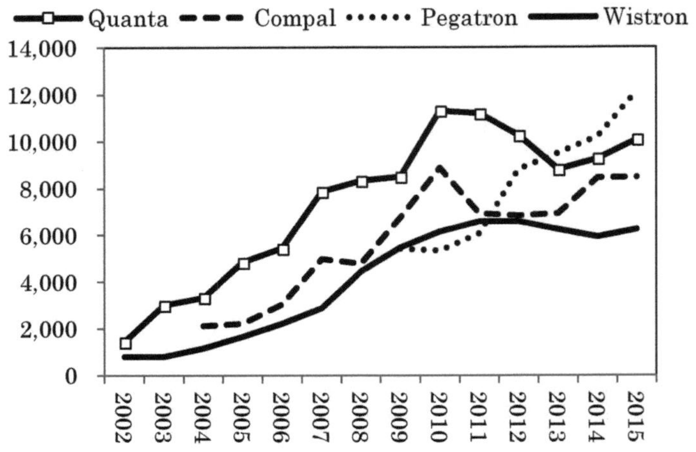

Fig. 4.5 Changes in sales of 4 major Taiwanese ODMs (Billion Taiwan Dollars). *Source* Annual Report of Taiwanese ODMs

and Foxconn, we focus on the other four major Taiwanese ODMs to look at the background of relocation to the western region.

After the financial crisis, production structure changed in PC market. Demand for iPad released from 2010 increased sharply and the mainstream of the PC market tended to change the product with high technology. In this way, it began to enter the post PC era and demand for PCs that expanded to date had declined from 2012. Under such circumstances, Taiwanese ODMs were greatly influenced.

First, we consider the fluctuation of sales of the four major Taiwanese ODMs. Figure 4.5 shows us that except Pegatron other three ODMs tended to decrease after 2010.[12] However, sales of Quanta and Compal tended to recover from 2013, and sales of Wistron was still sluggish. Pegatron was contrary to the other three ODMs, and sales continued to grow since 2010.

Next, we consider the fluctuation of profits of the four major Taiwanese ODMs. As shown in Fig. 4.6, profits of three ODMs except Quanta declined from 2010. Pegatron recovered in 2011, Compal and Wistron recovered from 2013. Profit of Quanta repeated the decrease and recovery from 2009 to 2015. On the other hand, profit of Pegatron grew rapidly from 2011.

Overall, sales and profits of Taiwanese ODMs declined around 2010, however, Pegatron was considered to have less impact from the financial crisis than the other 3 ODMs.

Under the influence of the global financial crisis, it seems that Taiwanese ODMs faced difficulties since 2010 and needed some change to stay in business. Taiwanese ODMs implemented two types of countermeasures to recover profits. One was to further reduce the production cost while expanding the conventional PC business,

[12]Pegatron is an independent company from the manufacturing department of PC brand company ASUS.

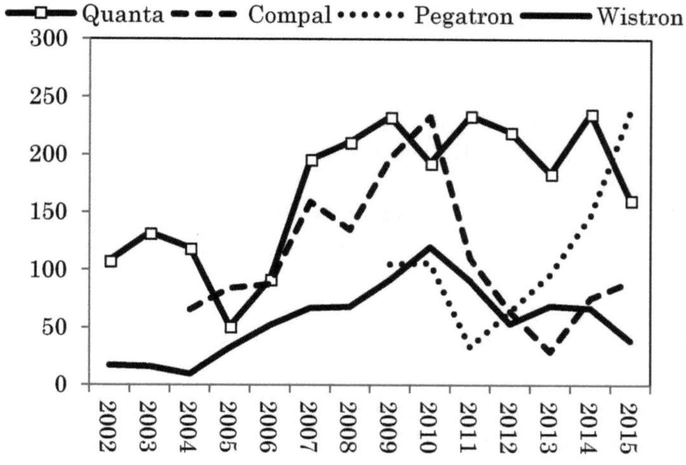

Fig. 4.6 Changes in profit of 4 major Taiwanese ODMs (Billion Taiwan Dollars). *Source* Annual Report of Taiwanese ODMs

another is to develop new business other than PC manufacturing.[13] According to Table 4.2, Pegatron launched the non-PC manufacturing business at an early stage than other three ODMs, that was why Pegatron had less impact from the financial crisis and recovered rapidly.

4.3.2 Factors to Relocate Taiwanese ODMs to Chongqing

4.3.2.1 Chongqing's Economy[14]

Chongqing is the upper reaches of the Yangtze River and the junction of midland and west China. Due to the development of traffic infrastructure, Chongqing is the only water, land, and air transport network region in the upper reaches of Yangtze River and the transport center of southwest China. The area of Chongqing is 82,400 km^2 (2.4 times the total of Beijing, Shanghai, and Tianjin), although the central district is 647 km^2, and administration units include total 19 wards and 19 counties. In 2013, the population of Chongqing is 29.1 million, however, 12.1 million people reside in rural areas. Chongqing is the city with the largest population and the most administrative units in China. In 1997, Chongqing became the fourth municipality directly under the central government and the other three are Beijing, Shanghai, and Tianjin. Since

[13]There are statements that "Put more emphasis on reducing production costs" (2009) and "Reduce production and transportation costs to the utmost" (2010) in Annual Report of Quanta.

[14]In this paper, we focus on location of Taiwanese in Chongqing for the reason that most of the Taiwanese ODMs located in Chongqing and Chongqing is the backward region compared to Chengdu.

2000, Chongqing developed rapidly as the important area of Western Development Policy.

In 2014, GDP per capita of Chongqing was 47,850 yuan ($US7,788), while the national average was 46,507 yuan ($US7,570). Chongqing exceeded the national average for the first time in 2012. The disparity between Chongqing (west) and other three municipalities (coast) was still significant. In 2014, GDP per capita of Shanghai and Beijing were 97,370 yuan ($US15,849) and 99,995 yuan ($US16,276). Thus, Chongqing was relatively a backward region compared to the other municipalities.

4.3.2.2 Process for Relocating Taiwanese Firms to Chongqing

The relocation of notebook PC's Taiwanese ODMs to Chongqing began with the investment by Hewlett-Packard (HP) in 2009. In 2009, Chongqing government obtained information that HP was planning to increase 40 million notebook PCs for the world market to recover the economic crisis. Therefore, Chongqing government proceeded negotiation with HP to present conditions for the construction of infrastructure for export, compensation for distribution cost, and guarantee 80% local procurement of parts for the establishment of HP production of notebook PC and orders for 40 million PC. In this way, Chongqing succeeded in getting the order from HP. Since then, Chongqing government attracted Taiwanese major ODMs with the order of HP, and as a result, Foxconn and Inventec and Qunata began to relocate to Chongqing since 2010.

In 2011, Acer the Taiwanese brand company located to Chongqing with Wistron, Compal, Pegatron[15] (Table 4.3). According to Table 4.3, under a competitive relationship between PC brand companies and a collaboration between PC brand companies and ODMs, Taiwanese ODMs relocated to Chongqing in a short period of time.

In addition, group movement between Taiwanese ODMs and parts suppliers also happened in relocation to Chongqing. For example, Wistron moved to Chongqing followed with 15 parts suppliers including battery, loudspeakers, and chassis. In 2012, about 300 parts suppliers contract with Quanta planned to transfer production process to Chongqing and about 60 already started production in the same year.

Thus, accumulation of notebook PC manufacturing industry was formed by 5 PC brand companies, 6 Taiwanese ODMs, and 875 parts suppliers by the end of 2014. As a result, there was a rapid increase in production of the notebook in Chongqing since 2011. Table 4.4 shows us evidently that production volume of Chongqing and Chengdu grew rapidly and exceeded that of Shanghai and Jiangsu in 2014. In 2014, production volume of notebook PC in Chongqing was 63.4 million of which exports were 58.5 million (92.3%). According to Table 4.4, it is clear that Taiwanese ODMs moved to Chongqing and Chengdu in short time and made Chongqing–Chengdu region become the second notebook PC production base in China.

[15]Quanta sells to HP, Lenovo, Acer, Dell. Compal sells to Acer, Dell and Lenovo. Wistron sells to Acer and Lenovo. Pegatron sells to ASUS and Acer.

Table 4.3 Location of Taiwanese ODMs and PC brand companies in Chong Qing and Chengdu

Time	Chongqing	Chengdu
2009.8	HP (brand)	
2009.8	Foxconn (Mfg. PC)	
2009.10		Foxconn (electronic product)
2009.12	Inventec	
2010.1	Qunata	
2010.9		Dell (brand)/Compal
2010.10		Lenovo (brand)
2010.11		Wistron
2010.12	Acer (brand)	
2011.1	Pegatron	
2011.4	ASUS (brand)	
2011.5	Wistron	
2011.6	Compal	

Source Based on newspaper report

Table 4.4 Regional production of Notebook PC in China

Region	Brand company	ODMs	Production (million unit)			
			2014	2013	2012	2011
Shanghai	Lenovo, HP, ASUS	Quan, Inven, Pega	44.7	61.9	73.0	89.5
Jiangsu	Samsung, Acer, Hasee	Wis, Com, Pega	61.4	68.3	74.9	89.0
Chongqing	HP, Acer, ASUS	Quan, Inven, Wis, Com, Fox	63.5	54.7	40.3	24.1
Chengdu	Lenovo, Dell	Wis, Com	74.3	59.2	43.8	23.6

Source Intelligence Research Group, www.zhiyan.org
Note 1 Full name of ODMs refer to note of Table 4.1
Note 2 The data is the total of notebook PC and tablet PC and data of Chengdu is mostly production of tablet PC

4.3.2.3 Factors to Move the Computer Industry into Chongqing

The question we should ask is that why Taiwanese ODMs relocated to Chongqing so fast. As mentioned in Sect. 4.3.2.1 that Chongqing is relatively backward region compared to coastal region. Why Taiwanese ODMs relocated to the relatively backward region Chongqing in west China and not Southeast Asian countries? According to the relocation to the coastal area and the situation around 2010 of Taiwanese ODMs, let us suppose that the reason for Taiwanese ODMs' relocation to Chongqing was cost reduction. In 2010, GDP per capita of Chongqing was 4076 $US and that of Philippine and Vietnam was 2155 and 1297 $US.[16] It is clear that production cost in these regions was much cheaper than Chongqing. It seems that Taiwanese ODMs did not choose Philippine and Vietnam but choose Chongqing an inland region which is 2000 km from Shanghai (coast) was an unreasonable choice. It went against the behavior of the movement of Taiwanese PC companies in China. Therefore, there must be some other factors for Taiwanese ODMs of the relocation to Chongqing not only the cost.

In this section, we approach the factors of Taiwanese ODMs' relocation to Chongqing in both demand side and supply side.

Demand Side

As mentioned in Sect. 4.3.2.2 that Chongqing attracted HP and succeeded in locating notebook PC production base of 40 million. This attraction activity could be considered in "the exchange strategy of market and investment" by Chongqing government.[17] There were some exchange conditions that priority of access market in Chongqing, export infrastructure to European market, supplement the distribution cost, the guarantee of 80% locally procured parts. Furthermore, Chongqing government attracted Foxconn, Inventec and allocated 20 million, 10 million, and 10 million units to each order. On the other hand, Chongqing government required each ODM company promise to locate with parts supplier and establish research and development department in Chongqing.

There is a problem that why Chongqing government could guarantee 80% of local parts procured although there were not any PC industry sectors until 2009. The reason is that Chongqing government used the group relocation of Taiwanese PC companies by the experience of relocation to Yangtze River Delta. Hence, Chongqing government attracted Taiwanese ODMs by providing order from HP and required the group relocation with parts suppliers. Indeed, for Taiwanese ODMs which faced the difficult situation around 2010 (see Sect. 3.1.2), distribution of orders from the brand company by Chongqing government was attractive.

In this way, "the exchange strategy of market and investment" by Chongqing government was implemented successfully under the division of labor structure of Taiwanese PC industry and international production network.

Supply Side

However, even if there is demand, conditions on the supply side are cannot be ignored by Taiwanese ODMs which need to further reduce cost since 2010.

According to the location to Yangtze River Delta of Taiwanese ODMs, we shall pay attention to the cost and export convenience of Chongqing on the supply side.

(1) **Labor**

---

[16] World Economic Outlook Data bases http://www.imf.org/external/ns/cs.aspx?id=28.

[17] See Kin (2010).

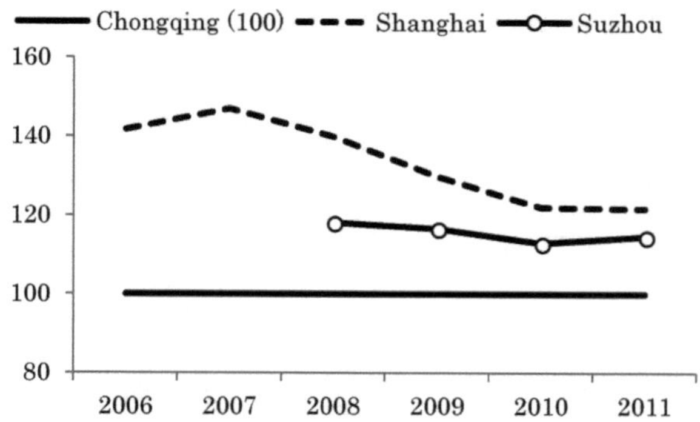

Fig. 4.7 Per capita average wage index of urban manufacturing industry in Chongqing, Shanghai and Suzhou. *Source* Chongqing Statistical Yearbook, Shanghai Yearbook, Jiangsu Statistical Yearbook

First, let us have a look at the condition of human recourses in Chongqing. As shown in Fig. 4.7, the difference between Chongqing and Yangtze River Delta in the average wage of city manufacturing tended to shrink, however, Chongqing was also nearly 20–30% cheaper than Shanghai and Suzhou. Traditionally, Taiwanese ODMs concentrated on Suzhou not only for low labor costs but also be able to use Shanghai's infrastructure and resources. However, as the average wage level of Yangtze River Delta increased in recent years in Suzhou, the pressure of labor costs increased for Taiwanese ODMs. In contrast, Chongqing's labor cost was nearly 20% cheaper than Suzhou, due to this cheap labor, Chongqing could be considered as a big attraction for Taiwanese ODMs.[18]

(2) **Industry Zone**

In Chongqing, industry zone which had the same function with Yangtze River Delta was constructed in 2008. Lianglucuntan Free Trade District includes both port and airport (He 2010). It is the third state-level economic development zone in China that was constructed after Shanghai Pudong and Tianjin Binghai. Lianglucuntan Free Trade Port locate in the center of Chongqing, nearby financial center area and also the starting point of logistics route, hence the logistics convenience of is high and logistics cost can be saved.

Moreover, resources of electricity, water, and natural gas in Chongqing are abundant and the price is cheaper than Yangtze River Delta. The total production cost is about 30% cheaper than Yangtze River Delta around in 2010.

(3) **Logistics**

Guarantee of logistics cost to the market was one of the conditions provided to HP by Chongqing government. In 2009, Chongqing government faced the logistics problem to international when attracted HP, due to this, Asian–Europe railroad passage was planned.[19] Until now the international freighting route from Chongqing used

[18]Deng et al. (2014) did a field study of human resources of PC manufacturing in Chongqing in detail.

[19]See Chongqing Government (2009).

Table 4.5 International trade passages

	Time (days)	Distance (km)	Route	Cost ($US)
New Eurasia railway	17	11,380	Chongqing–Kazakhstan–Russia– Belarus–Roland–Germany Duisburg	8,900
River and sea	40	22,000	Chongqing–(Yangtze River)–Shanghai-(Pacific)–Rotterdam in the Netherlands	4,000
Railway and sea	30	20,000	Chongqing–Myanmar–(Indian Ocean)–(Mediterranean Sea)–(Atlantic)–Rotterdam in Netherlands	5,900
Airway	1	8,126	Chongqing–Germany Duisburg	156,000

Source Chongqing Government (2011), and Xia et al. (2014)

waterway which is shown in Table 4.5 In 2009, the new Eurasia railway was planned and opened since 2011. Table 4.5 shows us that the new Eurasia railway takes less time than the waterway and the train-sea routes, moreover it is much cheaper than air transport.

Not only the new Eurasia railway was opened but also the airport in Chongqing was developed rapidly. In the attraction activity of Chongqing to HP, Chongqing government promised extended the runway by 400 meters so that Boeing 747 can take off and land at Chongqing's International Airport.

In this way, inland region Chongqing changed from region with poor geographical condition to the hub in western China and the hub between China and Europe by the geographical advantage that is closer to Europe than Shanghai. Since Chongqing became the new hub between China and foreign country, the potential of export convenience in Chongqing is getting close to that of Shanghai.

4.4 Concluding Remarks

In this chapter, we consider the relocation of Taiwanese PC companies from Taiwan to coastal region of China, and from coastal region to inland of China. Due to the changes in PC industry and the relationship between PC brand companies and Taiwanese ODMs, Taiwanese PC companies tended to relocate to the region with low production cost and export convenience for maintaining the competitive of cost and shipping speed. This point is found in the relocation of Taiwanese PC companies to Yangtze River Delta and Chongqing. However, the difference of twice relocation for Taiwanese PC companies is that the latter case is led by demand provided by Chongqing government. In summary, Chongqing government not only changed

Chongqing's geographical condition close to that of Yangtze River but also created demand for Taiwanese PC companies. That is the reason that Taiwanese PC companies related rapidly to Chongqing and made Chongqing became the PC production base as an inland region. This case gave a suggestion to the foreign investment attracting and industrial development of the inland region.

References

Asamoto, T. 2011. *Economic development of Taiwan: Formation process of catch-up type high-tech industry*. Tokyo: Keiso Shobo.

Chongqing Government. 2009. *National logistics industry coordination and promotion plan.* Government Document of Chongqing, No. 108.

Chongqing Government. 2011. *The 12th 5-year plan for domestic economy and society development of Chongqing*. Government Document of Chongqing, No. 108.

Deng, Z., X. Liang, and K. Kang. 2014. On the talent demand and training strategy of notebook computer industry. *China Information Management*, 17 (6):105–105.

He, Y. 2010. The policy of opening up markets was moved to inland: Development strategies and investment environment of Chongqing. *JC Economic Journal* 202: 30–33.

JETRO. 2011. *China data File*. Tokyo: Japan External Trade Organization.

Kin, J. 2010. *New development of Chongqing the engine of China Western Development Policy* (*China Research Report*, No. 136). Tokyo: Fujitsu Research Institute.

Kawakami, M. 1998. Inter-company disintegration and development of industry: Case of Taiwanese personal computer industry. *Asian economy* 39 (2): 2–28.

Kawakami, M. 2012. *Compressed industrial development: Growth mechanism of Taiwan notebook computer companies*. Nagoya University Press.

Kika, K. 2006. Multi-Level Economic Integration in East Asia: Cross-border production networks and industrial agglomeration in China. *Bulletin of Tokai University* 37: 161–180.

Seki, M. 2005. *Integration of Taiwan IT industry of Yangtze River Delta in China*. Tokyo: Shinhyoron.

Sun, Y. and Y. Taniguchi. 2015. Economic vitalization strategy of Chongqing, China. In *Firm's location selections and regional policy in the global economy*, ed. Ishikawa. T, 247–266. Japan: Springer.

Wang, Y., J. Luo, and X. Tong. 2003. Comparative analysis of Taiwanese PC industry in Dongguan and Suzhou. *Study Report of China Geological University* 3 (2): 6–10.

Xia, W., G. Jin, and S. Han. 2014. SWOT analysis of countermeasures in development of Chongqing-Xinjiang-Europe International Railway Logistics Line. *Logistics Technology* 33 (1): 1–4.

Yang, Y. 2000. The competitive advantage of personal computer industry in Taiwan. *Rokkondai Research Papers* 47 (1): 111–127. Kobe University.

Yang, Y. 2001. Industrial cluster of disintegration network in Taiwanese PC corporation. *Rokkondai Research Papers* 48 (2): 55–71. Kobe University.

Zhu, Y. 2003. *Development of Taiwan IT industry in China: development of investment and local production and impact on the world* (*Chinese Research Report,* No. 156). Tokyo: Fujitsu Research Institute.

Zhuang, X. 2004. *Management strategy of Taiwan IT industry: case of Acer*. Tokyo: Soseisya.

Chapter 5
Corporate Income Tax System as Location Factors: Case of Japan

Jumpei Ito

Abstract This chapter is a review of some impacts of corporate tax on location decision of MNEs in Japan. The corporate income tax system affects multinational corporations through various routes such as tax rates, tax base, and tax risk. Our issues can be summarized into three. The first is to observe the public data and to clarify the problems of the Japanese tax system. Second, how much Japanese multinationals care about tax issues. Lastly, how are the tax systems that determine the tax base affecting the location decision. In conclusion, it turns out that the tax system affects the location of multinationals through various channels, this finding indicates that, in order to realize relaxation of tax competition, it is necessary to examine from various viewpoints of taxation.

Keywords Corporate income tax · Location decision · Corporate tax asymmetries · International taxation · Transfer pricing regulations

5.1 Introduction

As corporate borderless transactions become more active, firm's tax avoidance behaviors have become more complicated. Established according to the purpose specific to each country, the tax system differs for each jurisdiction. This difference creates room for firms to transfer capital and profits internationally. The government will create new rules to fill the loophole of tax law which firms looking for and firms seek out new loopholes from that rule. This vicious spiral of governments and firms makes the tax system less transparent. What is important in such a situation is that each government cooperates to design a corporate tax system that lesser the opportunity of tax avoidance by firms. Therefore, it is necessary to make guidelines on how to implement corporate tax reform that does not create distortion of international

J. Ito (✉)
College of Community Studies, Shukutoku University, Chiba, Chiba, Japan
e-mail: junpei.ito@soc.shukutoku.ac.jp

T. Ishikawa (ed.), *Locational Analysis of Firms' Activities from a Strategic Perspective*, https://doi.org/10.1007/978-981-13-1684-5_5

capital allocation by clarifying the impact of a firm's international tax avoidance scheme.

Section 5.2 gives overviews of multinational activities and corporate income taxation status in Japan. Next, we discuss how much Japanese multinationals care about the tax issues in Sect. 5.3. In Sect. 5.4, we briefly review existing research on tax rate impact on location decision. And Sect. 5.5 discusses tax system of corporate tax asymmetries, international double taxation adjustment, and transfer pricing regulations. Section 5.6 briefly concludes.

5.2 MNEs and Tax System in Japan

Figure 5.1 shows the increase in foreign subsidiaries of Japanese firms and of outward FDI flows, and no big change at low level in inward FDI flows. This confirms that globalization of Japanese firms is progressing as in the other developed countries (see also Fig. 5.2), while the inflow of capital does not compensate for outflow.

In the context of international tax competition, government's interests are securing corporate tax revenue. Then, we will check how much tax base which is the target of tax revenue has been obtained. As shown Fig. 5.3, trend of taxable corporate income in Japan is not stable. It has been moving at a relatively high rate until the early 1990s. Along with the collapse of the bubble economy, it has shown a low percentage since the mid-1990s. And it has remained at a high level again except for around 2009 when the influence of the Lehman shock remarkably appeared.

While globalization becomes more active, corporate income tax (CIT) rate tends to decline. Japanese nominal CIT rate shows downward trend along with OECD trends (see Fig. 5.4). In addition, Fig. 5.4 also shows the transition of effective marginal tax rate (EMTR) calculated based on Devereux and Griffith (1998), which partially accounts for the impact of the tax base (e.g., depreciation allowance), and it is also

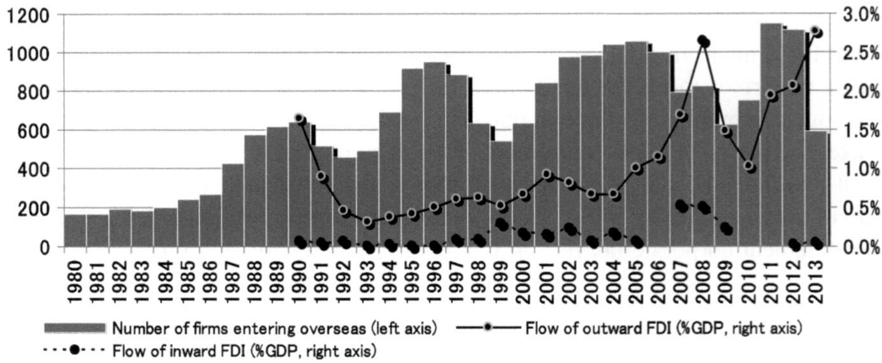

Fig. 5.1 Cross-border transactions of Japanese MNEs. *Source* Toyokeizai Shimposha, *A Directory of Japanese Firms' Foreign Investment*; OECD, *International Investment Statistics*

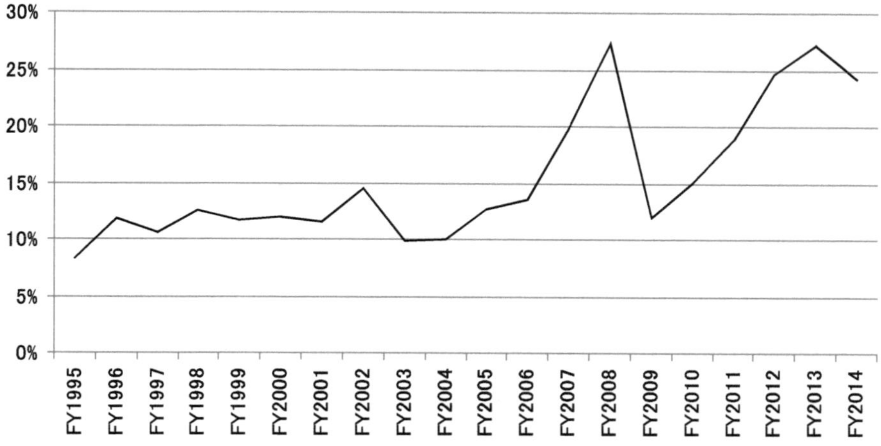

Fig. 5.2 Foreign capital investment ratio in Japan. *Source* METI, *Survey of Overseas Business Activity*

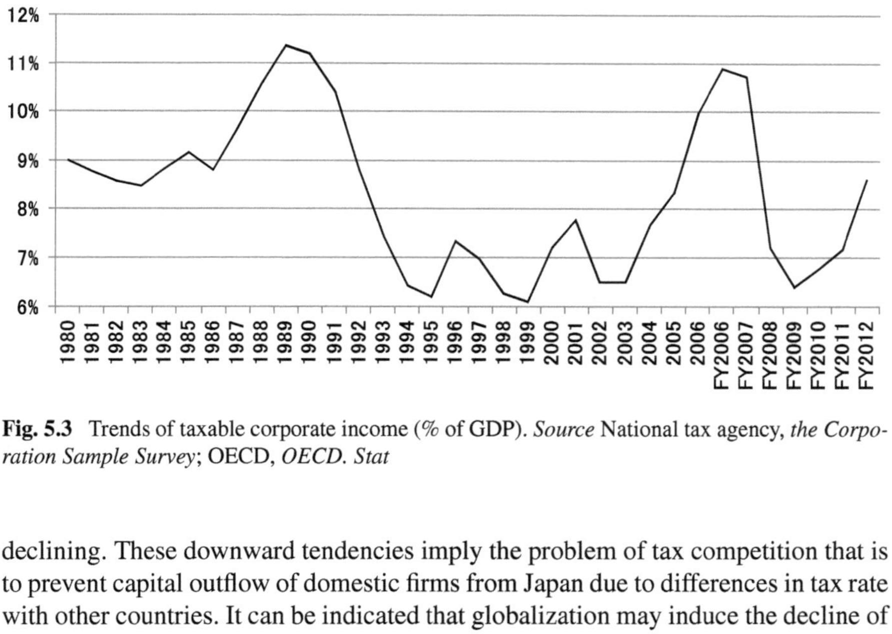

Fig. 5.3 Trends of taxable corporate income (% of GDP). *Source* National tax agency, *the Corporation Sample Survey*; OECD, *OECD. Stat*

declining. These downward tendencies imply the problem of tax competition that is to prevent capital outflow of domestic firms from Japan due to differences in tax rate with other countries. It can be indicated that globalization may induce the decline of tax revenue because of loss of taxable capital and decline of CIT rate.

Trends in CIT revenue per GDP are shown in Fig. 5.5. While the OECD average does not change greatly, CIT revenues in Japan show a gradual downward trend. Trend in Japan decreased to 3.1% in 2002, with the peak at 7.2% in 1988 during the bubble period. Since then, it has increased until 2007, it has declined to 2.6%, falling below the OECD average in 2009, since then it has increased. On the other hand, the OECD average is gradually increasing until the latter half of the 2000s, which is

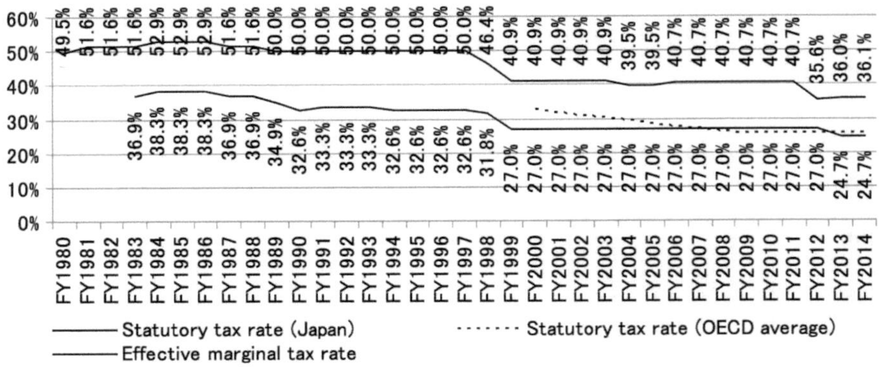

Fig. 5.4 Trends of CIT rate. *Source* PRI, *Financial Statistics of Japan*; OECD, *OECD Tax Database*; Oxford University Centre for Business Taxation, *CBT Tax Database*

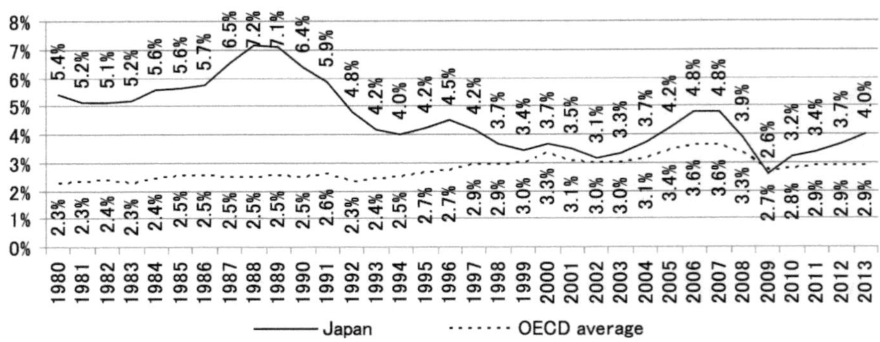

Fig. 5.5 Trends of CIT revenues (% of GDP). *Source* OECD, *OECD. Stat*

3.6% in 2007. And after the Lehman shock, it ranged from 2.7 to 2.9% and has not changed significantly.

It should be noted that level of Japanese CIT revenue has converged gradually to one of the OECD average, but as seen in Fig. 5.4, the tax rate still remains 10% higher than the OECD average. This may be because the expansion of Japanese tax base is quite smaller than that of other countries.

5.3 Are Firms Concerned with CIT?

Firms are able to transfer capital and the capital as a tax base will be lost from the domestic. Then, we will examine whether outflow of the tax base is attributable to the CIT system.[1] Table 5.1 shows the ranking of countries that the Japanese manufacturers cited as a potential location. And Fig. 5.6 is a summary of the number of

[1] Blonigen (2005) conduct detailed reviews on the factors of foreign location of firms.

Table 5.1 Ranking of countries cited as a potential location

	1st	2nd	3rd	4th	5th	6th	7th	8th	9th	10th
FY2005	China (393)	India (168)	Thailand (145)	Vietnam (126)	USA (96)	Russia (58)	Korea (51)	Indonesia (45)	Brazil (36)	Taiwan (31)
FY2010	China (394)	India (310)	Vietnam (165)	Thailand (132)	Brazil (126)	Indonesia (105)	Russia (75)	USA (58)	Korea (30)	Taiwan/Malaysia (29/28)
FY2015	India (171)	Indonesia (163)	China (162)	Thailand (128)	Vietnam (116)	Mexico (99)	USA (70)	Philippines (48)	Brazil (47)	Myanmar (34)

Note Values in parentheses are the number of responses
Source JBIC, *Report on Overseas Business Operations by Japanese Manufacturing Companies*

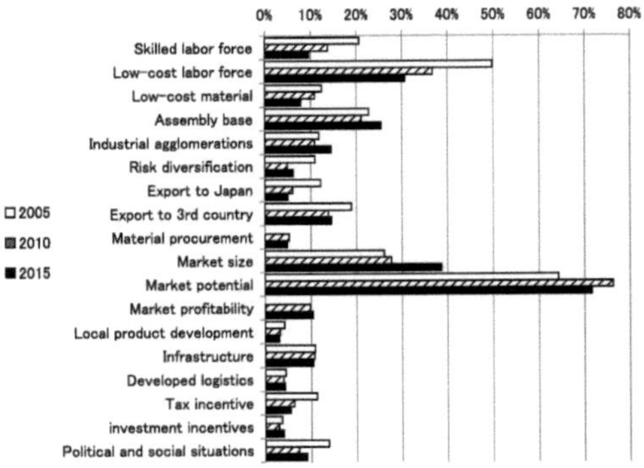

	2005	2010	2015
Skilled labor force	5 (9.8)	6 (9.3)	9 (19.6)
Low-cost labor force	2 (31.8)	2 (22.2)	3 (24.5)
Low-cost material	8 (10.7)	7 (13.4)	11 (9.6)
Assembly base	4 (1.6)	4 (2.2)	4 (5.6)
Industrial agglomerations	10 (3.1)	7 (15.9)	6 (10.1)
Risk diversification	12 (11.2)	15 (14.7)	12 (26.8)
Export to Japan	9 (10.3)	13 (8.5)	14 (11.8)
Export to 3rd country	6 (4.5)	5 (4.3)	5 (12.4)
Material procurement	-	14 (6.2)	15 (10.8)
Market size	3 (12.5)	3 (9.4)	2 (7.7)
Market potential	1 (0.9)	1 (0.2)	1 (0.2)
Market profitability	-	10 (8.8)	8 (4.9)
Local product development	15 (6.7)	17 (10.3)	18 (14.6)
Infrastructure	13 (23.6)	9 (21.4)	7 (18.9)
Developed logistics	14 (11.3)	16 (16.1)	16 (16)
Tax incentive	11 (6.8)	12 (17.8)	13 (21.8)
investment incentives	16 (3.8)	18 (4.9)	17 (5.7)
Political and social situations	7 (15.8)	11 (21)	10 (19.2)

Fig. 5.6 Reasons why the country is promising. *Notes* (1) The values on the left of the parentheses indicate the ranking in the promising 10 areas (11 areas in 2010). (2) Values in parentheses indicate standard deviation of response ranking in promising 10 areas (11 areas in 2010). *Source* JBIC, *Report on Overseas Business Operations by Japanese Manufacturing Companies*

answers of 18 reasons why the country you choose is promising. In this figure, the item with the most replies is the "market potential". In addition, since the standard deviation is extremely small compared to other items, it can be seen that firms have a large incentive to foreign location into market potential regardless of firm's characteristics. This practical result is consistent with knowledge of academic field that the market potential has a significant positive influence on the foreign location.[2]

Second, the items with many responses are "low-cost labor force" and "market size". "Low-cost labor force" has large standard deviation because the number of responses is biased towards developing countries. The response rate was the second highest response rate of 49.9% as of FY 2005, and it decreased to 3rd place to 30.6% in FY 2015. Then, respondents would have a great incentive to transfer downstream process of production to countries with low wages, as in the form of vertical direct investment. As for "market size", as of 2005, there were many responses, mainly in the developed countries including the United States, and the response rate was 26.0%, which is the 3rd place. With the rise of the Asian market, "market size" is increasingly important for companies in Asian region in FY 2015, and the response rate is positioned at second place, which is 38.7%. Incidentally, tax-related item is listed as "tax incentive". This ranks from the 11th place to the 13th place, and it is not so large. The response rate is decreasing from 11.3% in FY 2005 to 5.5% in FY 2015. For each country in Table 5.2, relative high response rates of "tax incentive" are in Southeast Asia region such as Thailand, the Philippines, and Myanmar, and since the response rate varies widely from region to region, the standard deviation is 21.8, which is a large value.

Next, we consider tasks in promising countries. Items with many responses in Fig. 5.7 are "highly competitive market", "increase in labor cost", "transparency of

[2]The impact of market potential on foreign activities is explained in detail in Bénassy-Quéré et al. (2005).

Table 5.2 Response rate of "tax incentive"

	India (%)	Indonesia (%)	Thailand (%)	Philippines (%)	Brazil (%)	Vietnam (%)	Malaysia (%)	Myanmar (%)	Mexico (%)	Russia (%)	China (%)	Taiwan	USA (%)	Korea (%)
2005	5.4	2.2	21.4	–	0.0	18.3	–	–	–	1.7	13.2	12.9	4.2	9.8
2010	2.6	1.9	15.9	–	5.6	8.5	25.0	–	–	6.7	6.3	0.0	1.7	3.3
2015	4.1	3.1	14.8	18.8	4.3	1.7	–	14.7	4.0	–	1.2	–	2.9	–

Source JBIC, *Report on Overseas Business Operations by Japanese Manufacturing Companies*

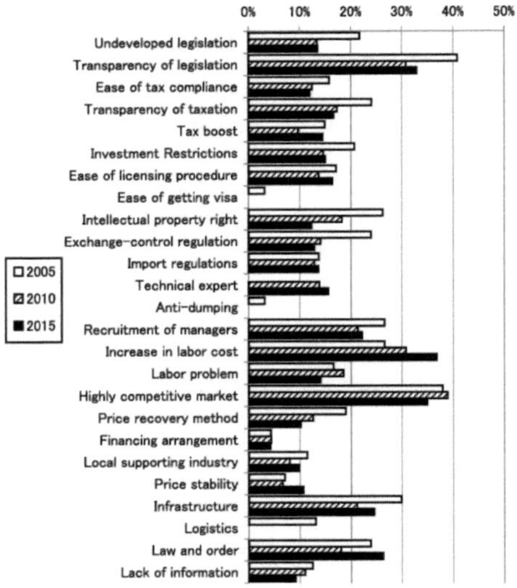

	2005	2010	2015
Undeveloped legislation	10 (30.5)	14 (20.3)	14 (22.3)
Transparency of legislation	1 (14.4)	2 (15.6)	3 (3.6)
Ease of tax compliance	15 (12.5)	17 (29.5)	17 (26.6)
Transparency of taxation	7 (12)	9 (6)	7 (6.1)
Tax boost	16 (72.1)	19 (50.5)	11 (24)
Investment Restrictions	11 (3.7)	10 (11.4)	10 (11.7)
Ease of licensing procedure	13 (13.2)	13 (9.9)	8 (11.1)
Ease of getting visa	23 (39.1)	-	-
Intellectual property right	6 (42.5)	7 (35.6)	16 (35.6)
Exchange-control regulation	8 (31.7)	11 (28)	15 (32)
Import regulations	17 (20)	15 (16.7)	13 (5.7)
Technical expert	-	12 (27.8)	9 (22.5)
Anti-dumping	23 (37)	-	-
Recruitment of managers	4 (21.8)	4 (15.5)	6 (15.5)
Increase in labor cost	4 (60.7)	2 (12.4)	1 (42.2)
Labor problem	14 (48.2)	6 (18.1)	12 (28)
Highly competitive market	2 (21.9)	1 (1.3)	2 (20.9)
Price recovery method	12 (38.5)	16 (22.6)	19 (28.8)
Financing arrangement	22 (23.8)	22 (24.9)	22 (11.4)
Local supporting industry	20 (20.5)	20 (11.3)	20 (32)
Price stability	21 (48)	21 (33.4)	18 (27.7)
Infrastructure	3 (29.8)	5 (26.4)	5 (35.6)
Logistics	18 (23.4)	-	-
Law and order	9 (39.9)	8 (40.5)	4 (31)
Lack of information	19 (57.4)	18 (30.6)	21 (29.4)

Fig. 5.7 Task in promising countries. *Source* JBIC, *Report on Overseas Business Operations by Japanese Manufacturing Companies*

legislation", "recruitment of managers", and "infrastructure". Many responses are given to market potential and labor costs which are similar to promising factors, but factors about infrastructure are also answered a lot. "Highly competitive market" maintained the response rate of 30% throughout the year, ranking first in 2010 and second in 2005 and 2015. And "increase in labor cost" increase gradually the response rate from 26.6% in FY2005 to 36.7% in FY2015. "Transparency of legislation" was the first in response rate at 40.8% in FY 2005, and decreased to the 30% level in FY 2010 and FY 2015 as it was improved. The response rate is maintained at the 20% level for "recruitment of managers". This item has little change in response rate over the years, and the response rate is not low in any country relatively. Then, it seems that securing human resources of manager class may be a chronic problem of foreign location wherever you choose. "Infrastructure" has been in the 20% range over the years and can be cited as a problem specific to developing countries. In China and India, the response rate is high, but in the developed countries such as the United States, South Korea, and Taiwan, the response rate is zero or close to zero.

From questionnaire results, it seems that the operation of the legislation can influence the decision on which country the company will enter. The items listed as tasks of tax legislation are "ease of tax compliance", "transparency of taxation", and "tax boost". "Ease of tax compliance" has been moving at the 10% level throughout the observation period, ranked 15th in FY 2005, 17th in FY 2010 and FY 2015. As shown in Table 5.3, the response in developed countries is low and in emerging countries such as India and Brazil is high. "Transparency of taxation" also has less response in developed countries, and high response in developing countries (see Table 5.4). And it is ranked relatively high position as well as "transparency of legislation" at 7th or

9th over the period. Then, development of several legal systems should be important factor of location decision. "Tax boost" responded about 14% in FY 2005 and FY 2015, and 9.6% in FY 2010. And the ranking has risen to 11th place in FY 2015, contributing the increase in response rate of 27.7% in China (see Table 5.5).

Overall, most of tax issues such as tax preference and the complexity of the system are not major obstacles to foreign location of firms, but uncertainties such as transparency and movements of tax boost have relatively high impacts. The lack of transparency may increase risk of additional taxation for firms which engage in tax avoidance. Movement of tax boost is also risk in that companies do not know how much to pay tax in advance. The uncertainty of the tax system creates a difference in interpretation between the taxation system of the government and the firm, and creates the risk that it may incur additional taxation beyond what was assumed by tax planning. According to Ernst and Young (2013), the issue that companies should emphasize most in transfer pricing operations is not the reduction of tax burden itself such as "effective tax rate optimization" or "cash tax optimization" but is a result that it is "tax risk management" (Table 5.6). As a result, it is conceivable that the tax system has a negative incentive in entering foreign market, and the most important concern is minimization of tax risks which are emerged in tax planning.

5.4 Impact of CIT Rate on Capital Movement

As mentioned above, governments tend to reduce corporate income tax burden in response to international tax competition. And, what each government should pay attention to is the impact of corporate income tax burden on firm's foreign location or FDI. As for this concern, there are many academic accumulations starting with Hartman (1984). De Mooij and Ederveen (2005) analyzed the tax rate elasticity of 427 obtained from existing empirical studies about the tax impact on FDI and resulted that direct investment shows a reaction of about −4% at a change of 1% of CIT rate. Also, at de Mooij and Ederveen (2005), it is confirmed that the tax rate elasticity is higher when using the Devereux–Griffith type effective tax rate than the nominal CIT rate in analyzing; especially, Devereux–Griffith type effective average tax rate is the highest value.

Since Devereux and Griffith (1998), the Devereux–Griffith type effective tax rate (effective marginal tax rate and effective average tax rate) has been applied in many studies on the impact of corporate income taxation on international capital flows. The effective tax rate used for empirical analysis can be categorized as backward-looking measure or forward-looking measure, and the Devereux–Griffith type effective tax rate is the latter one. Backward-looking measure is an index to calculate the effective tax burden using revenue data or financial data that was already recorded, while forward-looking measure is that an index to virtually obtain the effective tax burden paid when performing an investment project according to the local tax rule. According to Devereux (2007), backward-looking measure is affected by (1) past investment, (2) tax burden from multiple tax jurisdictions, (3) losses, and (4) past

Table 5.3 Response rate of "ease of tax collection"

	India (%)	Indonesia (%)	Thailand (%)	Philippines (%)	Brazil (%)	Vietnam (%)	Malaysia (%)	Myanmar (%)	Mexico (%)	Russia (%)	China (%)	Taiwan (%)	USA (%)	Korea (%)
2005	18.1	17.9	5.8	–	20.0	8.5	–	–	–	15.2	24.5	0.0	0.0	0.0
2010	24.5	4.1	5.5	–	21.7	4.5	0.0	–	–	7.0	12.7	0.0	3.8	0.0
2015	30.2	14.9	4.2	2.3	20.0	7.3	–	3.0	8.9	–	8.2	–	0.0	–

Source JBIC, *Report on Overseas Business Operations by Japanese Manufacturing Companies*

Table 5.4 Response rate of "transparency of taxation"

	India (%)	Indonesia (%)	Thailand (%)	Philippines (%)	Brazil (%)	Vietnam (%)	Malaysia (%)	Myanmar (%)	Mexico (%)	Russia (%)	China (%)	Taiwan (%)	USA (%)	Korea (%)
2005	21.3	23.1	7.8	–	16.7	14.9	–	–	–	21.7	40.0	8.0	0.0	9.1
2010	16.3	10.2	6.3	–	15.0	11.5	0.0%	–	–	18.3	31.8	7.1	0.0	3.3
2015	24.1	22.1	5.1	9.1	22.2	16.4	–	15.2%	11.1	–	22.6	–	0.0	–

Source JBIC, *Report on Overseas Business Operations by Japanese Manufacturing Companies*

Table 5.5 Response rate of "tax boost"

	India (%)	Indonesia (%)	Thailand (%)	Philippines (%)	Brazil (%)	Vietnam (%)	Malaysia (%)	Myanmar (%)	Mexico (%)	Russia (%)	China (%)	Taiwan (%)	USA (%)	Korea (%)
2005	6.3	5.1	16.5	–	3.3	4.3	–	–	–	4.3	21.8	24.0	19.2	12.1
2010	5.4	5.1	4.7	–	6.7	2.6	12.0	–	–	2.8	22.0	0.0	5.8	10.0
2015	14.2	17.5	9.3	13.6	11.1	6.4	–	3.0	10.0	–	27.7	–	12.9	–

Source JBIC, *Report on Overseas Business Operations by Japanese Manufacturing Companies*

Table 5.6 Highest priorities in transfer pricing strategy (parents)

	2007 (%)	2010 (%)	2012 (%)
Tax risk management	50	50	66
ETR optimization	22	18	11
Cash tax optimization		7	6
Alignment with management/operational objectives	18	20	14
Performance measurement	7	5	1
None of these	3	0	1

Source Ernst and Young (2013)

taxes. Because profits and tax burdens required for calculation are affected by past investment and capital stock, there is a possibility of generating serious endogenous bias when estimating capital movements by backward-looking measure. Due to these problems of backward-looking measure, Devereux–Griffith type forward-looking measure has been used in many previous studies on the impact of corporate income tax on capital movements. However, even Devereux–Griffith type measure has a problem that it is computed under the strong assumption to avoid complexity of calculation. Then, Devereux–Griffith type measure cannot sufficiently capture the impact of the system which decide tax base. Therefore, in order to measure the effect of the details of tax system, it is necessary to observe with a variable different from Devereux–Griffith type.

5.5 Impact of Corporate Tax Base on Capital Movement

How are the systems that determine the tax base affecting international capital flows? In this regard, we focus on three issues of tax treatment of loss, taxing method of foreign source income, and transfer pricing regulations. First, we consider the tax treatment of losses. The deficit can be offset against positive income by carryforward deduction or carryback refund at the time different from when it is recorded. Since negative income can be offset with some limits, not all tax losses are subject to tax refund as negative income. Due to these restrictions, effective tax rate is different between positive income and negative income, creating corporate tax asymmetries.

According to the average tax rate measured by Auerbach and Poterba (1987) and Auerbach (2007), it is found that the less negative taxation due to insufficient tax refund was the biggest factor to raise the average tax rate. Then, tax treatment of losses has a major influence on the substantial tax burden of companies and it is thought that it may influence the choise of whether the jurisdiction is suitable for location. In this context, there are few previous studies. Dreßler and Overesch (2013) analyze whether the tax treatment of losses will affect the investment of German multinational corporations. Dreßler and Overesch (2013) clarify that the offsetting system of loss among group companies promotes investment and the tax loss carryforward system lowers the tax rate elasticity for investment. This result suggests that the tax treatment of losses affects international capital flows. However, it is not clear that the detailed information of regulations such as the deadline and limit of carryforward/carryback are influential on location decision.

Second, how to tax foreign source income affects the after-tax profit of the business groups as whole. When foreign subsidiaries repatriate profits to the parent, how much tax is imposed on profits depends on whether jurisdiction is in accordance with residence principle or source principle. Under residence principle, governments generally adopt foreign tax credit method which means profit tax in home country and tax paid abroad is creditable. Under source principle, in contrast, it is suitable to adopt foreign income exemption method which treats foreign source income as not taxable.

Hartman (1984), Boskin and Gale (1987), and Young (1988) analyze the influence of inward foreign direct investment on the after-tax rate of return in the US which adopts the foreign tax credit method. Slemrod (1990) tried to analyze that the influence of tax on FDI varies depending on whether foreign tax credit method or foreign income exemption method, but clear differences could not be found.

Bénnasy-Quéré et al. (2005) also examined whether the impact of bilateral direct investment on the corporate tax rate varies depending on the adjustment method adopted by the investing country. As a result, when the home country adopts a foreign tax credit method, difference in bilateral tax rates has a significant influence on FDI only if the difference is sufficiently large. And when adopts foreign income exemption system, it is demonstrated that investment incentives for low tax rate countries will increase. This result leads to the suggestion that the influence of corporate tax rate on direct investment varies depending on how the home country sets up the double taxation adjustment method. From these results, it is considered that companies located in countries that adopt foreign tax credit method are more limited than direct investment in low tax rate countries compared to countries that adopt foreign income exemption method. In Japan, 2009 tax reforms have changed from foreign tax credit method to foreign income exemption method. If we inherit the results of Bénnasy-Quéré et al. (2005), the 2009 tax reform will promote foreign direct investment.

Third, it is worth considering that the impact of transfer pricing regulations on capital flows. Multinational companies have incentives to transfer profits from high tax rate countries to low tax rate countries by selling intermediate goods among group companies with transfer price which lower than the market price, because such transfer maximize the after tax profits of the group of companies. Setting transfer pricing regulations severely, the government can prevent firms' transfer of profit and prevent the hollowing out of capital, while lenient regulations will attract firms without lowering tax rates. In the survey of Luckhaupt et al. (2012), research on transfer pricing taxation is roughly divided into two categories. One is the study of whether opportunities for tax planning arise due to differences in bilateral tax rates, which will lead to profit transfer. The other is how the existence of transfer pricing affects double taxation risk and tax administration costs. Regarding the study of profit transfer, Grubert and Mutti (1991) analyzed whether erosion of tax base in high-tax countries is realized due to the transfer of profits to low-tax countries, measured by the impact on profitability, direct investment, and trade pattern. As a result, it was revealed that the effect of the transfer of profits was confirmed for each explanatory variable. Hines and Rice (1994) analyzed the impact of taxation on profit, capital, and labor on US companies located in tax haven, revealing that capital and labor are inversely correlated with the magnitude of the tax rate. Huizinga and Leaven (2008) analyzed how the difference in CIT rate between parent and subsidiaries or among subsidiaries affects profit shifting. It showed that the tax rate difference among subsidiaries significantly affects the transfer of profits as well as between parent and subsidiaries. As mentioned above, there is academic accumulation as to how the transfer pricing influences corporate behavior. However, there are still few researches on what kind of regulations influence corporate behavior, and it is not clear what effect the transfer pricing regulations have on capital flows.

5.5.1 *Impact of Corporate Tax Asymmetries on Location Decision*

The influence of carryforward and carryback on investment has been studied by Devereux et al. (1994), and Edgerton (2010). However, there are still unclear points about the effect of companies on international capital flows in these researches. Since how much losses can be offset with income is depending on different rules established each country, the rules of losses may affect borderless location decision because of tax system arbitrage. Therefore, in this section, we will examine the influence of the tax loss carryforward rule on the company's international location decision.[3]

Table 5.7 summarizes the rules from 2009 to 2014 on carryover and carryback deficits applicable when firms start their business overseas. For the carryover period (Table 5.7a), there is no major change throughout the observation period, and the number of countries with no period limitation is the largest. The second largest number is 5 years, then 3 years, and there are relatively many countries that have been set within a short period of five years or less. Most countries do not adopt the carryback deficit (Table 5.7b), and there is no country setting a long-term carryback period. There are few governments that have not set a period and are actively managing transfer losses.

In most cases, limits are restricted to carryforward or withdrawal of losses up to 100% of the positive earnings booked in that year, but in some countries even lower limits are set. Table 5.7c lists the number of countries for which the limit amount is set at less than 100% of income. Countries that have set quantitative limitation have a slightly increasing trend in both carryforward and carryback, but still only a few countries have adopted them. The country's carryforward period with a limit of less than 100% is summarized in Table 5.7d. Most countries have set a carryforward period of 5 years or indefinitely and only two countries have set a short period of

[3]This section is written based on Ito (2017).

Table 5.7 Treatment of carryforward and carryback

(a) Carryforward period

	2009	2010	2011	2012	2013	2014
None	5	6	6	6	5	5
2	0	0	0	1	1	1
3	17	16	17	18	19	20
4	5	6	7	6	7	7
5	41	36	40	41	41	44
6	5	5	4	4	4	5
7	3	5	4	3	4	3
8	2	3	3	3	1	1
9	2	2	2	3	3	3
10	6	9	10	10	10	11
12	0	0	0	0	0	1
15	1	1	1	0	0	0
18	0	0	0	1	1	1
20	5	6	6	6	6	6
No limit	44	44	44	43	45	44
Total	136	139	144	145	147	152

(b) Carryback period

	2009	2010	2011	2012	2013	2014
None	123	124	129	131	132	138
1	5	6	6	7	8	7
2	4	4	4	4	4	4
3	2	3	3	1	1	1
No limit	2	2	2	2	2	2
Total	136	139	144	145	147	152

(c) Limit amount

	2009	2010	2011	2012	2013	2014
Carryforward	11	11	11	14	17	18
Carryback	2	3	3	4	4	4
Observations	136	139	144	145	147	152

(d) Carryforward period with limit amount

	2009	2010	2011	2012	2013	2014
2	0	0	0	1	1	1
3	0	0	0	1	1	1
5	6	6	6	6	6	4
9	0	0	0	0	1	1
12	0	0	0	0	0	1
No limit	5	5	5	6	8	10
Total	11	11	11	14	17	18

Source Ernst and Young, *Worldwide Corporate Tax Guide*

Table 5.8 Estimation results

	I	II	III	IV
Statutory tax rate (Host country)	−0.581*** (0.116)	−0.517*** (0.141)		
EMTR (Japan)			−0.158 (0.162)	−0.086 (0.237)
EMTR (Host country)			−0.809*** (0.207)	−0.745*** (0.253)
GDP (Host country)	0.056*** (0.006)	0.054*** (0.007)	0.054*** (0.006)	0.053*** (0.007)
Constant	0.723 (0.539)	0.463 (0.66)	0.687 (0.545)	0.435 (0.688)
Observation	7748	4560	7748	4560
Log-likelihood	−3897.6	−2197.3	−3901.4	−2199.5

Notes [1]Standard deviation in parentheses, *significant at 10%, **significant at 5%, ***significant at 1%
[2]Estimated results of Japanese company dummy and time series dummy are omitted

3 years or shorter since 2012. In these two countries the offsetting system of deficit is severe. In Mongolia with a 2-year carryforward period, the carryforward deduction limit is 50% of the positive income. In order to completely offset the deficit with income in Mongolia, firms have to earn double the income of the deficit amount within 2 years.

There are countries that specially set a longer deadline for the carryover for establishments, and six countries set this special measure in 2014. It is considered that such preferential policies were designed with the intention of encouraging the establishment of new companies. Therefore, here we examine whether the length of the carryover period has an incentive to establish a new foreign subsidiary.

Shevlin (1990) and Graham (1996) calculated a unique marginal effective tax rate to observe how the existence of corporate tax asymmetry affects corporate tax burden. Ito (2017) measured the Shevlin-Graham type marginal effective tax rate as an explanatory variable representing the effect of corporate tax asymmetry on location decision in Japanese firm. Our binomial probit estimation employ foreign location dummy as dependent variable from firm-level data as Toyokeizai Shimposha "Kaigai Shinshutu Kigyo Soran (a directory of Japanese firms' foreign investment)". As a result of the estimation, it was revealed that the Shevlin-Graham type effective tax rate of host countries has a significant negative effect on the foreign location of firms. And the marginal effects of the effective tax rate are estimated to be −0.75 to −0.8, which is higher than that of the statutory tax rate (Table 5.8). Since the effective tax rate is an index obtained by deducting the effect of the asymmetry of corporate taxation from the nominal tax rate, the estimation result suggests that companies are affected by the asymmetry of corporate taxation.

5.5.2 Impact of Adjustment of International Double Taxation on FDI

Ito (2013, 2017) examine how the international double taxation adjustment method affects direct investment. Japan changed method of international double taxation adjustment from foreign tax credit to foreign income exemption in 2009 tax reform. Foreign income exemption method is a system that exempts 95% of the dividend gains received by the parent firm, which makes effectively out of scope of Japanese taxation on dividends from foreign subsidiaries (i.e., source principle). Then, before the 2009 tax reform corporate tax of host country affects subsidiaries only when they retained, but after the reform host country's taxation cover in both dividends and retained earnings. Although the previous studies in Japan on international location choice are mostly focused on tax rate itself, but there is little concern about the difference of the tax rate effect taking into account of international double taxation adjustment.

International Taxation Subcommittee (2008) surveyed the impact of system change to foreign income exemption method. According to this survey, the 2009 tax reform aims to promote foreign remittance to the domestic market, and make it funds for domestic investment in R&D and employment. In Tajika et al. (2014) and Hasegawa and Kiyota (2017), it is shown that tax reforms affected remittance to the domestic market when the demand for funds was high or the foreign retained income was large. Although it was proved that subsidiary remittance to the home country was prompted by tax reform, it is not demonstrated whether domestic investment will be promoted as the International Taxation Subcommittee (2008) asserts. Therefore, Ito (2013) analyzed how the system of international double taxation adjustment affects outward FDI. As a result, outward FDI was estimated to promote by 1% difference between host and home country's tax rate by changing to foreign dividend exclusion in 2009 (see Table 5.9). This result is the contrary to the prospect of the International Tax Subcommittee (2008), and the 2009 tax reform is considered to have caused the outflow of domestic capital.

5.5.3 The Impact of Transfer Pricing Regulations on the Location Decisions

In a situation where governments do not harmonize their corporate tax rates and there are differences in the tax rate among countries, multinationals have incentives to shift their tax bases among group firms. Multinationals could potentially use profit shifting, debt shifting, and/or earnings stripping as a method for tax base shifting. Regardless of whether they are home or host countries, governments highly care about tax base being shifted abroad because of potential losses of their tax revenue. For contracting profit shifting, debt shifting, and earnings stripping, the governments implement transfer pricing regulations, thin capitalization rules, and earnings stripping rules, respectively. Transfer pricing regulations are very complex. While the

Table 5.9 Estimation results

	I	II	III
Dependent variable	Foreign direct investment		Foreign direct investment/domestic investment
Tax rate difference	0.607 (20.177)	−1.415 (22.432)	−0.053 (0.077)
2009 dummy	−5.279*** (1.754)	−5.3*** (1.756)	−0 02*** (0.007)
Tax rate difference X 2009 dummy	−32.941** (14.074)	−33.024** (14.077)	−0.149*** (0.053)
GDP (Host country, Log)	1.529 (4.175)	1.419 (4.208)	−0.002 (0.016)
Unit labor cost (Host country)	0.369*** (0.125)	0.375*** (0.128)	0 **(0)**
Education years (Host country, Log)	109.725*** (26.216)	112.254*** (28.941)	0.218** (0.099)
Ease of funding (Host country)	1.023 (1.024)	1.052 (1.034)	0.006 (0.004)
Property rights (Host country)	0.404 (1.629)	0.413 (1.63)	−0.003 (0.006)
Internal investment (Log)		0.385 (1.87)	
Constant	−249.358** (100.207)	−259.995** (112.7)	−0.422 (0.38)
Observations	102	102	102
R2			
AIC	544.796	546.754	−592.382

Notes Standard deviation in parentheses, **significant at 5%, ***significant at 1%

governments can use OECD guideline for establishing rules, the rules are not completely harmonized among countries. Lohse et al. (2012) provide a comprehensive summary of transfer pricing regulations of 44 countries from 2001 to 2009. In the literature, profit shifting and transfer pricing have received considerable attention. However, the extent to which multinationals can use transfer prices for profit shifting is not considered an important factor in the location decisions of multinationals. Because the worldwide net profits of multinationals theoretically depend not only on tax rates but also on the difficulty of profit shifting, the difficulty of profit shifting should be added to the determining factors of location decisions.[4] Thus, Ito and Komoriya (2015) investigate how transfer pricing regulations affect FDI incentives.

[4]Amerighi and Peralta (2010) examine theoretically the role of the difficulty of profit shifting in the location decisions of multinationals.

Ito and Komoriya (2015), following Lohse et al. (2012), investigated the implementation of nine type of regulations, pricing methods, priority of methods, documentation requirements, advance pricing agreements (APA), penalties, secret comparables and statute of limitations, and estimated the impact of regulations on FDI using simple gravity model. In Table 5.10, as a result, among several elements in the regulations, APA have significant effects on FDI incentives. "An advance pricing arrangement (APA) is an arrangement that determines, in advance of controlled transactions, an appropriate set of criteria (e.g. method, comparables and appropriate adjustments thereto, critical assumptions as to future events) for the determination of the transfer pricing for those transactions over a fixed period of time.[5]" Once APA is contracted, as far as taxpayers comply with APA, taxpayer can avoid double taxation risk significantly. Then, the results suggest that firms would prefer to pay cost in compliance with transfer pricing regulations rather than be afraid of double taxation risk, and that transfer pricing regulations play an important role in the location decisions of multinationals.

5.6 Conclusions

This chapter reviews impact of tax system on location decision mainly in Japan. Until the middle of the 2000s, this series of research focused mainly on tax rates typified by Devereux and Griffith (1998). As can be confirmed in Sect. 5.3, firms do not pay much attention to the tax rate at location decision. Then we focused on several tax systems of corporate tax asymmetries, international double taxation adjustment method, and transfer pricing regulations. Because all of these systems may affect location decision, it is inferred that tax competition is a phenomenon occurring not only from the tax rate but also from various channels. To alleviate tax competition in Japan should be achieved not only by lowering the tax rate but also by multiple measures, such as alleviation of tax loss carryforwards and of transfer pricing regulations, reconsidering of residence principle.

[5] OECD (2010, p. 168).

Table 5.10 Estimation results

	OLS	2SLS	OLS	2SLS	OLS	2SLS
Control variables						
ln(GDP)s	0.493*** (6.11)	0.442*** (5.90)	00570*** (8.50)	0.573*** (9.91)	0.496*** (6.12)	0.459*** (5.92)
ln(GDP)f	0.560*** (8.58)	0.580*** (10.11)	0.467*** (5.89)	0.486*** (6.45)	0.484*** (6.15)	0.511*** (6.55)
ln(GDP per capita)s	1.156*** (7.32)	1.099*** (6.84)	1.282*** (9.32)	1.311*** (9.95)	1.170*** (7.38)	1.129*** (6.88)
ln(GDP per capita)f	0.462*** (3.43)	0.423*** (3.56)	0.494*** (3.11)	0.377** (2.48)	0.519*** (3.25)	0.410*** (2.65)
Exchange rate	0.000 (0.59)	0.000 (0.64)	0.000 (0.72)	0.000 (0.39)	0.000 (0.53)	0.000 (0.55)
Transfer pricing opportunity						
Difference of Nominal Tax Rates	0.043*** (3.63)	0.044*** (3.76)	0.034*** (2.74)	0.030** (2.52)	0.040*** (3.16)	0.038*** (2.83)
Home country regulations						
Statue of limitation	0.000 (0.09)	0.002 (0.52)			0.000 (-0.05)	0.001 (0.27)
Documentation	−0.350** (−2.36)	−0.206 (−1.15)			−0.353** (−2.38)	−0.208 (−1.16)
APA	0.412** (2.16)	0.903*** (3.29)			0.418** (2.19)	0.892*** (3.24)
Secret comparables	−0.147 (−0.94)	−0.237 (−1.58)			−0.140 (−0.90)	−0.233 (−1.56)
Host country regulations						
Statue of limitation			−0.003 (−1.07)	−0.002 (−0.49)	−0.004 (−1.23)	−0.002 (−0.67)
Documentation			−0.153 (−1.01)	−0.365** (−2.04)	−0.146 (−0.97)	−0.347* (−1.93)
APA			0.341* (1.67)	0.241 (0.92)	0.340* (1.67)	0.235 (0.90)
Secret comparables			0.118 (0.75)	0.132 (0.89)	0.109 (0.70)	0.121 (0.81)
Constant	−38.95*** (−12.00)	−37.45*** (−11.93)	−41.44*** (-12.60)	−40.08*** (−12.81)	−39.19*** (−11.53)	−36.85*** (−11.02)
Obs.	2747	2038	2747	2038	2747	2038
R squared	0.235	0.234	0.233	0.229	0.238	0.237
F test	F(734,2002) = 2.23 $P = 0.000$	F(731,1 297) = 0.74 $P = 1.000$	F(734,2002) = 2.25 $P = 0.000$	F(731,1297) = 0.31 $P = 1.000$	F(734, 1998) = 2.21 $P = 0.000$	F(731,1294) = 0.13 $P = 1.000$
Hausman test	chi2(10) = 15.77 $P = 0.1063$	chi2(9) = 1.08 $P = 0.999$	chi2(10) = 6.88 $P = 0.737$	chi2(8) = 0.42 $P = 1.000$	chi2(14) = 17.21 $P = 0.245$	chi2(12) = 0.34 $P = 1.000$
Breusch–Pagan LM test	chibar2(1) = 240.22 $P = 0.000$		chibar2(1) = 249.18 $P = 0.000$		chibar2(1) = 235.54 $P = 0.000$	

Notes [1] *t*-values in parentheses, *significant at 10%, **significant at 5%, ***significant at 1%, P refers to *P* values
[2] The variable subscript s represents the home country and f represents the host country

References

Amerighi, O., and S. Peralta. 2010. The proximity-concentration trade-off with profit shifting? *Journal of Urban Economics* 68: 90–101.

Auerbach, A.J. 2007. Why have corporate tax revenues declined? Another look. *CESifo Economic Studies* 53 (2): 153–171.

Auerbach, A.J., and J.M. Poterba. 1987. Why have corporate tax revenues declined? In *Tax policy and the economy*, vol. 1, ed. L. Summers, 1–28.

Bénassy-Quéré, A., L. Fontagné, and A. Lahrèche-Révil. 2005. How does FDI react to corporate taxation? *International Tax and Public Finance* 12 (5): 583–603.

Blonigen, B.A. 2005. A review of the empirical literature on FDI determinants. *Atlantic Economic Journal* 33: 383–403.

Boskin, M.J., and W.G. Gale. 1987. New results on the effects of tax policy on the international location of investment. In *The effects of taxation on capital accumulation*, ed. M. Feldstein, 201–222.

de Mooij, R.A., and S. Ederveen. 2005. Explaining the variation in empirical estimates of tax elasticities of foreign direct investment. Tinbergen Institute Discussion Papers 05–108/3.

Devereux, M.P. 2007. The impact of taxation on the location of capital, firms and profit: A survey of empirical evidence. Working Papers 0702, Oxford University Centre for Business Taxation.

Devereux, M.P., and R. Griffith. 1998. Taxes and the location of production: Evidence from a panel of US multinationals. *Journal of Public Economics* 68: 335–367.

Devereux, M.P., M. Keen, and F. Schiantarelli. 1994. Corporation tax asymmetries and investment: Evidence from U.K. Panel Data. *Journal of Public Economics* 53 (3): 395–418.

Dreßler, D., and M. Overesch. 2013. Investment impact of tax loss treatment—Empirical insight from a panel of multinationals. *International Tax and Public Finance* 20: 513–543.

Edgerton, J. 2010. Investment incentives and corporate tax asymmetries. *Journal of Public Economics* 94 (11): 936–952.

Ernst & Young. 2013. *Navigating the choppy waters of international tax: 2013 global transfer pricing survey.*

Graham, J.R. 1996. Debt and the marginal tax rate. *Journal of Financial Economics* 41: 41–74.

Grubert, H., and J. Mutti. 1991. Taxes, tariffs and transfer pricing in multinational corporation decision making. *Review of Economics and Statistics* 73: 285–293.

Hartman, D.G. 1984. Tax policy and foreign direct investment in the United States. *National Tax Journal* 37 (4): 475–487.

Hasegawa, M., and K. Kiyota. 2017. The effect of moving to a territorial tax system on profit repatriation: Evidence from Japan. *Journal of Public Economics* 153: 92–110.

Hines Jr., J.R., and E.M. Rice. 1994. Fiscal paradise: Foreign tax havens and American business. *Quarterly Journal of Economics* 109: 149–182.

Huizinga, H., and L. Laeven. 2008. International profit shifting within multinationals: A multi-country perspective. *Journal of Public Economics* 92 (5–6): 1164–1182.

International Taxation Subcommittee. 2008. Waga Kuni Kigyo no Kaigairieki no Shikinkanryu ni tsuite –Kaigaikogaisha karano Haitou ni tsuite no Ekikinfusannyusido no Dounyu ni mukete (Remittance of foreign source income to Japan: Proposal for introduction of foreign income exemption method).

Ito, J. 2013. Kokusaikazeiseido to Houjinzei-ritsu niokeru Taigaichokusetsutoshi eno Eikyou (Effects of international taxation system and corporate tax rate on outward FDI). *International Public Economy Studies* 24: 9–19.

Ito, J. 2017. *Houjinshotokukazei ga Kigyo no Kaigaitenkai ni Ataeru Eikyo (Impact of coroporate income taxation on location decision)*. Ph. D. thesis, Chuo University.

Ito, J., and Y. Komoriya. 2015. The impact of transfer pricing regulations on the location decisions of MNEs. In *Firms' location selections and regional policy in the global economy*, ed. T. Ishikawa, 81–106.

Luckhaupt, Hagen, Michael, Overesch, and Ulrich, Schreiber. 2012. The OECD approach to transfer pricing: A critical assessment and proposal. In *Fundamentals of international transfer pricing in law and economics*, ed. Wolfgang Schön and Kai A. Konrad, 91–121.

Lohse, Theresa, Nadine, Riedel, and Christoph, Spengel. 2012. The increasing importance of transfer pricing regulations—A worldwide overview. Oxford University Centre for Business Taxation Working Paper 12/27.

OECD. 2010. *Transfer pricing guidelines for multinational enterprises and tax administrations*. OECD Publishing.

Shevlin, T. 1990. Estimating corporate marginal tax rates with asymmetric tax treatment of gains and losses. *The Journal of the American Taxation Association* 12: 51–67.

Slemrod, J. 1990. Tax effects on foreign direct investment in the US: Evidence from a cross-country comparison. In *Taxation in the global economy*, ed. A. Razin and J. Slemrod, 79–122.

Tajika, E., M. Hotei, and K. Shibata. 2014. The effects of dividend-exemption method on repatriation of income from abroad: The case of 2009 Japanese Tax Reform. *Economic Analysis* 188.

Young, K.H. 1988. The effects of taxes and rates of return on foreign direct investment in the United States. *National Tax Journal* 41: 109–121.

Part II
Economic Functions of City Systems in Regions

Chapter 6
City System Based on the Rank-Size Rule

Hiroyoshi Kozu

Abstract This paper proves to have a specific law about the size of the exponent for the rank-size model in the population system of the city. It has been said that an exponent of approximately 1 in the empirical evidence takes between 3 from 0.1 with the development of the computer software. Simon (Biometrica, 425–440, 1955) explained the exponent using the probabilistic theory and Krugman (The self-organizing economy, Blackwell, 1996) pointed out that it was difficult for us to understand Simon's story. Therefore, without using the probabilistic theory, we clarify the implication of the range of the exponent for the rank-size model by supposing the case that migrants concentrate on the city having maximum population in a metropolis in one country, the case that migrants form a new city, and the case that migrants are distributed in proportion to the population of each city.

Keywords Rank-size rule · Exponent · City system · Metropolitan area

6.1 Introduction

In regional science, the rank-size model based on Zipf's law (1946) has been applied on a city scale in urban areas. Isard (1956) explained the implications of the rank-size rule applied to regions, and geographers and urban economists have used this approach to study the formation of cities. Specific models were constructed by Berry and Horton (1970). On the other hand, Christaller (1933) constructed a central place model using geometry, Lösch (1940) explained the spatial demand curve under microeconomics, and Beckmann (1959) constructed an urban hierarchy model using geometric progression. More recently, Krugman (1996) and Allen (1997) explained self-organization using the rank-size rule. Furthermore, Krugman (1996) referred to the power law in the rank-size rule, following Simon (1955). Among a large number of studies on the rank-size rule, Simon (1955) explained Zipf's law using

H. Kozu (✉)
Faculty of Business Administration, Aichi University, Aichi, Japan
e-mail: kozu@vega.aichi-u.ac.jp

T. Ishikawa (ed.), *Locational Analysis of Firms' Activities from a Strategic Perspective*, https://doi.org/10.1007/978-981-13-1684-5_6

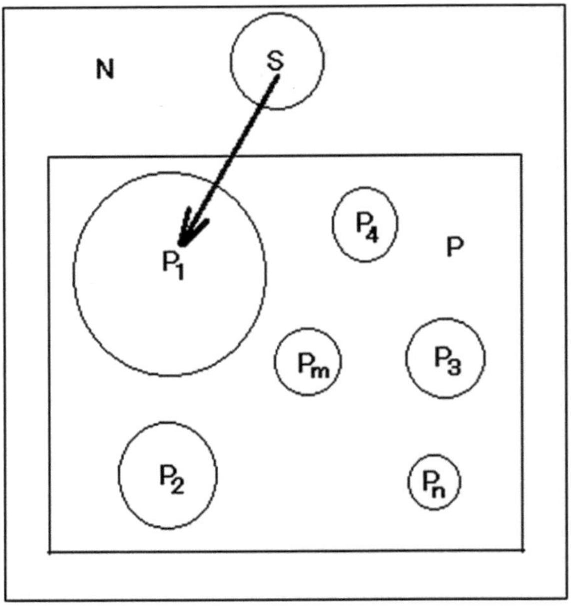

Fig. 6.1 Concentration of migrants in a city of rank 1 cited from Kozu (2013, p.5)

the probability that a new city is formed from one or more lumps and suggested some implications of the power law that had been derived from empirical studies. In this paper, from relative relationships between migrant and resident, we derive the implications of the power law for the rank-size rule.

6.2 The Rank-Size Rule in Metropolitan Areas

We consider the following three cases: case (1) supposes that migrants are concentrated in a city of rank 1 in a metropolitan area, case (2) supposes that migrants form a new city in a metropolitan area, and case (3) supposes that migrants are distributed in proportion to the population of the city in a metropolitan area.

(A) Comparison between case (1) and case (2)

The total population of a metropolitan area can be represented as

$$T = P + S, \tag{6.1}$$

where T is the total population, P is the number of residents, and S is the number of migrants.

When migrants are concentrated in a city of rank 1 (see Fig. 6.1), the total population can be represented as

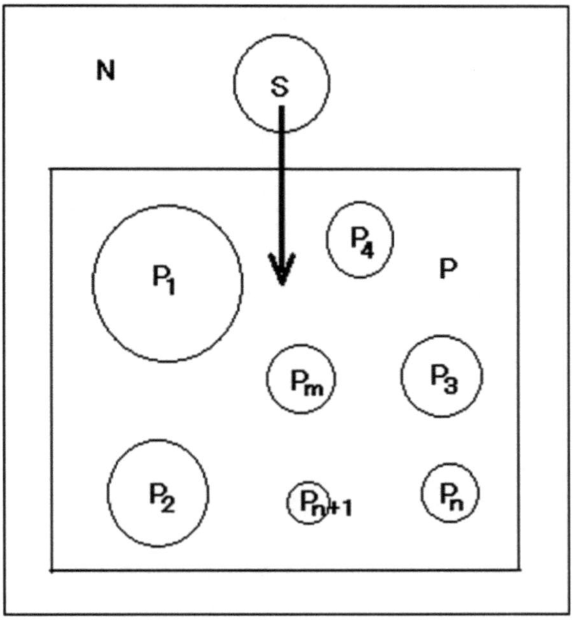

Fig. 6.2 Formation of a new city by migrants cited from Kozu (2013, p.5)

$$T = \int_{1}^{m} \frac{P_1 + S}{n^{\alpha}} dn, \tag{6.2}$$

where p_1 is the population of city 1, n is the rank of the city (for Japan, Tokyo is 1, Yokohama is 2), and α is an exponent.

When a new city that is not of rank 1 is formed by migration in a metropolitan area is formed by migration (see Fig. 6.2), the total population can be represented as

$$T = \int_{1}^{m+1} \frac{P_1}{n^{\beta}} dn, \tag{6.3}$$

where β is an exponent.

When we assume that both the number of residents in the metropolitan area and the number of migrants are constant, the total population can be represented as

$$\int_{1}^{m} \frac{P_1 + S}{n^{\alpha}} dn = \int_{1}^{m+1} \frac{P_1}{n^{\beta}} dn. \tag{6.4}$$

Dividing Eq. (6.2) by the national population N, we obtain

$$\frac{P}{N} + \frac{S}{N} = \left(\frac{P_1}{N} + \frac{S}{N}\right) \int_1^m \frac{1}{n^\alpha} dn. \tag{6.5}$$

We can rewrite Eq. (6.5) as

$$\frac{\pi_p + \pi_s}{\pi_1 + \pi_s} = \frac{1}{1-\alpha}(m^{1-\alpha} - 1), \tag{6.6}$$

where $\pi_p = \frac{P}{N}$, $\pi_1 = \frac{P_1}{N}$ and $\pi_s = \frac{S}{N}$.

Equation (6.6) can be simplified to

$$A = \frac{1}{1-\alpha}(m^{1-\alpha} - 1), \tag{6.7}$$

where $A = \frac{\pi_p + \pi_s}{\pi_1 + \pi_s}$.

Furthermore, dividing Eq. (6.4) by N gives

$$\frac{P}{N} + \frac{S}{N} = \left(\frac{P_1}{N}\right) \int_1^{m+1} \frac{P_1}{n^\beta} dn. \tag{6.8}$$

We can rewrite Eq. (6.8) as

$$\pi_p + \pi_s = \frac{\pi_1}{1-\beta}\left[(m+1)^{1-\beta} - 1\right], \tag{6.9}$$

which can then be simplified to

$$B = \frac{1}{1-\beta}\left[(m+1)^{1-\beta} - 1\right], \tag{6.10}$$

where $B = \frac{\pi_p + \pi_s}{\pi_1}$.

Here, we can find the scope of exponent α by comparing the relative numbers of migrants and residents in a city of rank 1.

Consider the cases $1 < \frac{\pi_s}{\pi_1}$ and $\frac{\pi_s}{\pi_1} < 1$.

First, if $1 < \frac{\pi_s}{\pi_1} = \frac{B}{A} - 1$, then $B > 2A$.

Therefore,

$$\frac{1}{1-\beta}((m+1)^{1-\beta} - 1) > \frac{2}{1-\alpha}(m^{1-\alpha} - 1). \tag{6.11}$$

We assume that self-organization is stable in the long term under a large number of cities, so that if $\alpha \approx \beta$ and $m \approx m+1$, then $m^{1-\alpha} < 1$ from Eq. (6.11).

Hence $1 < \alpha$.

Second, if $\frac{\pi_s}{\pi_1} = \frac{B}{A} - 1 < 1$, then $B < 2A$.

Therefore,

$$\frac{1}{1-\beta}\left((m+1)^{1-\beta}-1\right) < \frac{2}{1-\alpha}\left(m^{1-\alpha}-1\right). \tag{6.12}$$

Under the same assumptions as above, we have $1 < m^{1-\alpha}$ from Eq. (6.12). Hence $0 < \alpha < 1$.

In short, if the number of cities is very large, self-organization is stable, the proportion of the population of the biggest city with respect to the nation is very small, and a new city is formed by migrants, then $1 < \alpha$. If not, then $0 < \alpha < 1$.

(B) Comparison between case (2) and case (3)

Here, we compare the creation of a new city with the case that migrants are distributed in proportion to the size of the cities in a metropolitan area.

The total population of the metropolitan area including residents and migrants can be represented as

$$T = P + \sum_{i=1}^{n} \frac{P_i}{P} S = P(1+W), \tag{6.13}$$

where $W = \frac{S}{P}$, P_i is the population of city i, P is the total number of residents, and S is the total number of migrants.

In the case that migrants are distributed in proportion to the size of the cities in the metropolitan area, the total population can be represented as

$$T = P + S = \int_{1}^{m} \frac{P_1(1+W)}{n^{\alpha}} dn. \tag{6.14}$$

In the case that a new city is created by migrants, the total population can be represented as

$$T = P + S = \int_{1}^{m+1} \frac{P_1}{n^{\beta}} dn. \tag{6.15}$$

From Eqs. (6.14) and (6.15), we obtain

$$\int_{1}^{m} \frac{P_1(1+W)}{n^{\alpha}} dn = \int_{1}^{m+1} \frac{P_1}{n^{\beta}} dn. \tag{6.16}$$

From Eq. (6.16), we have

$$W = \frac{\frac{1}{1-\beta}\left((m+1)^{1-\beta} - 1\right)}{\frac{1}{1-\alpha}\left(m^{1-\alpha} - 1\right)} - 1. \tag{6.17}$$

Because $W = \frac{S}{P}$, we can rewrite Eq. (6.17) as

$$W = \frac{S/N}{P/N} = \frac{\pi_s}{\pi_p} = \frac{\frac{1}{1-\beta}\left((m+1)^{1-\beta} - 1\right)}{\frac{1}{1-\alpha}\left(m^{1-\alpha} - 1\right)} - 1. \tag{6.18}$$

Consider the relative numbers of migrants and residents in the metropolitan area. Assume that $\alpha \approx \beta$ from self-organization in the long term. From Eq. (6.18),

If $W > 1$, then $\frac{\pi_S}{\pi_P} = \frac{(m+1)^{1-\alpha}-1}{m^{1-\alpha}-1} - 1 > 1$, and hence $1 > 2m^{1-\alpha} - (m+1)^{1-\alpha}$.

If $W < 1$, then $\frac{\pi_S}{\pi_P} = \frac{(m+1)^{1-\alpha}-1}{m^{1-\alpha}-1} - 1 < 1$, and hence $1 < 2m^{1-\alpha} - (m+1)^{1-\alpha}$.

Furthermore, when we assume that there are a large number of cities in the metropolitan area, that is, $m \approx m + 1$, then

(a) if $\frac{\pi_S}{\pi_P} > 1$, then $1 > m^{1-\alpha}$ and hence $1 < \alpha$;

(b) if $\frac{\pi_S}{\pi_P} < 1$, then $1 < m^{1-\alpha}$ and hence $0 < \alpha < 1$.

In case (a), when the number of migrants is larger than the number of residents, we find that the difference in city scales in the metropolitan area is larger, that is, $1 < \alpha$.

In case (b), when the number of residents is larger than the number of migrants, we can show that the difference in city scales in the metropolitan area is smaller, that is, $0 < \alpha < 1$.

Putting (A) and (B) together yields the following.

If $1 < \frac{\pi_S}{\pi_1}$ and $1 < \frac{\pi_S}{\pi_P}$, then $1 < \alpha$. If $\frac{\pi_S}{\pi_1} < 1$ and $\frac{\pi_S}{\pi_P} < 1$ then $0 < \alpha < 1$.

These results show that if the proportion of migrants relative to the population of a city of rank 1 is large and the proportion of migrants relative to the national population is large, then $1 < \alpha$. Otherwise, $0 < \alpha < 1$.

6.3 Conclusions

We have found that city scale differences in a metropolitan area with a supercity are smaller in nations with a small number of migrants. It is possible to explain the city scale differences by regarding metropolitan areas as nations. For example, before World War 2 in 1940s Japanese economy was slow and there were a number of migrations. In this period the exponent which reveals the difference coefficient of the city scale is approximately 1.068. While in 1960s when Japanese economy was enjoying high economic growth, the exponent is approximately 0.963. And then in 2013 when the migration was with stable, the value of exponent is approximately 0.808 (These exponents are estimated from national census data for Japan). Incidentally, the exponent for the United States of America in 2013, which is one of the representative countries as a developed country, is 0.882, and the exponent for

Brazil in 2013 as a fairly-developed country is 0.918 (These exponents are estimated from data taken from World Statistics 2013, from the Ministry of Internal Affairs and Communications Statistics Bureau).

The changes from case (A) to case (B) seem to explain the changes in the difference scale of major cities in urban areas in Japan between World War 2 and the present. In the future, we plan to estimate the exponents based on the rank-size rule to investigate changes in population differences for cities around the world.

References

Allen, P. M. 1997. *Cities and Regions as Self-Organizing Systems*. Taylor & Francis.

Beckmann, M.J. 1959. City hierarchies and the distributions of city size. *Economic Development and Cultural Change* 6 (1959): 243–248.

Berry, B. J. L., and F. E. Horton. 1970. *Geographic Perspectives on Urban Systems*. Prentice Hall.

Christaller, W. 1933. *Die zentralen Orte in Suddeutschland*, 331S. Jena: Gustav Fischer.

Isard, W. 1956. *Location and Space-Economy*. M IT Press.

Kozu, H. 2013. Order and Complexity in a City. *The Keiei Sogo Kagaku* (*Journal of managerial research, Japanese*). Institute of Managerial Research, Aichi University, pp. 1–24.

Krugman, P. 1996. *The Self-Organizing Economy*. Blackwell.

Lösch, A. 1940. *Die raumlich Ordnung der Wirtschaft*. Stuttgart: G. Fisher.

Simon, H. 1955. On a class of skew distribution functions. *Biometrica*, pp. 425–440.

Zipf, G.K. 1946. *The* P_1P_2/D hypothesis on the intercity movement of persons. *America Sociological Review* 11: 677–686.

Chapter 7
An Analysis on Regularity of City Population Distribution in City System

Toshiharu Ishikawa

Abstract The city system transfigures in response to the spatial changes of economic activities in the globalized economy. The analysis of the relationships between the city system and performance of the regional economic activity is indispensable for analyzing the influence of broadening economic activity on the city systems in regions. Distribution of city population is considered as a phenomenon expressing the characteristics of a city system. And the rank-size rule is widely used as a theory on city population distribution. The primary purpose of this paper is to introduce a method to describe in detail the change in city population distribution from the viewpoint of the rank-size rule. After an explanation of the derivation methods of the rank-size rule, an analytical framework is proposed which connects the population change of the cities constituting the city system and the largest city. Then it is analyzed on this framework how the city population fluctuation changes the ranks of the cities in the city system. In this analysis, an improved method is introduced to grasp how much the position of a city relatively changes in a city system even if the city remains in the same rank in the city system.

Keywords Rank-size rule · Distribution of city population · City system Dynamics

7.1 Introduction

Globalization of the economic activities has been accelerating from the end of the twentieth century. This has caused great spatial structural changes in the cities and city systems. As the movement of various kinds of goods becomes easier on a global scale, consumers' preference for diversity of the consumer goods has increased. As a result, the consumers' directionality towards a few larger cities has increased. Eventually, the many mid-sized cities in regions have declined, and many city systems

---

T. Ishikawa (✉)
Faculty of Economics, Chuo Unversity, Hachioji, Tokyo, Japan
e-mail: ishiy@tamacc.chuo-u.ac.jp

T. Ishikawa (ed.), *Locational Analysis of Firms' Activities from a Strategic Perspective*, https://doi.org/10.1007/978-981-13-1684-5_7

in regions have been formed by one large city and many small cities. In the early twenty-first century, however, some of the cities of the medium or second rank which tended to decline in the city system are attracting attention of the city developers and planners again: In many advanced industrialized countries, the governments' plans are drafted to achieve even greater growth of the regional economy or to establish new industries in regions; when new production activities establish in the regions, the large cities are in a marginal state in the supply of land and workers; and many small cities are vulnerable in production and living base. On the other hand, in the medium or the second ranked cities, the production and living base are developed to some extent, and they have experience in industrial production.[1] It is considered in this context that the medium-sized cities are suitable place to attract new industries. It would be said that the city systems transfigure complexly in response to the changes in economic activities in the globalized economy.

In the above situation, the analysis of the relationships between economic activity and city system may be indispensable for analyzing the influence of broadening economic activity on the city systems. Distribution of city population is considered as a phenomenon expressing the characteristics of a city system. And the rank-size rule is widely used as a theory on city population distribution. The purpose of this paper is to explain a method to describe the change of the city population distribution from the viewpoint of the rank-size rule. After an explanation of the derivation method of the rank-size rule, a method is proposed to grasp how much the position of a city relatively changes in a city system even if the city is in the same rank in the city system.

The structure of this paper is as follows. In the next section, the rank-size rule in population distribution is derived from the entropy theory. And then, using actual city population data in Japan, the rule is briefly inspected. Section 7.3 derives the rank-size rule from a viewpoint of the dynamic analysis; an analytical framework connecting the population change of the cities constituting the city system and the largest city is built. It is shown that the newly derived rank-size rule provides more detail information of the change in city's position in a city system. Section 7.4 summarizes the results of the analyses.

7.2 Analysis of Regularity of City Population Distribution

7.2.1 Derivation of the Rank-Size Rule from Examination of Population Distribution

Considering the population size of the cities in regions, it is possible to find certain regularity in population size distribution. Attempts to formulate the regularity of

[1] See Camagni et al. (2016). Related references are Papers in Regional Science, Vol. 95 No. 1 March 2016, which features the relationship between city systems and accumulated economies.

the city population distribution have long been accumulated, and the analysis by Auerbach (1913) is representative. He ranks the population of a city from the largest to the smallest and shows that the product of the city's rank and its population is almost constant. If city's rank is r and its population is Pr, $r \bullet Pr$ is the constant M. Auerbach's law is expressed by the following equation,

$$r Pr = M. \tag{7.1a}$$

Taking the logarithm of both sides of Eqs. (7.1a), (b) is derived

$$\text{Log}\, Pr = \log M - \log r\,. \tag{7.1b}$$

Similarly, Zipf (1941) shows the regularity in population distribution by the following expression:

$$\text{Log} P_r = \text{Log} P_1 - a\text{Log} r, \tag{7.2}$$

where P_1 is the population of the largest city and a is a positive coefficient. The city population at rank r is $1/r^a$ of the largest city population. The above formula (7.2) is well-known as the rank-size rule of city population.[2]

7.2.2 *Derivation of the Rank-Size Rule from Entropy Theory*

It is possible to derive the rank-size rule given by Eq. (7.2) from other viewpoints. Let us derive this rule based on the entropy theory. Sheppard (1982) conducts a clear analysis from this theory and derives the rank-size rule of city population as follows.

Let pr denote the ratio of the city population ranked r to the total urban population of the area in which N cities exist. By summing N population ratios, the formula (7.3) should hold,

$$\sum_{r=1}^{N} p_r = 1. \tag{7.3}$$

If there is no a priori information on city population, a reasonable estimate of the population distribution of N cities in the area is considered $p_r = 1/N$. This inference can be derived by maximizing the uncertainty amount H expressed by the following equation:

$$H = -\sum_{r=1}^{N} p_r L_N(p_r)\,. \tag{7.4}$$

[2] As a recent analysis of population distribution, there are works of Gabaix (1999) and Reed (2002).

When maximizing Eq. (7.4) under the condition of Eq. (7.3), its solution is $p_r = 1/N$, which supports the above conclusion.

The distribution of the actual city population shows bias to the largest city at various degrees. In one case where the city population is biased towards a specific city with a high degree of concentration, in other case the bias is weak, population distribution between cities is more leveled. It is, therefore, considered that there is a priori information on how much bias is present. The value of K in Eq. (7.5) is used as an index showing the deviation of the population distribution to the largest city. It is shown in Eq. (7.5) that the index K showing the bias of population distribution to the largest city is derived by multiplying the rank of the city by the population ratio as a weight.

$$K = (1/N)\sum_{r=1}^{N} p_r L_N(r) \tag{7.5}$$

The smaller the coefficient K indicating this bias is, the more the city's population distribution is biased towards the largest city, while, the larger the coefficient is, the more the distribution is leveled.

The population ratio of each city that maximizes the entropy under the conditions (7.3) and (7.5) can be obtained by maximizing Eq. (7.6),

$$H = -(1/N)\sum_{r=1}^{N} p_r L_N(p_r) + \lambda\left(1 - \sum_{r=1}^{N} p_r\right) + \mu\left(K - (1/N)\sum_{r=1}^{N} p_r L_N(r)\right). \tag{7.6}$$

The population ratios of the cities that maximize Eq. (7.6) can be derived by solving the following simultaneous equations:

$$\partial H/\partial p_r = -(1/N)L_N(p_r) + 1) - \lambda - (\mu/N)L_N(r) = 0 \tag{7.7i}$$

$$(r = 1 \ldots N)$$

$$\partial H/\partial \lambda = \left(1 - \sum_{r=1}^{N} p_r\right) = 0 \tag{7.8}$$

$$\partial H/\partial \mu = \left(K - (1/N)\sum_{r=1}^{N} p_r L_N(r)\right) = 0 \tag{7.9}$$

The population ratio of each city obtained by solving the above simultaneous equations shows the city population ratio that produces the most level city population size distribution under a given bias coefficient. Solving the system of simultaneous equations by analytical method gives the relationship shown by Eq. (7.10).

$$p_r = p_1/r^{(\mu/N)}. \tag{7.10}$$

Equation (7.10) is reexpressed by Eq. (7.11),

$$\mathrm{Log}p_r = \mathrm{Log}p_1 - (\mu/N)\mathrm{Log}_r\,. \tag{7.11}$$

Equation (7.11) shows that the population ratio p_r of the city of rank r is linked to the population ratio p_1 of the city with the first rank in the area, and Eq. (7.11) is an expression showing the rank-size rule of city population. The rank-size rule can be derived from the entropy argument. The value of μ can be derived by solving simultaneous Eqs. (7.7i)–(7.9) by numerical calculation after obtaining the value of K from Eq. (7.5).

It can be said that the rank-size rule indicated by $p_r = p_{1/}\mathrm{r}^{\ (\mu/N)}$ shows the city population ratios which make city population distribution the most level under the bias shown by the value of K.

7.2.3 Application Analysis of the Rank-Size Rule Derived from the Entropy Theory

This subsection applies the rank-size rule derived from the entropy theory to the actual city population distribution. As a city system of case studies, this subsection takes the populations of the 20 cities in Niigata prefecture in Japan in 1964 and 1994. Table 7.1 shows the population and the ratio of each city in each year.[3] From Eq. (7.5), the index K in each year is derived as shown in Table 7.2.

If the value of K is known, the population ratio of each city that maximizes the entropy, which is shown by Eq. (7.12), can be obtained by solving simultaneous equation system composed by from Eq. (7.7i) to (7.9) above. The population ratio of each city that maximizes entropy in 1964 can be derived by solving simultaneous composed by the following 22 equations with respect to p_r ($r = 1, 2, \ldots 20$), λ, and μ.

[3]The data is obtained from Data book (Chiiki Keizai Soran, Japanese,1974, 1995)

Table 7.1 City population in Niigata prefecture in 1964 and 1994

City, 1964	Population	Ratio	City, 1994	Population	Ratio
Niigata	344,846	0.246215	Niigata	479,185	0.300141
Nagaoka	152,194	0.108664	Nagaoka	186,843	0.11703
Joetsu	121,947	0.087068	Joetsu	129,950	0.081395
Kashiwazaki	77,895	0.055616	Kashiwazaki	88,382	0.055359
Shibata	74,128	0.052926	Sanjo	86,824	0.054383
Sanjo	73,582	0.052536	Shibata	80,324	0.050311
Niitsu	56,689	0.040475	Niitsu	66,349	0.041558
Tokamachi	50,207	0.035847	Toyosaka	48,147	0.030157
Ojiya	48,331	0.034508	Tokamachi	45,596	0.028559
Mitsuke	41,223	0.029433	Tsubame	44,205	0.027688
Tsubame	40,592	0.028982	Mitsuke	44,107	0.027627
Itoigawa	40,218	0.028715	Ojiya	43,292	0.027116
Kamo	39,480	0.028188	Gosen	39,670	0.024848
Goson	38,911	0.027782	Shirane	38,471	0.024097
Tochio	37,229	0.026581	Kamo	34,752	0.021767
Shirane	34,952	0.024955	Itoigawa	33,360	0.020895
Atai	34,506	0.024637	Murakami	31,860	0.019956
Toyosaka	32,823	0.023435	Arai	28,483	0.017841
Murakami	32,441	0.023162	Tochio	27,546	0.017254
Riyotsu	28,395	0.020274	Riyotsu	19,189	0.012019
Total	1,400,589	1	Total	1,596,535	1

Table 7.2 Values of K of Niigata prefecture in 1964 and 1994

	1964	1994
K	0.0709	0.0634

$$H = -(1/20)\sum_{r=1}^{20} p_r L_N(r) + \lambda\left(1 - \sum_{r=1}^{20} p_r\right) + \mu\left(0.0709 - (1/20)\sum_{r=1}^{20} p_r L_N(r)\right) \tag{7.12}$$

$$\partial H/\partial p_r = -(1/20)(L_N(r)+1) - \lambda - (\mu/20)L_N(r) = 0 \tag{7.13r}$$

$$(r = 1 \ldots 20)$$

Table 7.3 City's population ratio derived from entropy theory in 1964 and 1994

City, 1964	Derived ratio	Derived population	City, 1994	Derived ratio	Derived population
Niigata	0.22126	309894.32	Niigata	0.27125	433060.1
Nagaoka	0.12456	174457.37	Nagaoka	0.13753	219571.5
Joetsu	0.089	124652.42	Joetsu	0.09158	146210.7
Kashiwazaki	0.07012	98209.301	Kashiwazaki	0.06973	111326.4
Shibata	0.05828	81626.327	Sanjo	0.05603	89453.86
Sanjo	0.0501	70169.509	Shibata	0.04687	74829.6
Niitsu	0.0441	61765.975	Niitsu	0.04029	64324.4
Tokamachi	0.03947	55281.248	Toyosaka	0.03535	56437.51
Ojiya	0.0358	50141.086	Tokamachi	0.0315	50290.85
Mitsuke	0.03281	45953.325	Tsubame	0.02841	45357.56
Tsubame	0.03031	42451.853	Mitsuke	0.02588	41318.33
Itoigawa	0.02821	39510.616	Ojiya	0.02376	37933.67
Kamo	0.02639	36961.544	Gosen	0.02197	35075.87
Gosen	0.02483	34776.625	Shirane	0.02043	32617.21
Tochio	0.02345	32843.812	Kamo	0.01909	30477.85
Shirane	0.02222	31121.088	Itoigawa	0.01792	28609.91
Arai	0.02144	30028.628	Murakami	0.01689	26965.48
Toyosaka	0.02016	28235.874	Arai	0.01597	25496.66
Murakami	0.01927	26989.35	Tochio	0.01515	24187.51
Riyotsu	0.01847	25868.879	Riyotsu	0.0144	22990.1
λ	0.5084		λ	0.3046	
$\mu/20$	0.8289		$\mu/20$	0.97996	

$$\partial H/\partial\lambda = \left(1 - \sum_{r=1}^{20} p_r\right) = 0 \tag{7.14}$$

$$\partial H/\partial\mu = \left(0.0709 - (1/20)\sum_{r=1}^{20} p_r L_N(r)\right) = 0 \tag{7.15}$$

As shown in the above equations, $N = 20$ and $K = 0.0709$ in 1964. Table 7.3 shows the population ratios and population of each city and the Lagrangian λ and μ that maximize entropy in 1964 and 1994.

From Table 7.3, the city population distribution that maximizes the entropy in 1964 is expressed by Eq. (7.16) and that in 1994 is expressed by Eq. (7.17)

$$\mathbf{LogP_r = Log(309894) - 0.8289Log_r} \tag{7.16}$$

$$\mathbf{LogP_r = Log(433068) - 0.97996Log_r} \tag{7.17}$$

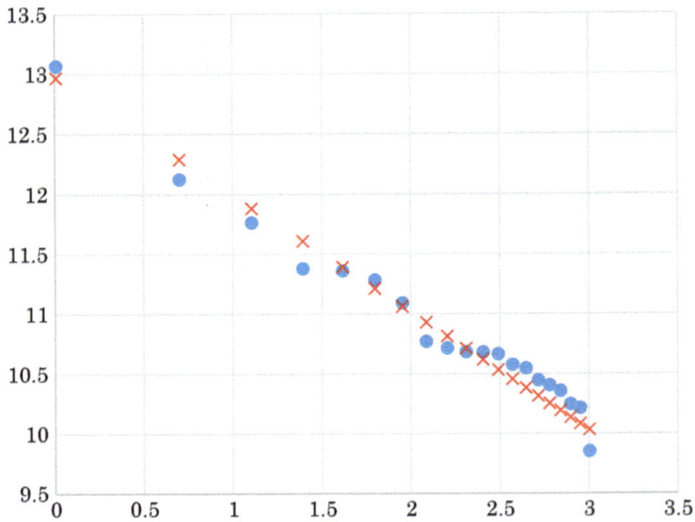

Fig. 7.1 Actual population and population that maximizes entropy in 1994 Mark ●: actual population, ×: population derived from entropy maximization

Table 7.4 Divergence Index in 1964 and 1994

	1964	1994
D	0.0132	0.0126

Figure 7.1 shows the actual city population distribution (logarithmic representation) in 1994 and the city population distribution derived from the theory of maximization of entropy.

Divergence index *D* expressed by Eq. (7.18) shows the difference between the actual city population distribution and that derived from the entropy theory. As shown in Table 7.4, the divergence between the two city population distributions has shrunk in 30 years from 1964 to 1994.

$$\mathbf{D} = \sum_{\mathbf{r}=1}^{\mathbf{20}} (\mathbf{P_{2r}} - \mathbf{2P_{2rE}})^{\mathbf{0.5}}/\mathbf{20}, \tag{7.18}$$

where $\mathbf{p}_{\mathbf{rE}}$ is population ratio of ranked *r* city which is derived from the entropy theory.

Analysis of this subsection shows the following thing: In the 30 years from 1964 to 1994, the city population of Niigata Prefecture in Japan has increased, and the bias of its distribution towards the biggest city Niigata City is increased. The medium part of the actual city population distribution is lower than that of the city population distribution derived from the theory of maximizing entropy, and this trend does not change in 30 years.[4]

7.3 Analysis of Rank-Size Rule of City Population Distribution from Dynamics

7.3.1 Derivation of Rank-Size Rule from a Viewpoint of Dynamics

This subsection examines the formulation of the rank-size rule and change of the rank of a city from a dynamic viewpoint. In examination from this viewpoint, there is a clear study by Kozu (2004). Thus, by partly expanding his analysis framework, this subsection develops the rank-size rule to increase its applicability in the real world.

First, the symbols used in the analysis here are explained. There are N cities in a certain area. r indicates the rank by city population. $r = 1$ represents the largest city and $r = N$ implies the smallest city. As the city population declines, the value of r increases. P_r is the population of the rank r. ΔP_r and Δr represent the increment of city population and increment of rank, respectively.

Supposing that the change in city's population and the change in its rank is linked, the following equation holds:

$$\Delta P_r / P_r = -\phi \Delta \mathbf{r} / \mathbf{r} \tag{7.19}$$

where ϕ is a positive parameter.

By integrating both sides of the above equation with r, Eq. (7.20) is obtained

$$\int_{1}^{N} \Delta P_r / P_r \, dr = -\phi \int_{1}^{N} \Delta r / r \, dr \, . \tag{7.20}$$

N in Eq. (7.20) indicates the number and rank of all cities in the area as described above. N is assumed to be a real number. Then, N can take a value such as 1.1. Now, Eq. (7.20) can be expressed by the following equation:

[4]The conclusions presented here only suggest a direction for future economic analysis. An analysis of what kinds of economic factors generate these phenomena is very interesting.

$$\mathrm{Log}P_N - \mathrm{Log}P_1 = -\phi \mathrm{Log}N \tag{7.21}$$

Equation (7.21) can be expressed as Eq. (7.22), which coincides with rank-size rule,

$$\mathrm{Log}P_r = \mathrm{Log}P_1 - \phi \mathrm{Log}r. \tag{7.22}$$

7.3.2 Analytical Analysis on the Change in Rank Order of City Population

This subsection develops the rank-size rule from a viewpoint of dynamics. By differentiating Eq. (7.22) with Log$r$, Eq. (7.23) is obtained.

$$d\mathrm{Log}P_r/d\mathrm{Log}r = -\phi \tag{7.23}$$

Equation (7.22) is expressed as follows:

$$\Delta P_r/P_r/(\Delta r/r) = -\phi \tag{7.24}$$

Now, if time is denoted by t, the growth of the largest city population of the first rank and the growth of the city population of rank r are expressed as the following two formulas:

$$\mathrm{P}_1 = \mathrm{e}^{\alpha t} \tag{7.25}$$

$$\mathrm{P}_r = \mathrm{e}^{\beta t} \tag{7.26}$$

These two equations can be rewritten as Eqs. (7.27) and (7.28).

$$\mathrm{Log}P_{\mathbf{1}} = \alpha t \tag{7.27}$$

$$\mathrm{Log}P_r = \beta t \tag{7.28}$$

From Eqs. (7.27) and (7.28), Eqs. (7.29) and (7.30) can be derived

$$\dot{P}_1/P_1 = \alpha \tag{7.29}$$

$$\dot{P}_r/P_r = \beta. \tag{7.30}$$

$\dot{P}_1$ and $\dot{P}_r$ represent the change in the population of the city ranked *1* and the city ranked r by time. From the above development, the following relationship can be obtained:

$$\beta t = \alpha t - \phi \mathrm{Log}\, r \quad (7.31)$$

And this equation is shown as Eq. (7.32).

$$\beta = \alpha - \phi(\dot{r}/r) \quad (7.32)$$

And this equation is shown as Eq. (7.32).

$$(\beta - \alpha)/(-\phi) = \left(\dot{P}_r/P_r - \dot{P}_1/P_1\right)/((\Delta P_r/P_r/(\Delta r/r))) = (\dot{r}/r) \quad (7.33)$$

Eventually, from the above equation, the following relationship is obtained:

$$(\alpha - \beta)/(-\phi) = \left(\dot{P}_1/P_1 - \dot{P}_r/P_r\right)/((\Delta P_r/P_r)/(\Delta r/r)) = (\dot{r}/r) \quad (7.34)$$

From Eq. (7.34) the following conclusions are obtained: if the population increase of the city of the rank r is smaller than that of the largest city of rank 1, the ranking of city of the rank r is lower (the numerical value of r is higher). Conversely, if the population increase of the city of the rank r is larger than that of the largest city, the ranking of the city of the rank r is higher (the numerical value of r is lower). These changes are larger in response to changes in population of the rank elasticity. In addition, the ranking of cities is represented by real numbers, which means that it is possible to grasp in detail the extent to which cities' own positions have relatively changed in the city system.

7.4 Concluding Remarks

Since the latter half of the twentieth-century economic activity has become globalized, and production activities have expanded on a global scale. In response to the globalization, the production activities in a city have diversified dramatically. According to these changes, the content of the production activity in each city is greatly varied, and the roles of cities are influenced by the position of the individual cities in the city system. It could be said that the economic role of the city systems in regions is increasing in importance in the twenty-first century. In the analysis of the city systems, it is indispensable to obtain the methods to describe the city systems and to elucidate the mechanism of the influence of broadening economic activity on the city systems.

Against this background, this paper deals with the rank-size rule expressing the city population distribution from two perspectives and shows how to describe the relation between the changes of city's rank and size within the city system. This analysis shows that the fluctuation of the rank of a city within the city system is also related to the fluctuation of the population of the largest city in that city system. And a method to grasp the relative position of a city in a city system in more detail is elucidated in the analysis. This paper does not intend to analyze the formation of the city system and the mechanism of transformation of the city system from an economic viewpoint. But, it is expected that the method derived in this paper provides a suggestion on the direction of economic analysis of the relationships between city system and regional economy.

References

Auerbach, F. 1913. *Das Gesetz der Bevolkerungs konzentration*, Petermanns Mit-teilungen, 59 Jahrg., Gotha.

Camagni, R., R. Capello, and A. Caragliu. 2016. The rise of second rank cities: What role for agglomeration economies? *European Planning Studies* 23: 1069–1089.

Gabaix, X. 1999. Zipf's law for cities: An explanation. *Quarterly Journal of Economics* 114: 739–767.

Kozu, H. 2004. "Spatial analysis on information and tourism—rank-size model and economic theory-" (Japanese). *The Keiei Sogo Kagaku* (*Journal of Managerial Research*). Institute of Managerial Research, 25. Japan: Aichi University,.

Reed, W.J. 2002. On the rank-size distribution for human settlements. *Journal of Regional Science* 42 (1): 1–17.

Sheppard, E. 1982. City size distributions and spatial economic change. *International Regional Science Review* 7 (2): 127–151.

Toyo Keizai, Shinposha. 1974. *Chiiki Keizai Soran* (Data book).Tokyo.

Toyo Keizai, Shinposha. 1995. *Chiiki Keizai Soran* (Data book).Tokyo.

Zipf, G.K. 1941. *National Unity and Distribution*, Bloomington: Principia Press.

Chapter 8
The Relationship Between City System and Regional Economic Performances: An Empirical Study Based on Shandong, China

Na Wang

Abstract With the development of economic globalization and urbanization, the formation of the city system is the product of the development of regional urbanization to a certain stage. First, this chapter is to verify the relationship between the city system index and regional economic development of all provinces based on the analysis of the city system index of 278 cities in China. Then, we can confirm the relationship between Shandong's city system and regional economic performances based on the analysis of panel data of 17 prefecture-level cities in Shandong.

Keywords City system index · Regional economic performances
Rank-size index · City primacy index · Panel data analysis

8.1 Introduction

The formation of city system is the product of regional urbanization development to a certain stage. Since the industrial revolution, with the city function appear, the role of urban agglomeration has been continuously strengthened. The urban population has increased rapidly, and the scale of the city has expanded rapidly. A large number of large cities and megacities have emerged and have gradually merged into a multilevel and open city system. At the same time, the development and improvement of city system have promoted the development of regional economy, society, and culture, and its theoretical research and application have attracted extensive attention.

For a country or region, cities with different size of the population constitute a city system. City size distribution constitutes an important feature of city system (Henderson 2005), and it has an important impact on economic growth (Henderson et al. 2001; Henderson 2003). The earliest research on the development of regional economy by city system structure can be traced back to Berry (1961). After the study of city size distribution, along with the economic growth, city population distribution

N. Wang (✉)
School of Public Administration, Shandong Normal University, Jinan, Shandong, China
e-mail: wangna@sdnu.edu.cn

T. Ishikawa (ed.), *Locational Analysis of Firms' Activities from a Strategic Perspective*, https://doi.org/10.1007/978-981-13-1684-5_8

was the change trend of the inverted U type (Alonso 1980; Wheaton and Shishido 1981; Junius 1999; Henderson 2000, 2003). The empirical results of China's domestic data also show that the city primacy degree and economic growth have the inverted U type relationship (Xie and Wang 2012). The excessive concentration of cities leads to the inefficiency of human and material capital investment and then affects the regional economic development (Henderson 2003). Therefore, it can be concluded that there is a close relationship between city population size distribution and regional economic development. By testing the impact of city population (or employment) size (Hanson 2005; Au and Henderson 2006; Mao and Pan 2012; Ke and Zhao 2014; Chen and Zhou 2016; Wang et al. 2017) or city population density (Ciccone and Hall 1996; Fan 2006; Liu 2009) on economic output or labor productivity, we can measure the impact of city system on regional economic development. In the city system, the city size distribution will affect the external function of the whole city system and will eventually affect the regional economic growth.

In summary, to measure the relationship between city system and regional economic development, more is the city population size to represent the city system structure, the research object is in the prefecture-level city for Chinese units to carry out the empirical analysis, in terms of the area and population of all the provinces in China, each province can be regarded as an independent city system.

In view of the deficiencies of previous research, the purpose of this chapter is to identify the relationship between city system and regional economic performances. This chapter is based on the national scope around prefecture-level cities, to measure the relationship between the city structure of each province and regional economic development by the city system index, and select the typical representative of Shandong province as an example, through the empirical analysis to verify the relationship between the city system and regional economic performances of Shandong.

8.2 Theoretical Analysis of City System and Regional Economic Development

8.2.1 Rank-Size Rule

The rank-size rule examines the size distribution of a city system from the relationship between city size order and city population size, reflects the relationship between different city size and rank in the whole system, and can evaluate the distribution situation of a country or a regional city system. In a country or region, the rank order of city size has a significant negative correlation with its scale, the larger the number of position order, the smaller the scale. If the ordinal numbers of these cities can establish a regular functional relationship with their sizes, the distribution based on this function is called the rank-size distribution of cities. The population size and the city rank of the regional city system are in accordance with the following formula:

$$\ln P_i = \ln P_1 - q \ln R_i \tag{8.1}$$

In Eq. (8.1), P_i is the population of the city of i, P_1 is the largest city population, R_i is the rank of the city of i, and the parameter q which reflects the size structure of the city is usually called Zipf index. Among them, in Eq. (8.1), when $q = 1$, it shows that the ratio of the primate city to the smallest is just the number of cities in the whole city system, the city size distribution system is the regular distribution of sequence, which is the optimal distribution in the city system, namely the scale distribution, this is a special case; when $q > 1$, it shows that the city size is relatively centralized and the size distribution of cities is different, the primate city monopoly is stronger, namely the primate distribution; when $q < 1$, it shows that the city size distribution is relatively dispersed, a more balanced population distribution, the middle rank city is more than city for sequence distribution developed, namely the middle order distribution.

When the size of the city is compared for many years, if there is no change in q, it shows that the growth rate of cities at all levels in the city system is relatively uniform, and the proportion of city population at all levels to the total population of the city is basically no change; if q becomes larger, it indicates that the growth rate of larger cities is faster than that of smaller cities, while regional development tends to concentrate; otherwise, the growth rate of smaller cities is faster than that of larger cities, and regional development tends to disperse.

8.2.2 *City Primacy Index Theory*

The city size distribution law is summarized as Law of the Primate City by M. Jefferson (1939), that is, the proportion of the largest city population size and the second city population size in a country. This has become a commonly used index to measure the size distribution of cities, indicating the degree of difference between cities of different sizes in a country or region. Primacy degree reflects the concentration degree of the city population in the largest city in a city system, which can be used to analyze the evolution of agglomeration degree of regional population distribution. Because two-city index inspects less cities, it is easy to have one-sidedness, and then there are four-city index and eleven-city index. Four-city index refers to the ratio of the largest city population in a country or region to the sum of second to fourth city population, eleven-city index is the ratio of the largest city population in a country or region to the sum of second to eleventh city population. They can be used to explain the evolution of the size disparity of cities with larger population size, which can reflect the size structure of cities more comprehensively.

$$\text{Two city index } S_2 = P_1/P_2 \tag{8.2}$$

$$\text{Four city index } S_4 = P_1/(P_2 + P_3 + P_4) \tag{8.3}$$

$$\text{Eleven city index } S_{11} = 2P_1/(P_2 + P_3 + \ldots + P_{11}) \tag{8.4}$$

Among them, P_1, P_2, P_3, ... P_{11} are the city population size in the order of population size from large to small in the city system. According to rank-size rule Eq. (8.1), the distribution of the optimal size when $q = 1$, when the best index calculation of two-city index $R = 2$, let $P_1 = xP_2$, $q = 1$ can be obtained $P_1 = 2P_2$, the optimal city size distribution. When $S_2 > 2$, the city size distribution is more concentrated, the primacy city has a strong monopoly position and belongs to the high primacy type. When $S_2 < 2$, the city size distribution is dispersed, belonging to the low primacy type. Similarly, according to the above principles, it is also possible to introduce the best size distribution when S_4 and S_{11} are equal to 1.

8.2.3 Central Place Theory

Through the survey of the southern cities of Germany, Christaller (1933) pointed out the relationship between city size hierarchy, function and spatial structure of a region (country), and put forward the central place theory by establishing data model. The central place theory mainly includes triangle settlement distribution, hexagonal market area, and market network. In a central hierarchy, a certain level of center controls the center of the next level, and the control quantity is called the K value. According to the different levels of economic development, and according to the optimal market principle, the optimal traffic principle and administrative principle, where the different levels of the economic center are divided into three models of $K = 3$, $K = 4$, $K = 7$, show that the magnification range attracts senior economic center of the secondary center attracting scope.

8.3 The Relationship Between City System and Regional Economic Performances in China

This chapter uses the index of city system to verify the relationship between city system and regional economic development in China. Using the data of 278 prefecture-level cities in 23 provinces[1] of China in 2015, a simple regression analysis was carried out.

[1]There are 31 provinces, municipalities directly under the central government and autonomous regions in mainland China. This article does not include four municipalities (Beijing, Tianjin, Shanghai, and Chongqing), and Xinjiang, Hainan, Tibet, and Qinghai.

Table 8.1 City System Index of 23 Provinces in China (2015)

Province	City size	CSI	CD	ML
Guangdong	21	2.163	0.070	1.645
Heilongjiang	12	2.208	0.079	1.540
Gansu	12	2.279	0.095	1.259
Hubei	12	2.302	0.087	1.497
Liaoning	14	2.344	0.084	1.630
Jilin	8	2.437	0.090	1.650
Henan	17	2.516	0.089	1.780
Anhui	16	2.523	0.096	1.633
Shanxi	10	2.609	0.081	2.047
Zhejiang	11	2.637	0.096	1.808
Shanxi	11	2.648	0.099	1.769
Jiangxi	11	2.660	0.104	1.664
Guangxi	14	2.681	0.096	1.871
Hunan	13	2.699	0.100	1.813
Fujian	9	2.760	0.115	1.525
Jiangsu	13	2.782	0.108	1.746
Shandong	17	2.801	0.096	2.035
Sichuan	18	2.834	0.082	2.315
Hebei	11	2.934	0.098	2.185
Neimenggu	9	3.170	0.114	2.198
Yunnan	8	3.438	0.090	2.928
Guizhou	6	3.535	0.127	2.467
Ningxia	5	3.540	0.144	2.069

Source China City Statistical Yearbook 2016
Note City size is the prefecture-level cities, *CD* is the deviation coefficient, *ML* is the city density, and *CSI* is the city system index. Because in "China City Statistical Yearbook", this "City" as the city's administrative area, including city, county, and municipality; "municipal district" includes all districts, counties not included, this table calculation data are used "municipal district" data. Among them, the population data used in CD index is the registered population of the municipal district. The area of ML index uses the actual area of each province, and the nearest distance between cities is calculated by the nearest distance of the local people's government

8.3.1 City System Index

According to the city population distribution and city region density derived city system index (CSI),[2] city system index of 23 provinces in China is calculated, according to the CSI, they are arranged from small to large in sequence, as shown in Table 8.1.

[2]The derivation of the city system is explained by Ishikawa (2016).

For example, Shandong (GRP ranks the third in the 23 provinces) is the economic developed province of the eastern coastal areas. Its city deviation coefficient is 0.096, its city density coefficient is 2.035, and its city system index is 2.801, which means that the population size distribution of the inner cities of the province tends to be balanced, and the spatial distribution of city space is not concentrated. The same example is the eastern coastal economically developed regions of Jiangsu (GRP ranks the second in the 23 provinces). Its city deviation coefficient is 0.108, its city dispersion coefficient is 1.746, which means that city population size distribution in the province also tends to be balanced. On the contrary, Heilongjiang is the northeast economic underdeveloped province. Its city deviation coefficient is 0.079, its city intensity coefficient is 1.540, and its city system index is 2.208, which means that the population size distribution of the inner cities of the province is biased towards the largest cities, and the spatial distribution of city space is more concentrated. Another example, Gansu is a less developed province in the western inland region. Its city density coefficient is 1.259, which is the most densely concentrated province in the 23 provinces, and its city system index is 2.279, which is ranking the third among the 23 provinces.

In summary, the Chinese city system has the following characteristics. The city population size distribution of the economically developed provinces in the coastal areas tends to be balanced, and the distribution of city spatial size is scattered. The city population size distribution of the less developed provinces in the inland areas is relative to the largest cities in the province, and the distribution of city spatial size is more concentrated. The characteristics of the Chinese city system may be the result of the use of nonagricultural population to represent the size of the city population. As we all know, in China, the data of the nonagricultural population representing the size of the city population (the household registration population) and the resident population are inconsistent. Therefore, it is impossible to accurately reflect the characteristics of the city system.

8.3.2 The Relationship Between City System Index and Regional Economic Performances

This chapter makes a comparative analysis of the basic conditions of the provincial cities in Table 8.2 by CSI of Table 8.1 to investigate the economic significance of the city system indicators.

We can get the regression relationship between city system index (CSI) and gross regional product (GRP), fiscal expenditure, the number of industrial enterprises above designated size,[3] the ratio of the tertiary industry and the secondary industry. As shown in Fig. 8.1, the graph (1)–(4), the results show that there is no certain economic significance between the city system index and the economic development index of

[3]Industrial enterprises above designated size mainly refer to industrial enterprises whose annual main business income is above 20 million.

Table 8.2 The basic situation of 23 provinces in China (2015)

Province	Total land area adminis-trative region (km^2)	City population (ten thousand persons)	Gross regional product (billion yuan)	Expenditure of the local government (billion yuan)	Number of industrial Enterprises (numbers)	Tertiary indus-try/secondary industry
Hebei	186,535	1778	11,575	1850	3790	1.029
Shanxi	156,921	983	5689	929	888	1.576
Neimenggu	656,579	690	9299	980	1408	1.464
Liaoning	147,256	1913	16,230	2097	5665	1.032
Jilin	147,792	930	7752	1224	2323	0.784
Heilongjiang	390,382	1385	8893	1482	1752	1.171
Jiangsu	105,875	3509	42,351	516	23,579	1.105
Zhejiang	104,460	1798	23,442	3275	16,827	1.255
Anhui	140,282	2017	11,804	2231	6720	0.809
Fujian	124,160	1072	11,485	1654	5670	1.103
Jiangxi	168,025	1198	7600	1215	3039	0.879
Shandong	158,971	3231	30,635	3877	13,928	1.067
Henan	164,696	2070	11,843	2450	4890	1.104
Hubei	151,799	1586	16,065	2267	5430	0.942
Hunan	197,622	1391	13,618	2047	4061	1.031
Guangdong	179,749	4419	67,841	6530	35,300	1.206
Guangxi	238,576	1530	8877	1343	2520	0.944
Sichuan	193,156	2791	16,605	2284	5705	1.087
Guizhou	102,838	715	3995	550	905	1.579
Yunnan	194,910	648	4968	443	821	1.113
Shanxi	206,196	1346	8836	950	2128	1.041
Gansu	415,225	813	3702	740	842	1.440
Ningxia	61,588	279	1621	393	506	1.101

Source Same Table 8.1
Note Industrial enterprises include domestic enterprises, Hong Kong, Macao, Taiwan invested enterprises and foreign-invested enterprises. All of the data in this table are the data of the municipal district. City population refers to nonagricultural population in the municipal district, that is, the household population. If not specified gross regional product (GRP), refers to the nominal GRP, which is the same as below

each province. The reason is determined by the characteristics of the index of the city system of each province as shown in Table 8.1. That is to say, it is due to the reversal of the order of the city system index between the economically developed provinces and the less developed provinces.

With the above analysis, it is seen from CSI (Table 8.1) that Shandong is located in 23 provinces in seventeenth, in all eastern coastal provinces,[4] and CSI is 2.801. From Table 8.2, we can see that city population and GRP of Shandong is second only to Guangdong and Jiangsu, which is located in the third place in 23 provinces.

[4]The east coastal areas are different provinces in the eastern region, including Liaoning, Hebei, Shandong, Jiangsu, Zhejiang, Fujian, Guangdong, and Guangxi.

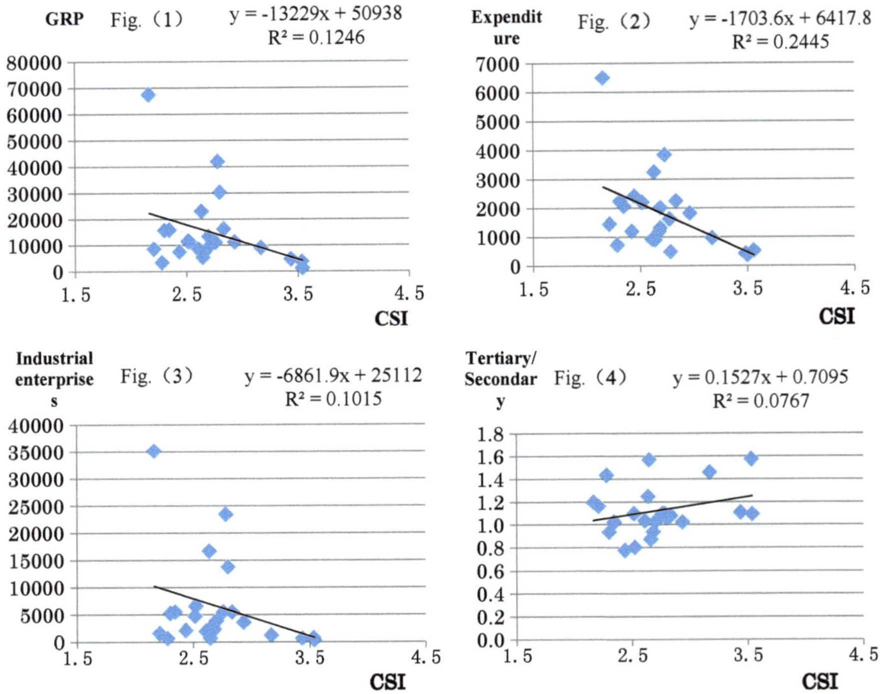

Fig. 8.1 Scatter diagram of regression relation between city system index (CSI) and each variable. *Source* same Table (8.1)

As an economically developed large population province, from the perspective of city system indicators, city population size distribution tends to be balanced, the spatial size distribution is dispersed, and the city density is not high. Therefore, Shandong can be regarded as a typical representative, and it is of great significance to analyze the relationship between its city system and regional economic development. In the following, first, we investigate the current situation of Shandong's regional economic development and the evolution of Shandong's city system and analyze the characteristics of its city system from other perspectives. On this basis, we further analyze the relationship between city system and regional economic development.

8.4 The Current Situation of Regional Economic Development in Shandong

At present, the eastern coastal areas of China mainly include the six large cities of the Mid-Southern Liaoning city agglomerations, the Beijing-Tianjin-Hebei city agglomerations, the Shandong peninsula city agglomeration, the Yangtze River Delta city agglomerations, the West Taiwan Strait city agglomerations, and the Pearl River Delta city agglomerations. Compared with Beijing-Tianjin-Hebei city agglomerations, Yangtze River Delta city agglomerations, Pearl River Delta city agglomerations, Shandong Peninsula city agglomerations has a wide gap in many aspects, and its competitiveness needs to be improved. The prefecture-level cities of Shandong Peninsula city agglomerations mainly include Jinan, Qingdao, Zibo, Dongying, Yantai, Weifang, Weihai, and Rizhao. Qingdao and Jinan, as the two core cities of Shandong Peninsula city agglomerations, play a leading role. Among them, Qingdao, as the economic center of Shandong, its economic strength occupies an absolute advantage in the Shandong peninsula city agglomeration, while Jinan, as the provincial capital city, is the political, cultural and educational center of Shandong, and Yantai and Weihai as a coastal tourist city of Shandong, the environmental advantages are obvious. This chapter expounds the current situation of regional economic development in Shandong from several aspects, such as natural endowments, economic development characteristics, traffic system, and the influence on the surrounding areas.

8.4.1 Natural Endowments

Shandong is rich in natural resources, and the reserves of petroleum and coal resources needed for industrial development are large. The transportation cost is low, which leads to the agglomeration of production factors such as labor and capital, which is beneficial to the development of scale economy. Industrial development has produced economic agglomeration effect because the agglomeration capacity is different under different levels of development, the evolution of city size is also different. Jining, Jining, Zaozhuang, and Dongying are rich in mineral resources, and the second industry dominated by mineral exploration and mining industry occupies a large proportion in the national economy. The agglomeration of mining workers also promotes the development of city systems in these areas.

8.4.2 Characteristics of Economic Development

In Shandong Peninsula area and central region of Shandong, the economic development is relatively fast, the city size is high, at the same time, the function structure specialization degree is high, and the spatial layout is more intensive. In contrast, the western regions with relatively low economic development level have lower city size, and the spatial layout is scattered compared with the eastern and central areas.

8.4.3 *Traffic System*

At present, the mileage of Shandong expressway network is more than 5710 km (as of the end of 2016), ranking eighth in the country. With the development of the traffic system, Shandong central railway and highway network with Jinan as its center, and Shandong Peninsula railway and highway network with Qingdao port as its center, which have been formed. Therefore, the city concentrated area with Jinan and Qingdao as the center is formed. The coastline of Shandong is long. The main port cities include the marine blue economic zone, Qingdao, Yantai and Weihai, Binzhou, Dongying and Weifang in the Yellow River Delta economic belt, and Rizhao City in Lunan economic zone. As a coastal port city, it has the advantages of natural traffic location, so the urbanization level of these cities is higher. But the western region is far away from Jinan and Qingdao, the two economic centers, the transportation cost is higher, the economic radiation is weak, and the city system development is slow.

8.4.4 *Influence on the Surrounding Areas*

The impact of the surrounding areas on a regional city system is mainly realized as regional spillovers, namely externalities. In an open economic environment, the development of any region will be affected by the surrounding areas. Direct foreign investment and the amount of foreign trade are often used as indicators to measure the impact of the surrounding areas. From the perspective of economic globalization, Shandong is close to the Bohai Sea and the Yellow Sea and is in the Circum Pacific economic circle. It is easy to be affected by the developed countries, and the level of economic and urbanization development is higher than that of inland provinces. Along with the change of industrial output layout in developed countries, Shandong has carried on a large number of transfer industries in Japan, Korea, and the United States, relying on the advantages of regional advantages. It has a great impact on the city system structure and regional economic development of Shandong. Since the reform and opening up, the coastal city in eastern Shandong to undertake a large number of Korean industrial transfer, the transition from labor-intensive industries to high-tech industries, the formation of the Shandong Peninsula city intensive areas. In the west of Shandong, the regional economic development level is relatively slow near Anhui and Henan, which are relatively backward in economic development level.

8.5 The Evolution of City System in Shandong

In the three decades of reform and opening, the level of urbanization in Shandong has been greatly improved. Especially after 2000, the urbanization of Shandong

Table 8.3 Basic situation of 17 prefecture-cities in Shandong (2012)

Prefecture -level city	County-level cities (numbers)	Population density (persons/km^2)	Nonagricultural population (ten thousand persons)	Gross regional product (100 million yuan)
Jinan	1	1081	352	3633
Qingdao	5	1105	280	4732
Zibo	0	940	162	2789
Zaozhuang	1	736	84	872
Dongying	0	254	67	1891
Yantai	7	662	137	2377
Weifang	6	709	162	1070
Jining	3	1175	95	855
Taian	2	761	72	726
Weihai	3	844	49	594
Rizhao	0	673	59	1033
Laiwu	0	562	65	631
Linyi	0	1084	162	1227
Dezhou	2	1129	46	473
Liaocheng	1	798	59	376
Binzhou	0	621	54	419
Heze	0	1063	73	381

Source China City Statistical Yearbook 2013

has entered an accelerated development stage. In the past 2000–2015 years, the urbanization rate in Shandong has been on the rise, from 38% in 2000 to 57% in 2015, with an average annual growth rate of 2.7%. The size of the city has changed accordingly. The nonagricultural population[5] of county-level cities in Shandong and above (including county-level cities and prefecture-level cities) increased from 9790 thousand persons in 1986 to 30,370 thousand persons in 2012, an increase of 3.1 times. Table 8.3 shows the basic situation of 17 prefecture-level cities in Shandong in 2012, including the number of county-level cities, population density, nonagricultural population, and GRP.[6]

In this part, the evolution process of Shandong city system will be expounded from the two aspects of city size hierarchy structure and spatial structure. The evolution of regional hierarchy can be explained from three aspects: the number of hierarchical cities, the rank-size rule, and the primacy of the city. All the data used are the data

[5]The population size of a city is usually measured by nonagricultural populations. The nonagricultural population refers to the registered population of the city.

[6]Due to the absence of nonagricultural population data in 2013 and 2014 of the Chinese City Statistical Yearbook, for the sake of unity, the data from the Shandong city system began to evolve, and the data presented below were closed until 2012.

of "People's Republic of China County National Population Statistics 1996–2013". In this data, the county-level cities of 17 prefecture-level cities in Shandong are also included, that is, 17 prefecture-level cities plus 31 county-level cities under city, a total of 48 cities.

8.5.1 *The Evolution of City Size Hierarchy*

According to the classification of city size, each country has different classifications and standards. According to the size of the city population, China mainly divides the city into five categories:

① Super megacities: more than 200 ten thousand
② Megacities: 100–200 ten thousand
③ Large cities: 50–100 ten thousand
④ Medium cities: 20–50 ten thousand
⑤ Small cities: less than 20 ten thousand

It can be seen from Table 8.4 that according to the city nonagricultural population division, by 2012, the city system of Shandong forms super megacities (2), megacities (4), large cities (11), medium cities (26), and small cities (5), which is a five-level size system.

According to Table 8.4 and Fig. 8.2, the number of small cities with less than 200 thousand nonagricultural population in Shandong decreased gradually during the period 1995–2012, and the number of 200–500 thousand nonagricultural population increased gradually in medium cities. First, in 2003, Jinan and Qingdao became the super megacities with a population size exceeding 2 million, and Jinan was more than 3 million in 2007, which fully highlighted the political, economic, and cultural center of the provincial capital cities. Second, the number of large cities and medium cities increased significantly, of which the number of medium cities increased from 18 in 1995 to 26 in 2012, becoming the largest proportion and the largest increase in the number of grades. The number of large cities increased from 4 in 1995 to 11 in 2012, such as Rizhao, Heze, Tengzhou, and other cities from medium cities to large cities. Third, the number of small cities reduced the most, from 22 in 1995 reduced to 5 in 2012, such as Zhaoyuan, Qufu, Zhucheng, and other cities from small cities to medium cities, which explains that the small cities of Shandong have achieved a great development. To sum up, the pattern of two grade differentiation of grade cities in Shandong has been gradually weakened, forming the size pattern centered on large cities and medium cities.

According to the distribution of city size hierarchy, Shandong has formed the central city agglomeration area with Jinan as the core, and the Shandong Peninsula city concentrated area with Qingdao as the core, which are the two major city agglomeration areas. According to Christaller's "Central Place Theory", the number of cities in the city system increases exponentially from the high to the low with the size order, and according to the principle of optimal market increase rate of $K = 3$, principle

Table 8.4 The change of city size hierarchy in Shandong

Year	Total city	City size hierarchy				
		Super mega cities	Mega cities	Large cities	Medium cities	Small cities
		>200 ten thousand	100–200 ten thousand	50–100 ten thousand	20–50 ten thousand	<20 ten thousand
1995	47	0	3	4	18	22
1996	48	0	3	4	19	22
1997	48	0	3	5	20	20
1998	48	0	3	5	19	21
1999	48	0	3	5	20	20
2000	48	0	3	6	23	16
2001	48	0	3	7	22	16
2002	48	1	2	7	25	13
2003	48	2	2	6	27	11
2004	48	2	2	6	27	11
2005	48	2	3	8	26	9
2006	48	2	3	9	26	8
2007	48	2	5	6	27	8
2008	48	2	4	7	27	8
2009	48	2	4	9	26	7
2010	48	2	4	10	27	5
2011	48	2	4	10	27	5
2012	48	2	4	11	26	5

Source People's Republic of China County National Population Statistics 1996–2013

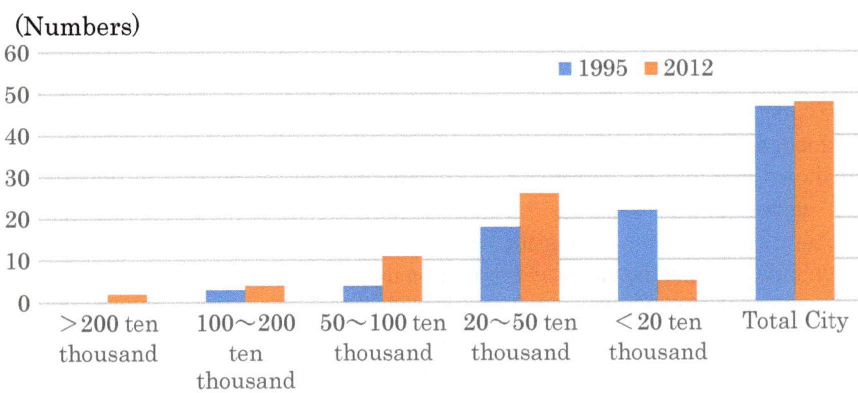

Fig. 8.2 The level of city population size comparison of Shandong. *Source* Same Table (8.4)

Table 8.5 The comparison between hierarchical structure of city size in Shandong and central place theory ideal structure (numbers)

Size grade	$K = 3$	$K = 4$		$K = 7$	Total	Shandong
1	1	1		1	1	2
2	2	3		6	2–6	4
3	6	12		42	6–42	11
4	18	48		294	18–294	31
5	54	192		2058	54–2058	1297

Source People's Republic of China County National Population Statistics 2013; Shandong Statistical Yearbook 2013

Note Size grade five includes the number of county-level cities, counties, and towns in Shandong

of optimal traffic growth rate of $K = 4$, and administrative optimal principle growth rate of $K = 7$, the number of grade centers varies regularly.

It can be seen from Table 8.5 that the city size hierarchy of Shandong is different from the theory of central place, and the number of cities in the first size is 1 in central place theory, while the number of cities with the first rank in Shandong is 2, Jinan and Qingdao, respectively. Therefore, the city size hierarchy of Shandong does not completely conform to the ideal structure of central place theory. However, from the size of grade one to five, the number of cities in each size of Shandong shows geometric change, which shows that hierarchical structure of city size is closer to the ideal structure of central place theory and city system presents a hierarchical structure.

8.5.2 The Evolution of Rank-Size Index

In this chapter, according to the data of Shandong city population size, the linear regression is used to simulate, and Zipf index fitting value q of 1995–2012 years is obtained, and the fractal dimension is calculated by value q. The calculation results are shown in Table 8.6 and Fig. 8.3. According to the calculation results, the city size segment of Shandong has fractal characteristics and conforms to the rank-size structure. Overall: first, during the period 1995–2012, Zipf index q is less than 1, which indicates that the city size distribution in Shandong is more dispersed, the city primacy is not obvious, the population distribution is more homogeneous, and the number of cities in the middle order is more uniform, the city system development is relatively mature. Second, during the period 1995–2012, Zipf index q showed a downward trend, indicating the size of city development in Shandong from the primacy of the city's strong monopoly situation to small and medium-sized cities as the main stage of evolution. In stages, during the period 1995–2005, Zipf index q showed a downward trend, an upward trend during the period 2005–2007, a downward trend again during the period 2007–2010, and an upward trend again after 2010.

Table 8.6 The rank-size distribution of city system in Shandong

Year	Rank-Size expression	*q*
1995	y = −0.803x + 5.547	0.803
1996	y = −0.808x + 5.605	0.808
1997	y = −0.811x + 5.624	0.811
1998	y = −0.812x + 5.628	0.812
1999	y = −0.813x + 5.644	0.813
2000	y = −0.810x + 5.676	0.810
2001	y = −0.798x + 5.683	0.798
2002	y = −0.807x + 5.758	0.807
2003	y = −0.797x + 5.804	0.797
2004	y = −0.798x + 5.843	0.798
2005	y = −0.772x + 5.941	0.772
2006	y = −0.779x + 5.979	0.779
2007	y = −0.813x + 6.111	0.813
2008	y = −0.800x + 6.096	0.800
2009	y = −0.775x + 6.043	0.775
2010	y = −0.748x + 6.038	0.748
2011	y = −0.756x + 6.063	0.756
2012	y = −0.763x + 6.095	0.763

It shows that the regional development of Shandong has experienced a process from decentralization to agglomeration, from agglomeration to decentralization, and from decentralization to agglomeration. Although the growth rate of cities is faster than that of small and medium-sized cities after 2010, the size of city development in Shandong is still in a decentralized state.

8.5.3 The Evolution of City Primacy Degree

Comprehensive Table 8.7 and Fig. 8.4 show that first, during the period 1995–2012, two-city index of Shandong was lower than 1.3, which is significantly lower than 2, while four-city index and eleven-city index are less than 0.65, which is significantly lower than 1. Therefore, the primacy degree of cities in Shandong is low and belongs to the low primacy type. The main reason is that the primacy city of Jinan development is not significant, while the sub-provincial city of Qingdao as the second largest population of the city, the gap between developmental level and size of Jinan is not large, which leads to the small city index of Shandong, so the primacy city is not obvious. Second, during the period 1995–2004, eleven-city index is slightly higher than four-city index. During this period, the size of Shandong's second to fourth

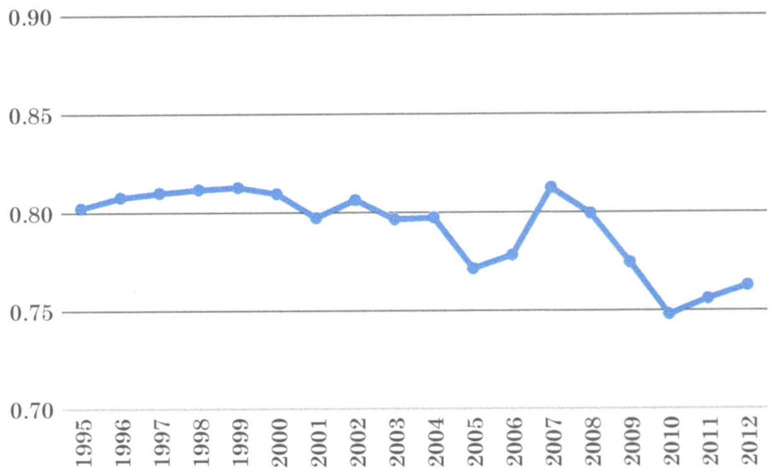

Fig. 8.3 Evolution of Zipf index (*q*) of city size in Shandong. *Source* Same Table (8.4). *Note* 47 cities in 1995, 48 cities during the period 1996–2012

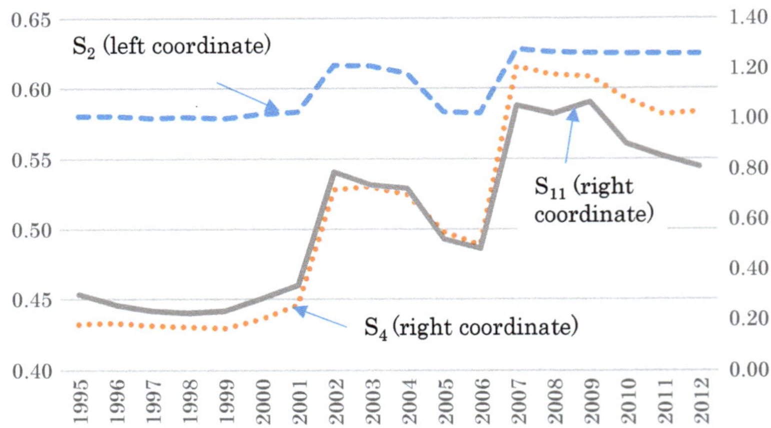

Fig. 8.4 The evolution of Shandong city primacy index. *Source* Same Table (8.5). *Note* *S*2 is two-city index, *S*4 is four-city index, and *S*11 is eleven-city index

cities is growing faster than that of fifth to eleventh cities, and the megacities and large cities in the province have been developing rapidly, and capital and labor force are gathering in large cities. But during the period 2005–2012, on the contrary, the city size of Shandong from second to fourth is slower than that of fifth to eleventh cities, and the population growth rate of the small and medium-sized cities in the province is increasing faster, and the population distribution tends to disperse.

Table 8.7 City Primacy Index in Shandong

Year	1995	1996	1997	1998	1999	2000	2001	2002	2003
S_2	1.011	1.011	1.004	1.006	1.002	1.019	1.027	1.215	1.214
S_4	0.433	0.433	0.432	0.431	0.430	0.436	0.446	0.528	0.531
S_{11}	0.453	0.446	0.441	0.440	0.441	0.450	0.460	0.541	0.531
Year	2004	2005	2006	2007	2008	2009	2010	2011	2012
S_2	1.182	1.027	1.022	1.280	1.268	1.264	1.263	1.261	1.260
S_4	0.525	0.498	0.489	0.616	0.610	0.609	0.592	0.581	0.583
S_{11}	0.529	0.493	0.486	0.587	0.581	0.590	0.561	0.552	0.544

Source Same Table 8.4

8.5.4 A Summary of the Size Structure of City System in Shandong

In conclusion, through the evolution of the number of hierarchy cities, the evolution of rank-size index, and the evolution of city primacy index, the characteristics of the city system in Shandong can be obtained.

Firstly, the primacy index of cities in Shandong is lower, the centrality of the primacy city is not obvious, and the dual-core structure is obvious. The size hierarchy level of city system in Shandong is on the rise, the city population continues to expand, and the size of Jinan and Qingdao gradually evolved into regional super megacities, But the phenomenon of population agglomeration in the primacy city is not obvious, and the gap between the largest cities and the cities from second to eleventh shows a narrowing trend.

Second, the size distribution of city system of Shandong tends to disperse. The distribution of city size in Shandong is dispersed, the population distribution is balanced, the number of cities in the middle order is more, and the city system is mature. Although the growth rate of the city phenomenon in recent years, overall, high-grade city size has a prominent decline, the population growth rate of small and medium-sized cities is faster than that of large cities, and the city population distribution tends to be balanced.

By comparing the characteristics of the regional city system and the level of regional economic development, we can get a relatively high level of city system structure in the economically developed areas, and at the same time, the regional city system structure with rapid economic growth is upgrading rapidly. Economic growth plays a role in city system structure through the division of labor effect, industrial agglomeration, and scale economy and so on.

8.6 An Empirical Study on the Relationship Between City System and Regional Economic Performances in Shandong

8.6.1 OLS Regression Analysis

From the summary of the city system scale structure of 48 cities in Shandong during the period 1995–2012, it can be seen that the city primacy degree is low, two city index, four city index and eleven urban index are on the rise. That is to say, the size of city system is increasing, but the population agglomeration in the primacy city is not obvious, while the rank-size Zipf index is declining. The population growth rate of small and medium-sized cities is faster than that of large cities, and the city population distribution tends to be in balance.

Table 8.8 OLS results

Variable	(12)	(13)	(14)
C	4.902**	7.657**	7.465**
$\ln(q)$	−15.235**	−12.802**	−14.677**
$\ln(S_2)$	3.036**		
$\ln(S_4)$		2.695**	
$\ln(S_{11})$			3.036**
Adjusted R-squared	0.8521	0.8933	0.8566
F-statistic	49.96**	72.18**	51.79**

Note * stands for $p < 0.05$, ** stands for $p < 0.01$

The relationship between city system scale structure and regional economic development is measured from the city primacy degree and the rank-size index. During the period 1995–2012, the primacy index of 48 cities in Shandong, and the rank-size index and gross regional product (GRP) are analyzed in a simple OLS regression analysis. In order to eliminate the heteroscedasticity, logarithms are taken for each variable. The explained variable is (ln(agrp))[7] of the actual regional GDP, and the explanatory variables are Zipf index ($\ln(q)$), two city index ($\ln(S_2)$), four city index ($\ln(S_4)$), eleven city index ($\ln(S_{11})$). Before OLS regression, there was no multicollinearity between the explanatory variables. After OLS regression, it is proved that there is no multicollinearity, heteroscedasticity and sequence correlation in the regression equation through heteroscedasticity test and sequence correlation test. Three regression models were established, which correspond to the regression equations, such as (8.5), (8.6) and (8.7):

$$\ln(\text{agrp})_{it} = 4.902 - 15.235\ln(q)_{it} + 3.036\ln(S_2)_{it} + \mu_{it} \tag{8.5}$$

$$\ln(\text{agrp})_{it} = 7.657 - 12.802\ln(q)_{it} + 2.695\ln(S_4)_{it} + \mu_{it} \tag{8.6}$$

$$\ln(\text{agrp})_{it} = 7.465 - 14.677\ln(q)_{it} + 3.036\ln(S_{11})_{it} + \mu_{it} \tag{8.7}$$

From the OLS regression of Table 8.8, we can draw the following conclusions.

First, both the two-city index and four-city index, or eleven-city index have a significant positive impact on gross regional product, while Zipf index has a negative impact on gross regional product. Therefore, it can be inferred that the higher the primacy degree of the city, the higher the concentration of the city population in the largest city will have a positive role in promoting regional economic development.

Second, the growth rate of small and medium-sized cities is faster than that of cities, that is to say, the more dispersed and balanced city population size is, the more it can promote the growth of regional economy. Accelerating the growth of the population to the largest city and speeding up the growth of small and medium-sized cities is conducive to the development of regional economy.

[7] Gross regional product (GRP) in 1995 as the base period calculation.

City system hierarchical structure of polarization in Shandong is not obvious, the population continues to focus on the two core cities of Jinan and Qingdao, and the agglomeration effect of large cities is increasing. This is mainly due to the two core cities of Jinan and Qingdao, and the large cities of Yantai and Weihai, as these cities not only undertake the transfer of the second industry in Japan and South Korea but also focus on the export-oriented manufacturing agglomeration, which increases the demand for labor and increases the absorptive capacity of rural surplus labor force. The population distribution of Shandong tends to be scattered, and the population growth rate of small and medium-sized cities is more than that of large cities. This is mainly due to the continuous improvement of infrastructure and public services in small and medium-sized cities and the transfer of rural labor force.

8.6.2 Panel Data Analysis

8.6.2.1 Variable Description and Data Source

In this chapter, using the data of 17 prefecture-level cities in Shandong during the period 2000–2012,[8] the panel data of the relationship between city system structure and regional economic development are analyzed. The data used are from the "China City Statistical Yearbook 2001–2013" and "People's Republic of China County National Population Statistics 2001–2013", and variable symbols are shown in Table 8.9, in order to avoid the impact of heteroscedasticity, and all variables are in logarithmic calculation.

In order to explore the relationship between city system and regional economic development, this chapter starts from two aspects. The influence of regional economic development on the evolution of city system, and the influence of the change of city system on regional economic development are discussed. The explanatory variables are selected on behalf of the city system changes in population density for the analysis of regional economic development on the influence of population size distribution; second, the actual gross regional product per capita and actual gross regional product were selected to measure the regional economic development, and the population size distribution is used to analyze the impact on regional economic development. In each panel data model, multiple variables that affect the city system and regional economic development are added as control variables. The control variables are selected from the perspectives of urbanization, industrial structure, human capital, domestic capital investment, foreign capital investment, finance and labor capital. The specific variables include the city level, industrial structure, human capital level,

[8]Municipal district data is not excluding counties and county-level cities under city data. As the statistics of "People's Republic of China National County Population Statistics 2001–2013" are only part of the population data, there are only 17 cities in Shandong province, but there are only statistical data of 17 prefecture-level cities of Shandong in "Chinese City Statistical Yearbook 2001–2013". Therefore, other variables representing economic significance corresponding to 48 cities in Shandong cannot be obtained.

Table 8.9 Variable symbol specification

Variable type	Variable name	Variable symbol	Data processing
Explained variable	Population size	popu	Population density in municipal district
	Actual GRP per capita	pgrp	In 1995 as the base period ratio of the actual GRP and the total population
	Actual GRP	agrp	In 1995 as the base period
Explanatory variable	Urbanization level	urb	The proportion of nonagricultural population in municipal district to the total population of city
	Proportion of foreign direct investment	fdi	The proportion of foreign direct investment in GRP
	Proportion of fiscal expenditure per capita	pfis	The ratio of fiscal expenditure to the total population of municipal district
	Proportion of fiscal expenditure	fis	The proportion of fiscal expenditure in GRP
	Proportion of investment in fixed assets per capita	pfci	The ratio of fixed assets investment to the total population of municipal district
	Proportion of investment in fixed assets[a]	fci	The proportion of fixed assets investment in GRP
	Index of industrial structure	ter-sec	The ratio between the tertiary industry and the secondary industry
	Proportion of the secondary industry	sec	The proportion of the secondary industry to GRP
	Proportion of the tertiary industry	ter	The proportion of the tertiary industry to GRP
	Proportion of employees in the secondary industry[b]	secem	The proportion of employees in the secondary industry to the total employed persons
	Proportion of employees in the tertiary industry	terem	The proportion of employees in the tertiary industry to the total employed persons
	Human capital level[c]	hum	Number of students in colleges

[a]Municipal district of investment in fixed assets mainly refers to various cities registered enterprises, institutions, administrative units and individuals in the plan a total investment of 500 thousand yuan and 500 thousand yuan of investment in construction projects. Occurred in the county and the area above the investment, direct leadership, governments at all levels and departments at or above the county-level management of construction projects and enterprises investment, and investment in real estate development

[b]Number of employees mainly refers to the number of employees at the end of the unit. Unit employees including all levels of state organs, party, and government organs, social organizations, enterprises, and institutions, and obtain all personnel labor remuneration. Including laid-off workers, reemployment of retirees, teachers and work in various units of foreign staff, part-time staff in Hong Kong, Macao, and Taiwan, personnel, borrowing unit personnel and second occupation. It does not include employees who leave their units and retain their labor relations

[c]Under normal circumstances, the human capital index using the number of college graduates will be more appropriate, due to the limitation of data, the number of college students used in this chapter

the proportion of investment in fixed assets, foreign direct investment, the proportion of fiscal expenditure, the proportion of the secondary industry and the proportion of the tertiary industry, the secondary industry and the tertiary industry proportion of employees.

8.6.2.2 Panel Data Model

Using Table 8.9 variables, a total of 5 models are established, such as Table 8.10. The random effects model (RE (1) and RE (2)) are used to measure the impact of regional economic development and related control variables on the city population size system, and the fixed effects model (FE (3), FE (4), and FE (5)) are used to measure the impact of city population size and related control variables on regional economic development.[9] In the random effects model RE (1) and RE (2), the explanatory variables are population density (ln(popu)). In the fixed effect model FE (3) and FE (4), the explanatory variables are actual gross regional product per capita (ln(pgrp)), and in the fixed effect model FE (5), the explanatory variables are actual gross regional product (ln(agrp)).

8.6.2.3 Panel Data Analysis

According to the panel data analysis of model (1) to model (5), the following conclusions are drawn.

First, model (1) and model (2) represent the impact of regional economic development on city population size system. In the model (1), the actual GRP, urbanization level, foreign direct investment, the proportion of fiscal expenditure, and the proportion of employees in the tertiary industry have a significant positive impact on the city population density, while the proportion of investment in fixed assets and the proportion of the secondary industry have a significant negative impact on the city population density. In the model (2), the actual GRP, urbanization level, foreign direct investment, the proportion of fiscal expenditure per capita, the proportion of employees in the tertiary industry, and the ratio between the tertiary industry and the secondary industry have a significant positive impact on the city population density, while the proportion of investment in fixed assets per capita has a significant negative impact on population density.

On the whole, the growth of the regional economy, the improvement of urbanization level, the increase in foreign capital investment, and the increase in financial expenditure attract the population to the city areas. In general, the average income of the technology intensive industries such as the financial industry, the electronic communications industry and the real estate industry in the tertiary industry is higher than the average income of the labor intensive secondary industry. Therefore, the increase of the proportion of employees in the tertiary industry will encourage the population

[9]The choice of random effect model and fixed effect model is the result of Hausman Test.

Table 8.10 Panel data analysis results

Variable	ln(popu)		ln(pgrp)		ln(agrp)
	RE(1)	RE(2)	FE(3)	FE(4)	FE(5)
ln(agrp)	0.08**	0.08*			
	(2.86)	(2.42)			
ln(popu)			−0.19**	-0.16**	0.30**
			(−3.57)	(−2.83)	(4.96)
ln(urb)	0.19*	0.22*	0.76**	0.81**	0.26*
	(2.25)	(2.43)	(9.90)	(11.09)	(3.06)
ln(fdi)	0.10**	0.08**	0.12**	0.11**	0.20**
	(4.84)	(4.00)	(6.42)	(5.95)	(6.54)
ln(pfis)		0.17**			
		(2.66)			
lb(fis)	0.40**		−0.48**	−0.51**	−0.89**
	(5.50)		(−8.07)	(−8.85)	(−8.66)
ln(pfci)		−0.23**			
		(−4.94)			
ln(fci)	−0.22**		−0.26**	−0.26**	−0.61**
	(−4.20)		(−4.24)	(−4.24)	(−5.55)
ln(ter-s)		0.36**			−0.42**
		(6.16)			(−4.59)
ln(s)	−0.42**		0.50**		
	(−2.62)		(3.70)		
ln(ter)				−0.25**	
				(−3.01)	
ln(secem)				0.64**	
				(7.46)	
ln(terem)	0.43**	0.29**	−0.49**		
	(3.69)	(2.75)	(−5.14)		
ln(hum)			0.09**	0.08**	0.29**
			(4.60)	(4.14)	(8.47)
c	5.87**	5.58**	9.77**	8.06**	4.72**
	(5.78)	(9.92)	(10.13)	(12.43)	(4.96)
Adjusted *R*-squared	0.4430	0.4964	0.9157	0.9172	0.8252
Observations	221	221	221	221	221

Note * stands for $p < 0.05$, ** stands for $p < 0.01$

to gather in the city and the region. Similarly, cities with the tertiary industry more than the secondary industry will also attract large numbers of people gathered to the city. In contrast, the increase of the proportion of the secondary industry will not bring more population agglomeration, and cannot bring the economies of size effect. In addition, although foreign capital accumulation will increase population density, domestic capital accumulation does not increase population density, instead it reduces population density. Therefore, it can be concluded that regional economic development has a positive impact on city population size, that is, regional economic development is conducive to the concentration of city population.

Second, model (3), model (4), and model (5) represent the influence of city population size on regional economic development. Model (3) and model (4) measure the impact of city population size and its control variables on the actual GRP per capita. Model (5) measures the impact of city population size and its control variables on the actual GRP. In model (3), urbanization level, the proportion of foreign direct investment, the proportion of the secondary industry, and human capital level have a significant positive impact on the actual GRP per capita, while the city population density and the proportion of fiscal expenditure, the proportion of investment in fixed assets, and the proportion of employees in the tertiary industry have a significant negative impact on the proportion of the actual GRP per capita. Similarly, in model (4), urbanization level, the proportion of foreign direct investment, the proportion of employees in the secondary industry, and human capital level have a significant positive impact on the actual GRP per capita, while the city population density, the proportion of fiscal expenditure, the proportion of investment in fixed assets, and the proportion of the tertiary industry have a significant negative impact on the actual GRP per capita. In model (5), city population density, urbanization level, the proportion of foreign direct investment and human capital level have a significant positive impact on the actual GRP, and the proportion of fiscal expenditure, the proportion of investment in fixed assets, and the ratio between the tertiary industry and the secondary industry have a significant negative impact on the actual GRP.

On the whole, it can be seen that the improvement of urbanization level and human capital level and the increase of foreign capital investment will promote the development of regional economy, and the reduction in population density can alleviate city crowding and increase GRP per capita. However, the increase in population density will increase GRP, that is, the concentration of city population will promote the regional economic growth. Since the proportion of the secondary industry in districts under cities of Shandong is still ahead of the tertiary industry, which occupies the dominant position,[10] therefore, the relative increase in the proportion of the secondary industry and the relative reduction in the proportion of the tertiary industry are conducive to the growth of the regional economy. On the contrary, the increase of employees in the secondary industry and the relative reduction of employees in the tertiary industry of the unit enterprises are also conducive to the growth of the regional economy. At the same time, the increase of the domestic capital investment

[10]In 2012, the proportion of the secondary industry to GRP was 52.9%, and the proportion of the tertiary industry to GRP was 44% in districts under cities of Shandong.

has not promoted the development of regional economy. In the above model (1) and model (2), the increase of the domestic capital investment has reduced the population density. It is proved that the investment in fixed assets in Shandong has been a trend of diminishing returns to factor inputs, the increase of capital investment will not lead to higher scale economic effect. That is, the economic model that depends on the input of extensive elements has not been able to meet the goals of economic growth. The pressure on the economic and social environment will only prevent the population concentration and the further development of the regional economy.

8.7 Conclusions

This chapter is based on the national scope around prefecture-level cities to measure the relationship between the city structure of each province and regional economic development by the city system index, and select the typical representative of Shandong province as an example, through the empirical analysis to verify the relationship between the city system and regional economic performances of Shandong. The main conclusions of this chapter are summarized as follows.

First, it is concluded that there is no clear relationship between the city system index and the indicators of economic development of all provinces based on the analysis of the city system index of 278 cities in 23 provinces of China. It is due to the reversal of the order of the city system index between the economically developed provinces and the less developed provinces.

Second, through the investigation of three aspects of Shandong's city size hierarchy, rank-size index, and city primacy index, we can draw the conclusion that Shandong's city system has the following characteristics: ①The city system of Shandong presents a hierarchical structure. ②The primacy index of cities in Shandong is lower, the centrality of the primacy city is not obvious, and the dual-core structure is obvious. The size of Jinan and Qingdao gradually evolved into regional super megacities. ③The size distribution of city system of Shandong tends to disperse. The size of high-grade cities is declining, the population growth rate of small and medium-sized cities is faster than that of large cities, and the city population distribution tends to be balanced.

Third, through the OLS regression analysis of size structure and regional economic development of Shandong's city system, the following conclusions are drawn: ①The higher the primacy of the city, the higher the concentration of the city population in the largest city, which will have a positive role in promoting regional economic development. ②The growth rate of small and medium-sized cities is faster than that of cities, that is to say, the more dispersed and balanced city population size is, the more it can promote the growth of regional economy.

Fourth, we can confirm that there is a close relationship between Shandong's city system and regional economic performances based on the analysis of panel data of 17 prefecture-level cities in Shandong during the period 2000–2012. On the one hand, regional economic, urbanization level, foreign capital investment, fiscal expenditure, the proportion of the tertiary industry, and the proportion of employees in the secondary industry, the increase of which can promote the aggregation of the population to the city and region. It can be concluded that regional economic development promotes the concentration of city population. On the other hand, urbanization level, human capital level, and foreign capital investment, the increase of which can promote regional economic development. It can be concluded that the concentration of city population has promoted the development of regional economy .

References

Alonso, W. 1980. Five bell shapes in development. *Chapters in Regional Science* 45 (1): 5–16.
Au, C.C., and J.V. Henderson. 2006. Are Chinese cities too small. *Review of Economic Studies* 73 (2): 549–576.
Berry, B.J.L. 1961. City Size distribution and economic development. *Economic Development and Culture Change* 9: 573–587.
Chen, J., and Q. Zhou. 2016. The synergy effects of city size and industrial structure on urban labor productivity in China. *Journal of Finance and Economics* 42 (9): 75–86. (in Chinese).
Christaller, W. 1933. *Central Places in Southern Germany.* [Jena: Fischer, in English by Carlisle W. Baskin]. London: Prentice-Hall.
Ciccone, A., and R.E. Hall. 1996. Productivity and the density of economic activity. *American Economic Review* 86 (1): 54–70.
Fan, J. 2006. Industrial agglomeration and difference of region labor productivity: Chinese evidence with international comparison. *Economic Research Journal* 11: 72–81. (in Chinese).
Hanson, G.H. 2005. Market potential, increasing returns, and geographic concentration. *Journal of International Economics* 67 (1): 1–24.
Henderson, J.V. 2000. *The effect of concentration on economic growth*, 7503. No: NEBR Working Chapter.
Henderson, J.V. 2003. The urbanization process and economic growth: The so-what question. *Journal of Economic Growth* 8 (1): 47–71.
Henderson, J. V. 2005. Urbanization and growth. In *Handbook of economic growth,* ed. P. Aghion, S. Durlauf, vol. 1, 1543–1591. North Holland: Elsevier.
Henderson, J.V., Z. Shalizi, and A. Venables. 2001. Geography and development. *Journal of Economic Geography* 1 (1): 81–105.
Ishikawa, T. 2016. *Dynamic location phases of economic activity in the globalized World*. Singapore: Springer.
Jefferson, M. 1939. The law of the primate city. *Geographical Review* 29: 226–232.
Junius, K. 1999. Primacy and economic development: Bell shaped or parallel growth of cities? *Journal of Economic Development* 24 (1): 1–22.
Ke, S., and Y. Zhao. 2014. Industrial structure, city size and urban productivity in China. *Economic Research Journal* 4: 76–115. (in Chinese).
Liu, X. 2009. Agglomeration economies and labor productivity: Evidence from Chinese urban panel data. *The Journal of Quantitative & Technical Economics* 7: 109–119. (in Chinese).
Mao, F., and J. Pan. 2012. Capital deepening, industry structure and labor productivity in Chinese cities. *China Industrial Economics* 10: 32–44.

Wang, Y., M. Nian, and C. Wang. 2017. Industrial structure, optimal size and the urbanization path in China. *China Economic Quarterly* 16 (2): 1–22. (in Chinese).
Wheaton, W.C., and H. Shishido. 1981. Agglomeration economies, and the level of economic development. *Economic Development and Cultural Change* 30 (1): 17–30.
Xie, X., and X. Wang. 2012. The evolution of city size distribution and economic growth. *South China Journal of Economics* 6: 59–73. (in Chinese).

Part III
Economic Analysis of Industrial Park in Regional Vitalization Process

Chapter 9
The Evolution of Economic Zones in the Philippines

Arianne Dela Rosa Dumayas

Abstract In the pursuit of industrial and regional development, many developing countries have established export processing zones (EPZ) and special economic zones (SEZ). In the Philippines, the first EPZ was established in 1969 with the aim of export-oriented industrialization and dispersal of economic activity away from capital region. As of 2016, the number of SEZs has expanded to 348 zones. This chapter examines the transformation of economic zone development in the Philippines. This chapter also presents key facts and figures about economic zones in the Philippines. This chapter also analyzes the impact of the evolution of economic zones on investments, exports, and employment. The economic zone development in the Philippines has undergone three main phases: government-led EPZ (1970–1994); private sector-driven SEZ (1995–1999); and Information Technology (IT) industry-centered SEZ (2000–present). The inclusion of private sector in development and management of economic zones has resulted to a significant boom in the number of economic zones and firms. The composition of economic activities within economic zones has shifted from manufacturing-based to services-based industries. The shift from the government-led EPZ to private-led SEZs enabled economic zones to become more instrumental in driving the overall growth in FDI and exports. On the other hand, the effect of economic zones on employment is relatively insignificant since only data on direct employment is considered.

Keywords Economic zones · Industrial development · Regional development IT parks/centers

A. D. R. Dumayas (✉)
Faculty of Economics, Chuo University, Hachioji, Tokyo, Japan
e-mail: ariannedumayas@gmail.com

T. Ishikawa (ed.), *Locational Analysis of Firms' Activities from a Strategic Perspective*, https://doi.org/10.1007/978-981-13-1684-5_9

9.1 Introduction

Export processing zones (EPZ) and special economic zones (SEZ) are often regarded as "panacea" to many development concerns such as industrial development, regional development, infrastructure unemployment, underinvestment, knowledge-transfer, and spillovers, etc. Given these promises of growth, development of EPZ or SEZ remains to be a popular development strategy of many developing countries. The rapid expansion of economic zones was in part driven by the globalization of trade and development that started in the 1970s and further intensified in 1990s and 2000s (Farole and Akinci 2011). The vertical and spatial fragmentation of manufacturing into highly integrated "global production networks" have propelled the growth of globalization and consequently, the rise of many economic zones around the world.

However, not all zones are alike. While some economic zones could contribute significantly to economic growth and development such as the experience of many industrialized countries, some have failed and became wasteful investment. Rodriguez-Pose and Hardy (2014) identify the dilemma that policy-makers in emerging economies with regards to the development of industrial parks or economic zones: the optimism of gaining benefit as evidenced by successful experiences of some countries; or the pessimism and caution based on the patchy record of economic zones in lagging regions.

The Philippines ventured into the development of EPZ in the late 1960s as part of the export-oriented industrialization strategy. The first EPZ was established in Bataan, a province around 170 km away from Manila. After almost half a century, the number of economic zones has expanded to 348 zones in 2016. Majority of these economic zones are Information Technology (IT) Parks and Buildings which houses mostly business process and outsourcing (BPO) firms.

In the light of the unprecedented growth of economic zones, this chapter seeks to examine how the economic zones in the Philippines have evolved over the past years. This chapter also presents key characteristics of economic zones in the Philippines. This chapter also analyzes the impact of the economic zone development on investments, exports, and employment. This chapter is organized as follows: Sect. 9.2 surveys the rationale behind the concentration of economic activity, various definition of economic zone, and assessment of zone performance. Section 9.3 presents the background information about economic zones such as definition, incentives, location, and management structure. Section 9.4 discusses the impact of transformation of economic zones on investments, exports, and employment. Section 9.5 concludes the paper and offers areas for further research.

9.2 Review of Related Literature

9.2.1 *Concentration of Economic Activity*

Marshall's theory of agglomeration economies is the earliest study that explains the rationale behind the concentration of economic activity in a geographical space. According to Marshall (1920), there are three factors that attract the firm to cluster in the same location: presence of skilled labor, availability of specialized input services, and knowledge or technological spillovers. The presence of skilled labor provides the firm's reductions in acquisition cost for both hiring and training. Firms can easily find qualified and easily trainable employees. The provision of specialized input services is more efficient when firms are clustered than dispersed. Knowledge or technological spillovers are sensitive to distance, firms that are in the same locations have easy access to each other's information or knowledge. Marshall also differentiated the two types of economies that can be derived from agglomeration: internal economies which occurred within the firm, and external economies which are based on larger changes outside the firm or the industry-level.

Meanwhile, the new economic geography (NEG) explains that the spatial configuration of economic activities is a result of two opposing forces: agglomeration (centripetal) forces, and dispersion (centrifugal) forces (Fujita et al. 1999). Agglomeration forces are a combination of three basic elements: first-nature, second-nature, and catalyst (Fujita 2008). First-nature refers to physical geographical features such as the presence of ports and river, natural resources, and weather conditions. Second-nature includes the key elements of heterogeneity in goods, increasing returns at the firm level, transport costs, and migration. Catalysts refer to the various factors that led to the growth of specific agglomeration such as historical conditions, accidents, and public policies. Dispersion forces are external diseconomies that are associated with concentration such as congestion, high price of land or rent, and environmental problems. Agglomeration forces attract different economic activities into one location, however, the same agglomeration forces will result to dispersion. Concentration of economic activity will likely lead to increased factor prices (land and wages), traffic congestion, overcrowding, and pollution. The balance between these forces determines the formation of economic agglomeration in a geographical space.

9.2.2 *Special Economic Zones: Definition and Transformation*

Special economic zones, industrial agglomeration, business park, science park, and technology centers are terms commonly used interchangeably to describe the concentration of industries in certain locations.

Markusen (1996) defines industrial agglomeration as "large, and spatially delimited area of trade-oriented economic activity that has a distinctive economic specialization, either resource, manufacturing, or service related." Markusen (1996) also distinguishes four types of industrial agglomeration: Marshallian-type, hub-and-spoke type, satellite platform type, and state-anchored type. Marshallian-type refers to industrial agglomeration that is found with small, locally owned firms with relatively small-scale economies for each firm and substantial intra-agglomeration trade among buyers and suppliers. Hub-and-spoke industrial agglomerations involve one or several large, vertically integrated firms and suppliers. Satellite platform refers to industrial agglomeration that has large, externally owned, and headquartered firms, with scale economies of core firms are moderate to high, and minimal intra-agglomeration trade between buyers and sellers. State-anchored industrial agglomeration involves one or several large government institutions, suppliers, and customers; with relatively high-scale economies in public sector; and intra-agglomeration trade among institutions and their suppliers.

Rodriguez-Pose and Hardy (2014) define industrial parks, in general, as concentration of specialized industries in particular location offering basic facilities, infrastructure, exemptions, and incentives. To understand the diversity of these park models, Rodriguez-Pose and Hardy (2014) outline a stylized classification of parks according to the degree of technological intensity and management support. Based on the classification, industrial parks have low technology level and low level of management support. On the other hand, technology park/center are often found to have high degree of management support and high-technological intensity. Rodriguez-Pose and Hardy (2014) argue that the rationale behind these industrial parks is to compensate regional inadequacies in terms of infrastructure, bureaucracy, fiscal regulations, and political barriers.

Carter and Harding (2011) and Farole and Akinci (2011) offer similar definition of special economic zones. Carter and Harding (2011) defines special economic zones as defined geographic area in which national, provincial or local government use policy tools such as tax holidays, improved, infrastructure, and less onerous or differentiated regulations and incentives other than those generally promote private, usually foreign, investment from enterprises which commit to create jobs and export their products or services to generate foreign currency for the host country. Meanwhile, Farole and Akinci (2011) distinguish special economic zone as demarcated geographic areas contained within a country's national boundaries where the rules of business are different from those that prevail in the national territory.

Meanwhile, Aggarwal (2010) identifies different types of SEZ and their transformation: trade-based SEZ, manufacturing-based SEZ, comprehensive SEZ, newer varieties' zone, and transnational zones. Trade-based SEZs are considered as the oldest form of SEZ which emerges way back in 1547 in Bay of Genoa in Italy (Meng, as cited in Aggarwal 2010). These trade-based SEZ are established to facilitate trade and are located near the ports. Manufacturing-based SEZ are first established in Spain in 1920s to increase value-added in exports. Meanwhile, the EPZ in Ireland in 1958 have become the model for subsequent manufacturing-based SEZ around the world. These EPZs are basically industrial estates that provides incentives and support to manufacturing and exporting activities. These zones have undergone significant transformation over the past years, specifically, in terms of composition of economic activity and level of technology. The first-generation zones are mainly involved in low-cost and labor-intensive activities, while the later zones have shifted to intermediate-high skill activities and high technology processes. Comprehensive SEZ can trace its roots to China's SEZ model in 1970s. These zones offer incentives not only to manufacturing and exporting firms but also encompasses different activities such as tourism, real estate, and retail. The newer varieties' SEZ which are more innovative and competitive, includes high-tech (science) parks, enterprise-specific zones, services, country-specific zones, and hybrid zones. Transnational zones are established in the border areas to increase economic and trade relations within the regions. One example is the cross-border SEZs promotion of China with Cambodia, Lao, and Vietnam.

FIAS (2008) identifies the common objectives of special economic zones: (1) Attract foreign direct investments (FDI); (2) Serve as pressure valves to alleviate large-scale unemployment; (3) Support of a wider economic reform strategy; (4) Experimental laboratories for the application of new policies and approaches. In line with these common objectives of development of special economic zones, Farole and Akinci (2011) outlines the three main issues regarding special economic zones: first, how to make economic zones successful in attracting firms that create jobs or the static measure of success; second, how to ensure that zones are economically sustainable and deliver positive externalities, including facilitating, upgrading and structural transformation, and catalyzing economic reforms or dynamic measure of success; and third, how to ensure that economic zones are sustainable from an institutional, social, and environmental perspective or social and environmental sustainability (Table 9.1).

As the economies moved toward liberalization, the role and significance of these economic zones have changed, thus prompting the countries to adjust their economic zone strategy Carter and Harding (2011) identifies the key transformation that has occurred with the economic zone strategy. First, economic zones are no longer strictly defined as geographic areas: single enterprises may obtain the privileges and benefits that were only given to economic zones such as the case of Togo, Senegal, Cameroon, and Nigeria. Some are also designed to meet the needs of specific industries: high technology and science-based industries (Malaysia, Korea, and India); financial services (Singapore, Malaysia, and Korea); petrochemicals (Singapore, Thailand). Second, economic zones are longer primarily government-initiated or government-operated, many are public–private or pure private. Third, economic zones no longer require foreign currency as some firms seek to trade in domestic market.

Aggarwal (2010) also observes similar development trends with the evolution in economic zones, specifically, in terms of zone configuration, incentives, ownership, objective, and composition of economic activity. In terms of objective, establishment of economic zones have developed from facilitating trade and generating employment to fostering high-skilled and high technological activities, stimulating economic activity, and diversifying export composition. The incentives have also evolved from traditional tax-related incentives to various incentives such as infrastructure, services, industrial policies, labor policies, and corporate taxation. Economic zone structure has also advanced from stand-alone industrial estates to integrated indus-

Table 9.1 Relevant definition of economic zones

Terms	Definition	Author
Industrial agglomeration	Large, and spatially delimited area of trade-oriented economic activity that has a distinctive economic specialization, either resource, manufacturing, or service related	Markusen (1996)
Industrial park/technology parks	Concentration of specialized industries in particular location with low/high level of technology and low/high level of management support	Rodriguez-Pose and Hardy (2014)
Special economic zones	Defined geographic area in which national, provincial or local government use policy tools such as tax holidays, improved, infrastructure, and less onerous or differentiated regulations and incentives other than those generally promote private, usually foreign, investment from enterprises which commit to create jobs and export their products or services in order to generate foreign currency for the host country	Carter and Harding (2011)
Special economic zones	Demarcated geographic areas contained within a country's national boundaries where the rules of business are different from those that prevail in national territory	Farole (2011)

Source Author's construction based on cited references

trial townships. The economic activity within economic zones has also evolved from trade-oriented and labor-intensive to capital-intensive and high technology intensive economic zones. Economic zones also started as government-created and owned but starting from the 1980s, privately developed and managed zones have begun to emerge. Economic zones location pattern also changed from areas that are located near the port areas to various parts of the country with the aim of integration with host economies.

9.3 Special Economic Zones in the Philippines

9.3.1 Definition and Incentives

In the Philippines, special economic zones are defined as selected with highly developed or have the potential to be developed into agro-industrial, industrial tourist/recreation, commercial, banking, investment, and financial centers. Through these special economic zones, the government aims "to encourage, promote, induce, and accelerate a sound a balanced industrial, economic, and social development of the country in order to provide jobs to the people especially those in the rural areas, to increase their productivity and their individual family income, and thereby improving the level and quality of their living condition through the establishment, among others, of special economic zones in suitable and strategic locations in the country and through measure that shall effectively attract legitimate and productive foreign investments (PEZA 1995)."

There are several types of special economic zones in the Philippines: industrial estates or manufacturing SEZ, export processing zones, free trade zones, tourism ecozones, agro-industrial SEZ, and IT Parks/Buildings.

- **Industrial Estates/Manufacturing SEZ**—tract of land developed for the use of industries. They have basic infrastructures such as road, water, and sewage systems, pre-built factory building, and residential housing.
- **Export Processing Zones**—zones whose locator companies are mainly export-oriented. EPZ incentives include tax and duty-free importation of capital equipment, raw materials, and spare parts.
- **Free Trade Zones**—areas in nearby ports of entry, such as seaports and airports. Imported goods maybe unloaded, repacked, sorted, and manipulated without being subject to import duties. However, if these goods are move into a non-free trade zone, they will be subjected to customs duties.
- **Tourism Ecozones**—tourism development zone/tourism estate declared as special economic zone suitable for development into an integrated resort complex with prescribed carrying capacities of tourist facilities and activities, such as, but not limited to, sports and recreation centers, accommodations, convention and cultural facilities, food and beverage outlets, commercial establishments and other special interest and attraction activities/establishments, and provided with the necessary infrastructure.
- **Agro-industrial SEZ**—large and suitable tract of land subdivided and developed in accordance with a comprehensive plan, with provision for basic infrastructures and utilities designed to host primarily agricultural and or natural resource-based processing activities which are export-oriented.
- **IT Parks/IT Buildings**—the whole or part of which has been developed into a complex capable of providing infrastructures and other support facilities required by IT Enterprises, including amenities required by professionals and workers involved in IT Enterprises.

There are also different firms engaged in various activities within the economic zone: export enterprise, free trade zone enterprise, service enterprise, domestic market enterprise, pioneer enterprise, utilities enterprise, facilities enterprise, tourism enterprise, ecozone developer/operator, and IT enterprise.

- **Export Enterprise**—manufactures, assembles, or processes products which are 100% exported, unless a lower percentage is approved by PEZA.
- **Free Trade Zone Enterprise**—imports and markets tax and duty-free gods within the free trade area in the ecozone. Goods bought outside the free trade area will be subject to customs and tariff duties.
- **Service Enterprise**—conducts in any one of a combination of the following activities: customs brokerage, trucking/forwarding, janitorial, security, insurance and/or banking, consulting, or any such service approved by PEZA.
- **Domestic Market Enterprises**—manufactures, assembles, processes goods which continually fails to export at least 50% of its total output for a period of three years if majority owned by Filipinos and at least 70% if majority owned by foreign nationals.
- **Pioneer Enterprise**—falls under any of the following conditions:
  - Manufactures, processes, or produces goods not produced in a commercial scale in the country.
  - Uses a design, formula, scheme, method, or process which is new and untried in the Philippines.
  - Produces nonconventional fuels or manufactures equipment that utilizes nonconventional sources of energy.
  - Develops areas for agri-export processing development.
  - Given such status under the annual IPP approved by the president.
- **Utilities enterprise**—provides light and power, water supply, and distribution, communications, and transportation system in the ecozone.
- **Facilities enterprise**—builds and maintains necessary infrastructure such as warehouse, buildings, road networks, ports, sewerage and drainage systems, and other facilities considered as necessary by PEZA in the development and operations of the ecozone.
- **Tourism enterprise**—operates sports and recreation center, accommodations, convention and cultural facilities, and other special interest and attraction activities/establishments with foreign tourist as primary clientele.
- **Ecozone Developer/Operator**—develops, operates, and maintains the ecozone, all component sectors (i.e., IEs, EPZs, Free Trade Zones, and Tourist Ecozones) and all related infrastructure (roads, light, and power systems, drainage facilities, etc.)
- **IT Enterprise**—provides or operates IT services. IT is the collective term for the various technologies involved in processing and transmitting information, which include computing, multimedia, telecommunications, microelectronics, and their interdependences. Also called "informatics" or "telematics," the term now often refers to the convergence of various information-based, broadcast, and mass media communication technologies.

The planning, developing, and operation of these economic zones are open to private sector as well as local government entities. However, each economic zone has specific area requirements and incentive scheme. In general, developers and firms are exempted from local and national taxes. In lieu of these taxes, five percent of the gross income shall be to national government (3%) and local government (2%). To avail this incentive, the developer must choose to locate outside the capital or in some economic zones like Information Technology Park and Center, outside Metro Manila or Cebu City (Table 9.2).

The incentives for the firms who choose to locate within economic zones are entitled to both tax-related and nontax-related incentives. Tax-related benefits includes: tax and duty-free importation of capital equipment, raw materials, spare parts, suppliers, breeding stocks, and genetic materials; income Tax Holiday of 4 years for nonpioneer projects or 6 years for pioneer projects; special tax rate of 5% of modified gross income in lieu of all national and local taxes after Income Tax Holiday; tax credit for import substitution Exemption from wharfage dues, export tax, and import fees; tax credit on domestic capital equipment, breeding stocks, and genetic materials; additional deduction for incremental labor expenses and training expenses; remittance of earnings without prior approval from the BSP[1]; exemption from local business taxes; exemption from Branch Profit Remittance Tax (BPRT) in the case of Philippines branches under 5% modified gross income. The nontax incentives include unrestricted use of consigned equipment; permanent resident status for foreign investors and immediate family; and employment of foreign nationals.

In addition to these tax-related and nontax-related incentives, the Philippines also offers the following advantages: fast-growing economy, favorable investment credit rating, large labor pool, liberalized and foreign investor-friendly policies, strategic location, low-cost of doing business, and high-class amenities for expatriates. The Philippines is currently one of the strongest economies in Asia with annual GDP growth rate of 6–7%. The Philippines is also granted a positive and stable investment grade by major credit rating agencies such as Standard and Poor's Financial Services (S&P), Fitch Ratings (Fitch), and Moody's Investor Service (Moody's). The Filipino workforce is considered as one among the best in the world: high literacy rate, proficient in English, easy to train, hardworking, and friendly. The Philippines have set up policies that allow 100% foreign ownership of companies and protects the basic rights of investors such as right to remit profits, right to pay foreign obligations, and right to repatriate investments. The Philippines is strategically located in Asia, within 4–5 h flying time to major capitals in the region. The Philippines also have relatively low wages, electricity, communication, and housing costs. The Philippines is also equipped with excellent amenities for expatriates such as business centers, housing, schools, hospitals, shopping malls, hotels and restaurants, beach resorts, and recreation centers.

[1]Bangko Sentral ng Pilipinas (BSP), the Philippines central bank.

Table 9.2 Area requirement and incentives to developers

Economic zone	Area requirement	Incentives to developers
Manufacturing	25 ha	5% Gross Income Tax (GIT)
Agro-industrial economic zone	5 ha	<25 ha: no incentive (except for sing locator economic zones >25 ha: 5%
Tourism economic zone	5 ha	<25 ha and located outside Boracay Island, Cebu city, Mactan Island, and Metro Manila: no incentive >25 ha and located outside Boracay Island, Cebu city, Mactan Island, and Metro Manila: 5%
Medical tourism park	1 ha	Within Metro Manila: no incentive Outside Metro Manila: 5% (only for new projects)
Medical tourism center	Within Metro Manila and Cebu city: 5 km^2 flr area	Within Metro Manila: no incentive
	Outside Metro Manila and Cebu city: 2 km^2 flr area	Outside Metro Manila: 5% (only for new projects)
Information Technology park	1 ha	Within Metro Manila and Cebu city: no incentive
		Outside Metro Manila and Cebu city including IT facilities enterprises: 5% (only for new projects)
	Within Metro Manila and Cebu city: 10 km^2 flr area	Within Metro Manila and Cebu City: no incentive
	Outside Metro Manila and Cebu city: 5 km^2 flr area	Outside Metro Manila and Cebu city including IT facilities enterprises: 5% (only for new projects)
Retirement Ecozone park	4 ha	5% GIT
	Within Metro Manila and Cebu city: 5 km^2 flr area	5% GIT
	Outside Metro Manila and Cebu city: 2 km^2 flr area	

Source Author's construction based on Philippines Economic Zones Authority (PEZA)

9.3.2 *Facts and Figures of Special Economic Zones in the Philippines*

As of July 2016, there are 348 special economic zones that are operating in the Philippines and additional 145 zones are being developed (Table 9.3). Almost 70% of active economic zones are IT Parks/Centers and around 20% manufacturing SEZs. IT Parks/Centers also constitute the largest number of planned economic zones.

One prominent characteristic of economic zones in the Philippines is the enormous number of private economic zones (Table 9.4). Except for economic zones that are managed by PEZA or by local government, almost all economic zones in the Philippines are developed and managed by the private sector. PEZA currently manages four manufacturing economic zones: Baguio City Economic Zone, Cavite Economic Zone, Mactan Economic Zone, and Pampanga Economic Zone. Meanwhile, the ownership or management structure within private SEZ varies. The developers of IT Parks/Centers are involved in the management of multiple number of IT Parks/Centers. The developers of IT Parks/Centers also happen to be the top real estate companies in the Philippines such as Robinsons Land Corporation, SM Prime Holdings, Ayala Land Inc., and Megaworld Corporation. On the other hand, developers or operators of manufacturing SEZ typically operate single zone, except for Carmelray Industrial Corporation and Laguna Technopark Inc.

As of August 2016, there are 3226 locator firms in economic zones (Fig. 9.1). Manufacturing SEZs have attracted the most number of firms than any other type of

Table 9.3 Operating and planned economic zones

Types of economic zones	Active	Planned
IT parks/centers	234	104
Manufacturing SEZ	72	29
Agro-industrial SEZ	21	6
Tourism SEZ	19	6
Medical tourism parks/center	2	
Total	348	145

Source Author's construction based on Philippines Economic Zones Authority (PEZA 2016a) statistics

Table 9.4 SEZ management, land area, and investments

Type of SEZ	Public	Private
IT parks/centers	6	228
Manufacturing SEZ	9	63
Agro-industrial SEZ	1	20
Tourism SEZ	0	19

Source Author's construction based on Philippines Economic Zones Authority (PEZA 2016a) statistics

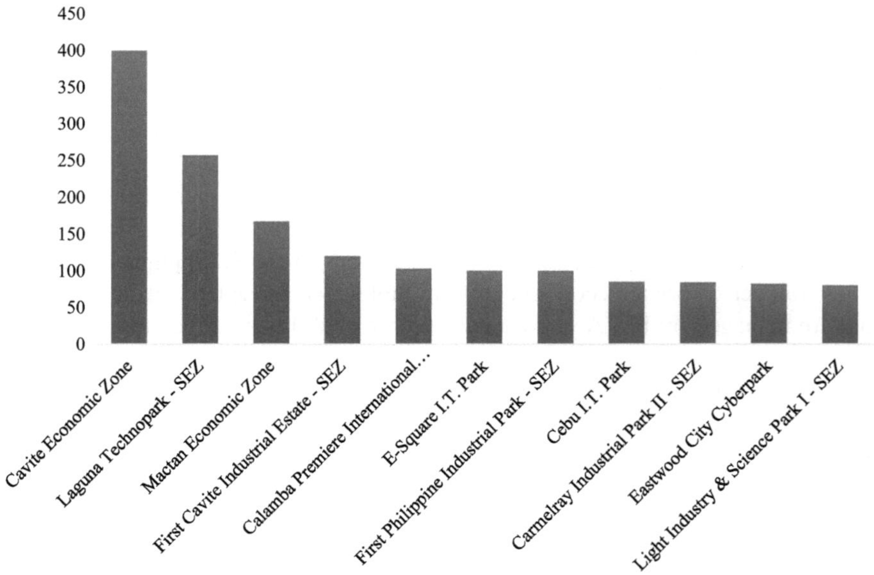

Fig. 9.1 Firms by SEZ location. *Source* Author's construction based on Philippines Economic Zones Authority (PEZA 2016a) statistics

SEZ. Interestingly, two public economic zones, Cavite Economic Zone and Mactan Economic Zone, remains to be a preferred location for many firms. Many of the firms are involved in exporting activities and IT services (Fig. 9.2). Other firms are engaged in different businesses such as facilities, logistic services, tourism, and utilities.

The geographical distribution of economic zones reveals an interesting pattern. IT Parks/Centers and Manufacturing SEZ tend to concentrate in few and relatively developed areas of the country. More than half of IT Parks/Centers are located within Metro Manila (Fig. 9.3). While several IT Center/Parks have chosen to locate in secondary or tertiary centers of Cebu Negros Occidental, Davao Del Sur, Laguna, and Iloilo. More second and third tier cities are being geared up to host IT Centers/Parks through Next Wave Cities(NWC) Program (ITBAP 2016). The NWC program is a joint effort by both government and public sector: Department of Science and Technology-Information and Communications Technology Office(DOST-ICTO) and IT Business Process Association of the Philippines (IBPAP).

Meanwhile, manufacturing SEZ is heavily concentrated in Southern Luzon and its neighboring regions of Metro Manila and Central Luzon (Fig. 9.3). A few manufacturing zones are dispersed in other regional growth centers of Cebu, Baguio, and Davao.

Agro-industrial SEZ and Tourism SEZ are relatively scattered across the country. Agro-industrial economic zones are mostly located in Mindanao island or Visayan island (Fig. 9.4). Tourism SEZ is dispersed in different locations but a couple of zones are located in Metro Manila, Cebu, and Palawan.

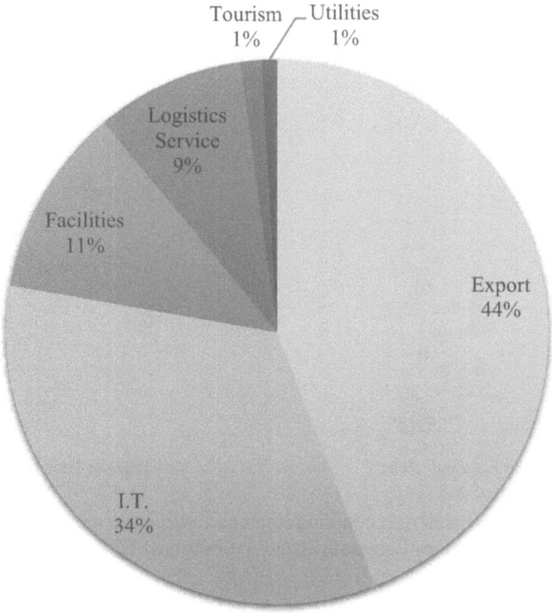

Fig. 9.2 Type of enterprises. *Source* Author's construction based on Philippines Economic Zones Authority (PEZA 2016a) statistics

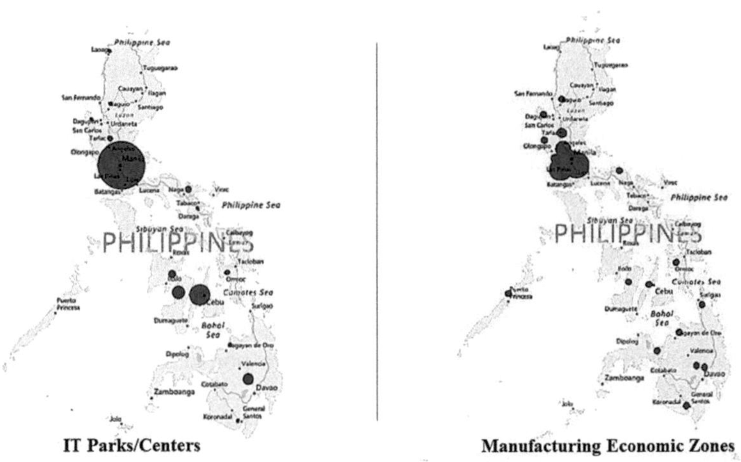

Fig. 9.3 Location of IT parks/centers and manufacturing economic zone. *Source* Author's construction based on Philippines Economic Zones Authority (PEZA 2016a) statistics

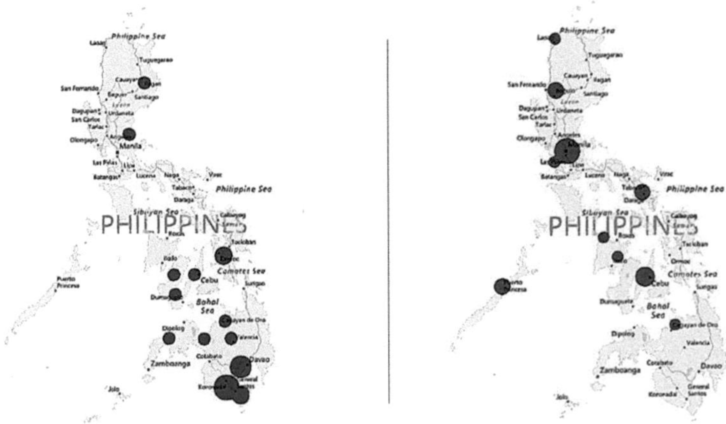

Agro-Industrial Economic Zone **Tourism Economic Zones**

Fig. 9.4 Location of Agro-industrial economic zones and tourism economic zones. *Source* Author's construction based on Philippines Economic Zones Authority (PEZA 2016a) statistics

9.4 Evolution of Economic Zones in the Philippines

9.4.1 Evolution of Economic Zones: From EPZ to SEZ

The special economic zones in the Philippines have undergone a significant transformation over the past decades. Like the development trends identified by Aggarwal (2010) and Carter and Harding (2011), the economic zones in the Philippines have undergone changes in terms of policy orientation, ownership or management structure, and types of activities. The evolution of economic zones in the Philippines can be categorized into three phases: government-led EPZ (1970–1994); private sector-driven SEZ (1995–1999); and Information IT industry-centered SEZ (2000–present).

As early as 1923, the Philippines Chamber of Commerce had plans to convert free ports into free trade zones (Castro 1982). However, this plan was shelved over the next decades until the government has pushed for export-oriented industrialization in the late 1960s.

The first phase of economic zone development (1970–1994) began in the late 1960s. RA 5490 or Export Processing Act in 1969 legislated the creation of the Mariveles, Bataan as the first free port zone. The same act also established the Foreign Trade Zone Authority which is mandated to develop and manage the zones. The Presidential Decree(PD) No. 66 has further pushed for the establishment of the first export processing zones of Bataan Export Processing Zone (BEPZ) in 1972. PD 66 also handed over the responsibility of managing the zones to Export Processing Zone Authority(EPZA). PD 66 envisioned the export processing zones as a means to encourage trade, strengthen foreign exchange position, support industrialization, and accelerate national development.

Three more public EPZ were inaugurated in the following years: Baguio City Export Processing Zone (BCEPZ) and Cavite Export Processing Zone (CEPZ) in 1980, and Mactan Export Processing Zone (MEPZ) in 1986. The production of the firms within these EPZs are mainly for export, however, given the special permissions from EPZA, 30% of the total production can be sold to domestic market. The establishment of these EPZs has paved the way for the integration of the Philippines into the global production networks. Consequently, the profile of main export products had shifted from traditional agricultural-based products to intermediate processed goods. On the other hand, like many first-generation of EPZs, the EPZs in the Philippines were heavily funded by the government and foreign loans. Unfortunately, in some cases, zones generated more costs than benefits (FIAS). For instance, the case of Bataan Export Processing Zone (BEPZ) is a typical example of zone which incurred higher cost than benefits (Warr 1989).

The government effort toward export-oriented industrialization intensified in the 1990s. The Calabarzon project was pursued under the Medium-Term Regional Development Plan for Region IV (1989–1992). Under this project, massive infrastructure projects such as superhighways, ports, and industrial estates were constructed in the five Southern Luzon provinces of Cavite, Laguna, Batangas, Rizal, and Quezon. The project aimed to further accelerate the industrialization and urbanization of these provinces. RA 7227 or the Bases Conversion and Development Act also enacted in 1992 to convert the former US military bases in Subic, Clark and Fort Bonifacio.

The second phase (1995–1999) of economic zone development started with the enactment of RA 7916 or the Special Economic Zone Act of 1995. The act enabled the private sector to participate in the development and management of economic zones. The act also expanded incentives to firms who firms engaging in non-export activities such as commercial/trade services, utilities and facilities, and real estates. The act also legislated the creation of distinct types of special economic zones with varying purposes such as industrial estates, export processing zones, and free trade zones (Manasan 2013). The same act also established Philippine Economic Zone Authority (PEZA), a government agency tasked to promote investments, provide assistance, and facilitate incentives to investors or locators within the special economic zones. PEZA took charge in management of the existing public EPZs.

The third phase (2000–present) of economic zone development commenced in 2000 when amendments were made to Special Economic Zones act to encourage and support the investments in IT industry through the establishment of IT Parks/Buildings and provision of incentives to IT enterprises. During this time, the IT and business processes outsourcing (IT-BPO) have just started to gain traction and government have started to take notice of its potential so appropriate incentives were provided. Subsequent board resolutions were approved to establish additional types of economic zones and activities: Tourism Economic Zones (2002), Medical Tourism Park/Center (2006), Retirement Ecozone Park/Center (2006), and Agro-Industrial Economic Zone (2007).

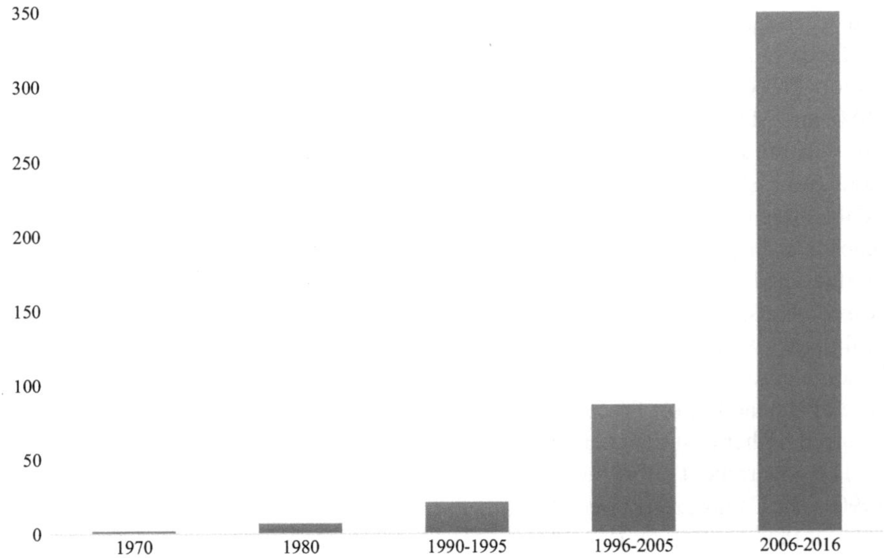

Fig. 9.5 Cumulative number of economic zones: 1970s–2016s. *Source* Author's construction based on Philippines Economic Zones Authority (PEZA 2016a) statistics

The shift from government-controlled and export-oriented EPZ to private-led zones with wide spectrum of activities has several significant consequences. First, number of economic zones has expanded significantly. Second, as result of larger number of zones, the number of firms has also surged. Third, the industrial composition of activities has changed from manufacturing dominated activities to services-based activities.

The number of economic zones has increased from two in 1970s to 348 in 2016 (Fig. 9.5). There is a remarkable increase in number of economic zones from 1996 after private sector was allowed and incentives were given to IT industry. Majority of the established economic zones from the 2000s to present are IT Parks/Buildings. Subsequently, the increasing number of economic zones has attracted more firms (Fig. 9.6). In particular, there is an unprecedented surge in number of firms from 2000s. Only a few number of firms which registered from 1970s to 1980s have remained.[2]

The main industrial composition of activities within economic zones has also changed from traditional manufacturing of export-oriented intermediate processed goods or semifinished products to IT services and real estate (Fig. 9.7). In 1970s–1980s, many of the firms were involved in producing wearing apparel,[3] radio,

[2]Please note that the number included are firms that are still in operation until now and registered as original project in PEZA.

[3]Classification based on Philippines Standard Industry Classification (PSIC).

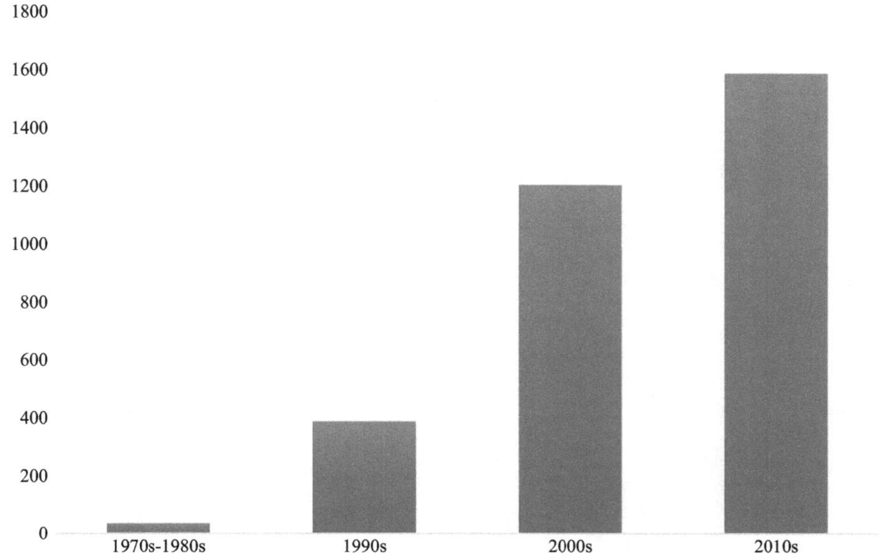

Fig. 9.6 Cumulative number of firms: 1970s–2016s. *Source* Author's construction based on Philippines Economic Zones Authority (PEZA 2016a) statistics

television, and communication apparatus. In 1990s, a huge number of the firms were still involved in producing intermediate goods such radio, television, and communication apparatus, electrical machinery and apparatus as well motor vehicles, trailers, and semitrailers. In 2000s, a remarkable shift from manufacturing activities to services have occurred. Majority of the firms are now involved in real estate activities, call centers, and warehousing and storage. In 2010s, many of the firms are engaged in IT-BPO activities such as business process outsourcing, software development, and call centers.

The changes in the industrial composition of activities within economic zones reflect of the overall structural transformation that has occurred in the Philippines (Fig. 9.8). In 1970s, the contribution of manufacturing and services to GDP were at the same level at 35%. In 1980s, the percentage of services have grown to 39%, while the manufacturing remained at almost the same level at 36%. Starting from 1990s, almost half of the total country's GDP were sourced from services with 47% and the percentage of the agriculture sector have fallen to 20%. In 2000s, the services sector remained as the top contributor of economic output with 53% share. The expansion of the services sector in 2000s–present can be attributed to rise of IT-BPO industry. In 2000, the revenue from BPO industry was only contributing 0.075% of the GDP but in a span of 10 years, it has turned into a multibillion-dollar industry and has contributed almost 5% share of country's economic production (Natividad 2015). In addition to this, BPO industry was almost employing almost 1 million full-time employees.

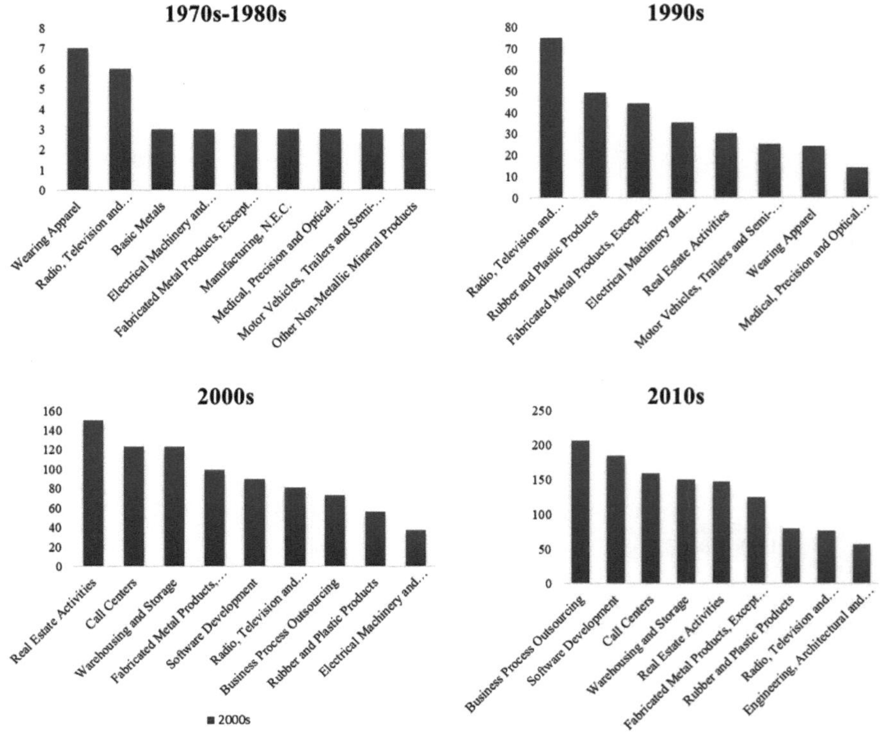

Fig. 9.7 Industrial composition: 1970s–2016s. *Source* Author's construction based on Philippines Economic Zones Authority (PEZA 2016a) statistics

9.4.2 Impact of Economic Zone Development on Investments, Exports, and Employment

The transformation in economic zone development is manifested in economic indicators of investments, exports, and employments. These three indicators are also known as static-outcomes and commonly used as measure of performance of economic zones, particularly, when economic zones are adopted as instruments of trade and investment policy (Farole 2011). Although, economic zone has existed from 1970s, the available data is only from 1980s. The figures for investments and exports are based on nominal values. The discussion focuses on the performance and contribution of economic zones during the three phases of SEZ development.

The flow of FDI at the national level from 1980 to 2015 is marked by a boom—bust cycle (Fig. 9.9). This erratic flow of FDI is commonly attributed to unstable political environment in the Philippines (Aldaba and Aldaba 2010). For instance, the 2001–2003 period which had the lowest level of FDI coincides with the overthrow of Estrada administration due to corruption charges and succession in power of Arroyo administration who was also frequently smeared by political scandals.

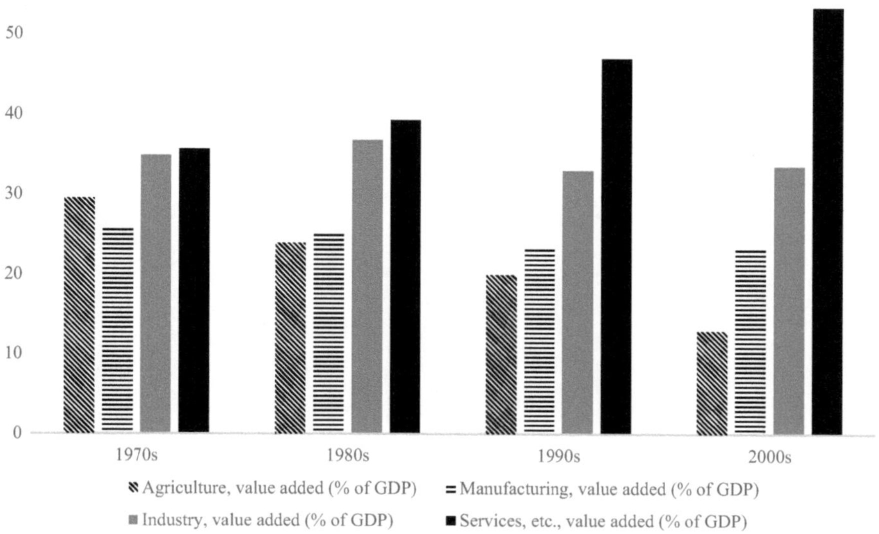

Fig. 9.8 Economic structure: 1970s–2000s. *Source* Author's construction based on Philippines Statistical Authority (PSA 2016a) statistics

Fig. 9.9 Total flow of FDI and share from economic zones (Million PHP) 1980–2015. *Source* Author's construction based on 1980–1994 (Remedia 1996); 1995–2015 (PEZA 2016b); total FDI (PSA 2016b)

In the early phase of economic zone development (1980–1994), economic zones have drawn an annual average of 794 million pesos. However, the contribution of FDI from economic zones to total FDI is negligible at 0.3%. In the second phase of

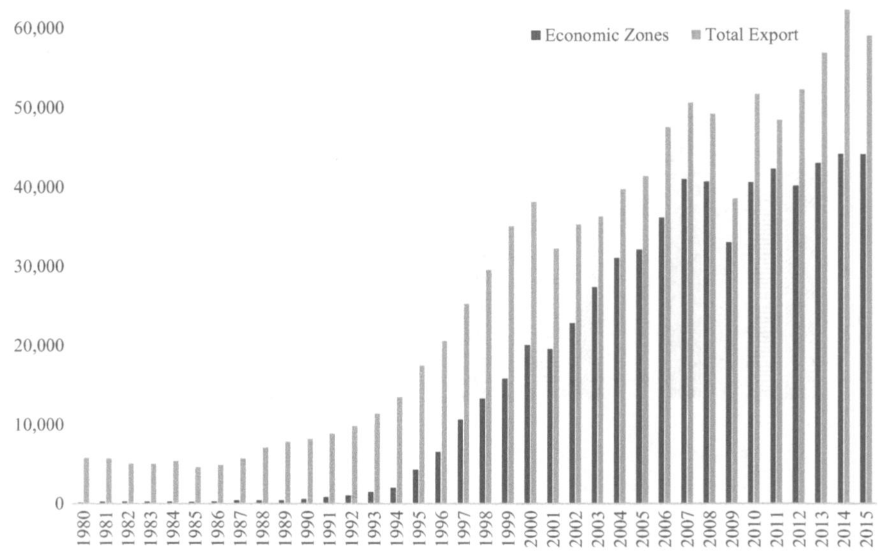

Fig. 9.10 Volume of total export and share from economic zones (Million USD) 1980–2015. *Source* Author's construction based on 1980–1994 (Remedia 1996); 1995–2015 (PEZA 2016b); total export (PSA 2016c)

economic zone development (1995–1999), the flow of FDI from economic zones has increased significantly with yearly average of 29,279 million pesos. Likewise, the impact on national level of FDI has expanded to 19%. In the third phase of economic zone development (2000–2015), FDI generated from economic zones has rapidly increased with an annual average of 95,829 million. Consequently, the share of FDI from economic zones has notably risen to 58%.

While the flow of FDI has been erratic, the value of exports has been expanding consistently from 1980–2015 (Fig. 9.10). The slight decline in exports in 2001 corresponds with political instability after the ouster of Estrada administration. The value of exports had also fell in 2009 after the global financial crisis of 2008.

In the first phase of economic zone development, economic zones have generated a yearly average of 588 million dollar. The exports from economic zones during this period constitute 7% of the total exports. In the second phase of economic zone development, exports from economic zones has significantly expanded with annual average of 10,098 million dollars. The share of exports from economic zone had become larger with 38%. In the third phase of economic zone development, economic zones produced a sizeable annual average of 34,781 million dollars. As a result, economic zones have become the most dominant source of exports in the country with 75% share.

Fig. 9.11 Total employment and share from economic zones (Millions) 1980–2015. *Source* Author's construction based on 1980–1994 (Remedia 1996); 1995–2015 (PEZA 2016b); total employment (PSA 2016d)

The number of employment generated at the national level has been gradually increase from 1980–2015 (Fig. 9.11). However, this growth in employment lags significantly behind rapid population growth. Moreover, despite recent strong economic growth of 6–7% annual GDP increase, unemployment rate of 5–6% remains the one of highest in Southeast Asia region (ASEAN Secretariat 2017).

In the first phase of economic zone development, the economic zones created annual average of 34,788 jobs and this constitutes a mere 0.2% of the total employment. In the second phase of economic zone development, the number of jobs generated from economic zones has increased to 494,800 and this accounts for 2% share of the total employment. In the third phase of SEZ development, economic zones have provided almost a million employment opportunities with 979,023 and contributes 3% share of the total employment. In contrast to investments and exports, the impact of economic zones on employment generation is relatively weak. The plausible reason behind the marginal effect of economic zones on employment is because the analysis only included data on direct employment. The data on indirect employment is incomplete and difficult to estimate so it was not considered in the analysis.

9.5 Summary and Areas for Further Study

This chapter presented some key characteristics of economic zones in the Philippines. Economic zones are defined as selected with highly developed or have the potential to be developed into agro-industrial, industrial tourist/recreation, commercial, banking, investment, and financial centers. IT Parks/Centers constitute the largest number of operating and planned economic zones. The development and management of economic zones are dominated by private sector. Majority of economic zones in the Philippines are private economic zones. The geographical distribution of economic zones demonstrates distinct patterns. IT Parks/Centers and Manufacturing SEZ tend to concentrate in few and relatively developed areas of the country. Meanwhile, Agro-industrial SEZ and Tourism SEZ are relatively scattered across the country.

This chapter analyzed the evolution of economic zone development in the Philippines. There are three main phases of economic zone development in the Philippines: government-led EPZ (1970–1994); private sector-driven SEZ (1995–1999); and Information Technology(IT) industry-centered SEZ (2000–present). The shift from government-controlled and export-oriented EPZ to private-led zones with wide spectrum of activities has several significant consequences. First, number of economic zones has expanded significantly. Second, as result of larger number of zones, the number of firms has also surged. Third, the industrial composition of activities has changed from manufacturing dominated activities to services-based activities.

This chapter examined the effects of transformation in economic zone development on investments, exports, and employment from 1980 to 2015. The shift from the government-led EPZ to private-led SEZs enabled economic zones to become more instrumental in driving the overall growth in FDI and exports. However, economic zones impact on employment is relatively negligible since available data only includes figures on direct employment.

Given the complex nature of economic zones, areas for further study can be identified. For instance, the examination of the impact of economic zone both at the national level and local level using econometric techniques. At the national level, the link between economic zones and structural transformation can be analyzed. This topic is significant, particularly, within the context of deindustrialization. Some scholars have argued that many developing countries experience premature deindustrialization, and this had negatively impacted the long-term economic growth. At the local level, the effect of economic zones on host location socioeconomic development, structure of urban system, and environmental condition can be assessed.

References

Aggarwal, A. 2010. Economic impacts of SEZs: Theoretical approaches and analysis of newly notified SEZs in India.*MPRA Paper* 20902. Munich: University Library of Munich, March 1, available at: https://mpra.ub.uni-muenchen.de/20902/2/. Accessed 10 Nov 2016.

Aldaba, R., and F. Aldaba. 2010. Assessing the spillover effects of FDI to the Philippines. *PIDS Discussion Paper Series No.* 2010–27. Makati City: Philippine Institute for Development Studies (PIDS).

ASEAN Secretariat. 2017. *ASEAN Statistical Yearbook* 2016/2017. Jakarta: Association of Southeast Asian Nations (ASEAN).

Carter, C., and A. Harding. 2011. SEZ: Policy incubators or catalysts for development? In *Special economic zones in Asian market economies*, ed. C. Carter and A. Harding. London: Routledge.

Castell, M. n.d. *Assessing the role of government institutions supporting industrial adjustment in the Philippines*: *The case of PEZA, CITEM and DBP*. Available at: http://www.dlsu.edu.ph/research/centers/aki/_pdf/_concludedProjects/_volumeII/Castell.pdf.

Castro, J. 1982. Philippines: The Bataan export processing zone. In *Exporting processing zones and industrial employment in Asia*, vol. 1, No. 1, 157–182.

Farole, T. 2011. *Special economic zones in Africa: Comparing performance and learning from global experiences*. Washington, D.C.: World Bank.

Farole, T., and G. Akinci (eds.). 2011. *Special economic zones progress, emerging challenges, and future directions*. World Bank: Washington, D.C.

FIAS. 2008. *Special economic zones: performance, lessons learned, and implications for zone development*. World Bank: Washington, D.C.

Fujita, M. 2008. Formation and growth of economic agglomerations and industrial clusters: A theoretical framework from the viewpoint of spatial economics. In *The flowchart approach to industrial cluster policy*, ed. A. Kuchiki and M. Tsuji. New York: Palgrave Macmillan.

Fujita, M., P. Krugman, and A.J. Venables. 1999. *The Spatial economies: Cities, regions, and international trade*. Cambridge, MA: MIT Press.

IT & Business Process Association of the Philippines (ITBAP). 2016. *Next Wave Cities Report 2016*. Taguig: IT & Business Process Association of the Philippines (ITBAP).

Manasan, R. 2013. Export processing zones, special economic zones: Do we really need to have more of them? *PIDS Policy Notes No.* 2013–15. Makati City: Philippine Institute for Development Studies (PIDS).

Markusen, A. 1996. Sticky places in slippery space: A typology of industrial districts. *Economic Geography* 72: 293–313.

Marshall, A. 1920. *Principle of economics*, 8th ed. London: Macmillan and Co.

Natividad, N. 2015. A history of the BPO industry in numbers, Rappler, August 31, available at: https://www.rappler.com/brandrap/stories/98207-bpo-philippines-timeline. Accessed 21 Jan 2018.

Philippines Economic Zone Authority (PEZA). 1995. Rules and Regulations to Implement Republic Act No. 7916 (The Special Economic Zone Act of 1995). Taguig City: PEZA.

Philippines Economic Zone Authority (PEZA). 2016a. *List of economic zones and economic zone locators*. Taguig City: PEZA.

Philippines Economic Zone Authority (PEZA). 2016b. Economic Indicators CY January 1995 to September 2016. Taguig City: PEZA.

Philippines Statistical Authority (PSA). 2016a. *Economic Structure (various years)*. Quezon City: PSA.

Philippines Statistical Authority (PSA). 2016b. *Foreign investments (various years)*. Quezon City: PSA.

Philippines Statistical Authority (PSA). 2016c. *Foreign trade statistics of the Philippines: Various years*. Quezon City: PSA.

Philippines Statistical Authority (PSA). 2016d. *Yearbook of labor statistics (various years)*. Quezon City: PSA.

Remedio, E.M. 1996. Export processing in the Philippines: A review of employment, working conditions and labor relations. *ILO Working Paper No.* 77. Geneva: International Labor Office.

Rodriguez-Pose, A., and D. Hardy. 2014. *Technology and Industrial Parks in Emerging Countries: Panacea or pipedream*. Heidelberg: Springer.

Warr, P. 1989. Export processing zones: The economics of enclave manufacturing. *World Bank Research Observer* 4 (1): 65–87.

Chapter 10
Trade Effects of ASEAN-Plus-China and -Japan Free Trade Agreements: With Focus on Production Stage and Machinery Industry

Hiroyuki Taguchi and Emiko Darcy Nishi

Abstract This article examines the trade creation and diversion effects of ASEAN-Plus-China (ACFTA) and -Japan (AJFTA) free trade agreements focusing on production stage and machinery industry by estimating the gravity trade model for the recent two decades between 1993 and 2015. The purpose for focusing on the trade flows by production stages (final goods and intermediate goods) and by industries (machinery and non-machinery) is to uncover the effects of ACFTA and AJFTA on the expanding international production networks in East Asia. The main findings are summarized as follows. First, regarding industry total, the trade creation effects of ACFTA and AJFTA are identified not in intermediate goods but in final goods. This might come from the larger tariff gaps between the Most Favored Nation (MFN) rates and the preferential rate for ASEAN in final goods than in intermediate goods, reflecting the structure of "tariff escalation". Comparing the effects of ACFTA and AJFTA, larger trade creation effects are found in ACFTA than in AJFTA, probably due to the larger tariff gaps as a result of higher MFN rates in China. As for the machinery industry, the trade creation effects are verifiable regarding ACFTA probably due to the large tariff gaps with the still-existing high MFN in China, while no trade creation effects are found with the implementation of the AJFTA because of no tariff gaps with almost zero MFN rates.

Keywords ASEAN-plus-China and -Japan free trade agreement · Production stage · Machinery industry · Trade creation and diversion effects

---

H. Taguchi (✉) · E. D. Nishi
Graduate School of Humanities and Social Sciences, Saitama University, Saitama, Japan
e-mail: htaguch@mail.saitama-u.ac.jp

T. Ishikawa (ed.), *Locational Analysis of Firms' Activities from a Strategic Perspective*, https://doi.org/10.1007/978-981-13-1684-5_10

10.1 Introduction

Since the early 2000s, regional trade agreements (RTAs) including free trade agreements (FTAs) have been in trend, particularly in the Asian area. As is shown in the list of all RTAs in force presented by the World Trade Organization (WTO) as of September 2017, the total number of RTAs has reached 298. Of the total 298 RTAs, 89 of them cover Asian economies, and 85 RTAs out of those 89 have been in force since the 2000s.[1] In this trend, the Association of South-East Asian Nations (ASEAN) has played a central role in forming FTAs. ASEAN itself initiated the ASEAN Free Trade Area (AFTA), which went into force in January 1993, and has extended its framework by adding in plus-one economies: ASEAN–China FTA (ACFTA, effective in January 2005), ASEAN–Japan FTA (AJFTA, effective in December 2008), ASEAN–Korea FTA (AKFTA, effective in January 2010), ASEAN–Australia–New Zealand FTA (AANZFTA, effective in January 2010), and ASEAN–India (AIFTA, effective in January 2010). Additionally, the comprehensive RTAs among ASEAN and the six countries above, named the Regional Comprehensive Economic Partnership (RCEP), is under negotiation at present.

The rising trend in RTA formations has also encouraged academic studies on RTAs from both theoretical and empirical viewpoints. The theoretical issue in this context is, for instance, whether regional trade blocs are viable through RTA conclusion. The literature has given mixed conclusions about regionalism and globalism: Yi (2000), for example, showed the possibility of the instability of global free trade, while Oladi and Beladi (2008) argued that not regional trade blocks but a global trade bloc can be stable. Regarding the empirical studies, the focus has been to investigate economic impacts of FTAs. When it comes to the issues of FTA effects on trade flows, the primary question has been about whether FTAs have "trade creation" and/or "trade diversion" effects, since Viner (1950) first argued these effects. Trade creation takes place when joining a FTA leads to the replacement of high-cost domestic production by imports from within the FTA members. In this situation, trade is increased and/or created within member countries. Trade diversion, conversely, occurs when joining a FTA leads to the replacement of cheap imports from outside the FTA members by more expensive imports from inside. Under this scenario, trade is reduced and/or even eliminated with nonmembers. To examine whether both trade creation and diversion effects take place in practice and which effects are dominant in the FTA formation, a number of empirical studies have conducted the estimation of the "gravity trade model", as Sect. 10.2 describes a literature review.

Other concerns of FTA effects have emerged in recent times, particularly in East Asia as follows. Trade integration has dramatically developed with the forming of international production networks since the 1990s. Kimura (2006) and Kimura et al. (2007) observed that the mechanics of international production networks in East Asia were closely linked with the "vertical" division of labor in intra-industries among a number of countries characterized by different income levels and that the mechanics were typically found in machinery industries that involved a large number of

[1] See WTO webpage: http://rtais.wto.org/UI/PublicAllRTAList.aspx.

multilayered vertical production processes. In terms of trade flows, the international production networks accompany active back-and-forth international transactions of parts and components, particularly, in machinery industries. The question then arises as to how the rising trend in RTA conclusion in East Asia affects these international production networks. To be specific, the research concerns could be on whether there are any differences in the trade effects of FTAs between production stages (final goods and intermediate goods), and between industries (machinery and non-machinery).

This article aims to examine the trade creation and diversion effects of ACFTA and AJFTA with focuses on production stage and the machinery industry by estimating the gravity trade model for the period between 1993 and 2015. The reason why this study targets ACFTA and AJFTA, and focuses on production stages and machinery industries lies in the fact that the international production networks have involved intensive trade flows of intermediate goods as well as final goods particularly in machinery industries, and that the networks have been still expanded upon in the area among Japan, China, and ASEAN at the timing of their FTA formations. It is the database named "RIETI-TID" that makes it possible to analyze trade flows by industries and by production stages. The RIETI-TID, which is produced by the Research Institute of Economy, Trade and Industry (RIETI) in Japan, covers all trade goods and classifies them according to each production stage based on the BEC (Broad Economic Categories) classification system developed by the UN Statistics Division.

The rest of the paper is structured as follows. Section 10.2 reviews the literature related to the FTA effects and clarifies this study's contribution. Section 10.3 conducts the empirics by estimating the gravity trade model, containing methodology, estimation results, and discussions. The last section summarizes and concludes.

10.2 Literature Review and Contribution

For assessing the trade effects of FTAs in an ex post manner, a number of empirical studies have done estimations utilizing the "gravity trade model". The model originated from Tinbergen (1962) and Pöyhönen (1963), which were the first to apply the "Newton's Law of Gravitation" to international trade flows. The original intent of the gravity trade equation was to explain bilateral trade flows by the economic size of two countries and the distance between them. Since Anderson (1979) assigned the model with theoretical underpinnings for the first time, the gravity trade model has been established as being consistent with trade theories based upon models of imperfect competition and with the Heckscher-Ohlin model (see, e.g., Helpman and Krugman, 1985; Deardorff 1998).

The gravity trade model has often proved as a useful instrument to assess the trade-integration effects of regional economic ties such as FTAs. The intensity of the trade integration caused by FTAs is usually measured by the coefficients of dummy variables, which are added to the gravity trade equation for the FTA partners during the FTA-in-force period. A positive and statistically significant coefficient for the dummy shows that the trade flows exceed the normal level predicted by the country's economic sizes and the distance between them, thereby implying an intensive trade-integration effect caused by the FTA.

Looking at the empirical literature on the FTA effects on trade flows, even after 40 years of accumulating estimations on gravity trade equations, there had seemed no clear and convincing empirical evidence, until Baier and Bergstrand (2007) presented a thorough empirical analysis on the FTA treatment effects.[2] They pointed out that trade policy is not an exogenous variable, and addressed econometrically the endogeneity of FTAs: the FTA dummy variable is correlated with the error term. They argued that standard cross-section techniques using instrumental variables and control functions did not provide stable estimates of the FTA effects in the presence of endogeneity. Instead, they utilized a theoretically motivated gravity equation using panel data with bilateral fixed effects. They finally concluded that, on average, an FTA approximately doubles two members' bilateral trade after 10 years, i.e., seven times the effect estimated using the standard cross-section techniques.

Based on the econometrical methodologies of Baier and Bergstrand (2007), Urata and Okabe (2014) examined the impacts of RTAs including FTAs on trade flows, focusing on their trade creation and diversion effects. They estimated the gravity trade equation covering 67 countries/regions for 27 years from 1980 to 2006 at a disaggregated level of 20 products. Their estimation addressed the problem of the RTA-endogeneity bias and zero trade flows by applying the panel-data analysis with bilateral fixed effects and the Poisson pseudo-maximum likelihood model as its estimating technique. Their main findings were that plurilateral RTAs produce trade creation for many more products compared to bilateral RTAs; RTAs among developed countries generate trade creation for a half of all products but not trade diversion for most of the products, whereas RTAs among developing countries give rise to trade diversion for many more products—probably due to high tariffs imposed on imports from nonmembers by developing countries.

When we focus on the literature on empirical studies of individual trade effects of ASEAN-plus-one FTAs, most of the studies have applied ordinary gravity trade equations but not addressed the problem of the FTA-endogeneity bias through the panel-data estimation with bilateral fixed effect. The following are the examples of those studies using ordinary gravity trade equations. Sheng et al. (2012) examined the impact of ACFTA on the members' trade flows and found that ACFTA leads to substantially higher bilateral trade between ASEAN and China. Yang and Martinez-Zarzoso (2014) also investigated the trade effects of ACFTA focusing on agricultural and manufactured products and showed the trade creation effect not only within ASEAN but also between ASEAN and China. A more comprehensive study of the trade effect of ASEAN-plus-one FTAs was done by Okabe (2015). It found that the trade creation effects of ACFTA and AKFTA appeared in industrial suppliers

[2]Baier and Bergstrand (2007) expressed the past unreliable estimates of FTA treatment effects as "fragile" estimates by citing Frankel (1997) and Ghosh and Yamarik (2004).

and capital goods between members, whereas the trade impact of AJFTA was not revealed in many cases, and suggested that the newer regional FTA such as RCEP needed to have a higher level of liberalization including not only tariff elimination but also such other measures as nontariff elimination, coordination of rules of origin and improvement of FTA usability.

It was Taguchi (2015) that estimated gravity trade model by applying the panel data with bilateral fixed effects to clear the FTA-endogeneity problem, to examine the trade creation and diversion effects of ASEAN-plus-one FTAs for the period between 1993 and 2013. It showed that the trade creation effect in ACFTA was much larger than those in AKFTA and AJFTA and that the trade diversion effects were commonly negative in ACFTA, AKFTA, and AJFTA. It also speculated that the larger trade creation effect in ACFTA might come from the wider gap between the general tariff rate and the preferential tariff rate for ASEAN in China.

This study extends the study of Taguchi (2015) by decomposing the total industry's trade effects of the FTAs into their trade effects by production stage and by industries. The contributions of this study to the literature above are summarized as follows. First, this study applies the panel data with bilateral fixed effects to the estimation of gravity trade model for the purpose of clearing the FTA-endogeneity problem, as in Baier and Bergstrand (2007), Urata and Okabe (2014) and Taguchi (2015). Second, this study deals with the trade flows by production stages (final goods and intermediate goods) and by industries (machinery and non-machinery), for uncovering the effects of AJFTA and ACFTA on the expanding international production networks in East Asia. Third, this study discusses the estimated trade effects of AJFTA and ACFTA by each category in connection with the gap between the general tariff rate and the preferential tariff rate for ASEAN in Japan and China.

10.3 Empirics

This section turns to the empirical analysis of the trade creation and diversion effects of ACFTA and AJFTA through estimating the gravity trade model. We first observe the trade flows of member countries, clarify the methodology of the gravity trade model, represent the estimation outcomes, and discuss them.

10.3.1 Observation of Trade Flows

This subsection simply observes the trade flows between ASEAN4 (Indonesia, Malaysia, Philippines , and Thailand) and China, and those between ASEAN4 and

Japan for 1993–2015. All the trade data are retrieved from RIETI-TID.[3] Figure 10.1 displays the trades of industry total (stage total, final goods, and intermediate goods) and machinery (final goods and intermediate goods).[4] The main findings are as follows. First, the increasing trends are steeper in the two-way trades between ASEAN4 and China than those between ASEAN4 and Japan in all the categories, and so the trade volumes between ASEAN4 and China overtook those between ASEAN4 and Japan during 1993–2015. Second, looking at the trade flows by production stages, in those between ASEAN4 and China in recent years, final goods are dominant in the exports from China to ASEAN4, while intermediate goods are dominant in the exports from ASEAN4 to China in industry total and machinery. This relationship might reflect the structure that China imports parts and components from ASEAN4 and exports final goods to ASEAN4 by processing them. Third, in the trade flows between ASEAN4 and Japan, final goods as well as intermediate goods are still dominant in the exports from Japan to ASEAN4 over the exports from ASEAN4 to Japan in machinery industries.

When we look at the trade share of machinery relative to industry total in 2015, it accounts for 69 and 50% in final goods and intermediate goods in the total trade between ASEAN4 and China, and 63 and 39% in final goods and intermediate goods in the total trade between ASEAN4 and Japan, respectively. These large trade shares of machinery might reflect the fact that the expansion of international production networks have involved intensive trade flows of intermediate goods as well as final goods in machinery industries, and justify the division of industry total into machinery and non-machinery industries in the subsequent estimation of gravity trade model.

From the simple observation above, however, we cannot judge whether ACFTA and AJFTA have accelerated the trade flows, since the trade flows would also be affected by other economic variables. The relationships between FTAs and trade flows should, therefore, be statistically tested by a more sophisticated manner, i.e., by the estimation of the gravity trade model.

10.3.2 *Methodology of Gravity Trade Model Estimation*

This subsection clarifies the methodology of the estimation of gravity trade model to investigate the trade creation and diversion effects of AJFTA and ACFTA. We follow the methodology presented by Baier and Bergstrand (2007), Urata and Okabe (2014) and Taguchi (2015), and specifically adopt a theoretically motivated gravity trade model using panel data with bilateral fixed effects and multilateral time-varying price resistance terms. The equation for estimation is specified as follows.

---

[3]The latest version is "RIETI-TID 2015". See the website: http://www.rieti-tid.com/trade.php.

[4]The "machinery" is the sum of general machinery, electronical machinery, household electric appliances, transportation equipment, and precision machinery.

[Industry Total, Stage Total]

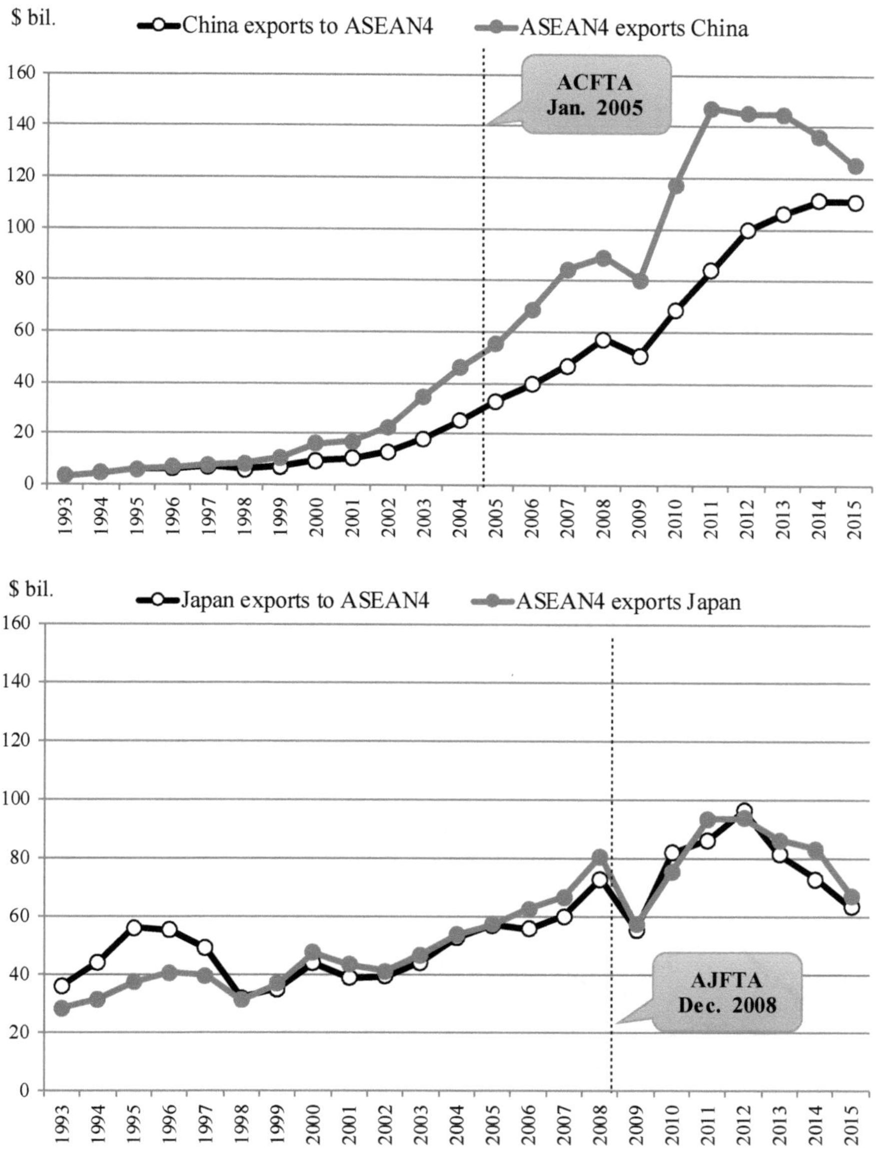

Fig. 10.1 Trends in trade flows. *Source* RIETI-TID2015

[Industry Total, Intermediate and Final Goods]

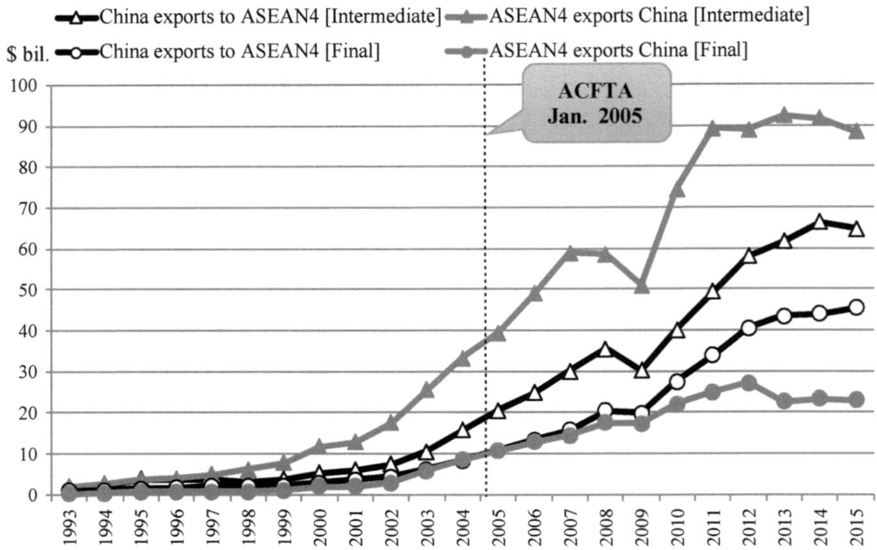

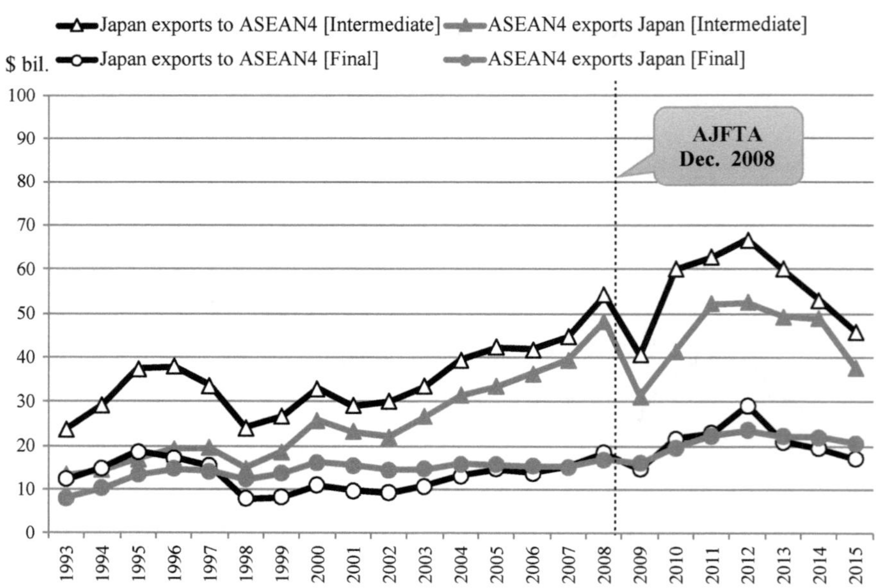

Fig. 10.1 (continued)

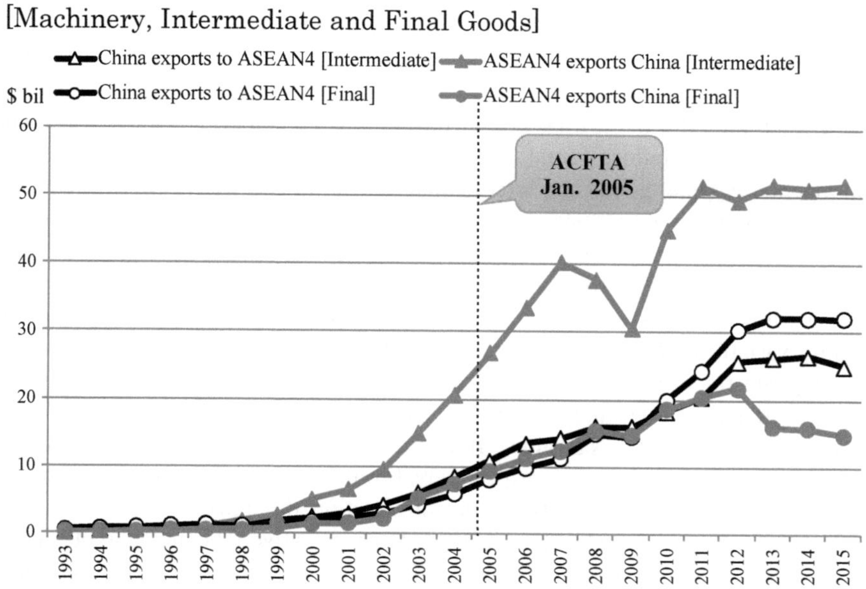

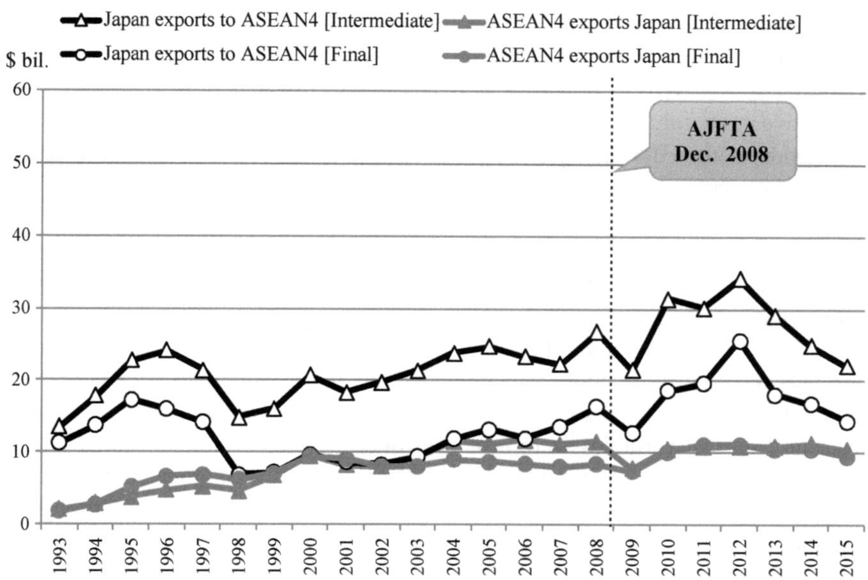

Fig. 10.1 (continued)

$$\ln\left[X_{ijt}/\left(\mathrm{GDP_{it}GDP_{jt}}\right)\right] = \alpha_0 + \alpha_1\mathrm{FTAC_{ijt}} + \alpha_2\mathrm{FTAD_{ijt}} + \alpha_3 D_{\mathrm{ij}} + \alpha_4\mathrm{rex_{ijt}} + \varepsilon_{\mathrm{ijt}}, \tag{10.1}$$

where X_{ijt} is the value of the trade flows from exporter *i* to importer *j*, which is decomposed into those of industry total (stage total, final goods, and intermediate goods) and machinery (final goods and intermediate goods) in this study; $\mathrm{GDP_{it}}(\mathrm{GDP_{jt}})$ is the level of nominal gross domestic product in country *i* (*j*); D_{ij} is a bilateral dummy variable between *i* and *j*; $\mathrm{rex_{ijt}}$ is a bilateral real exchange rate in the logarithm; and $\varepsilon_{\mathrm{ijt}}$ is an error term. We also insert the time dummy from 1993 to 2015.

Regarding the FTA effects on trade flows, the equation includes two kinds of dummy variables the same as in Urata and Okabe (2014). $\mathrm{FTAC_{ijt}}$, a variable for denoting the trade creation effect, takes a value 1 if both importer and exporter belong to the same FTA and 0 otherwise, and $\mathrm{FTAD_{ijt}}$, a variable for denoting the trade diversion effect, takes a value 1 if the importer is a member of the FTA, but the exporter is not and 0 otherwise, respectively. From the concept of trade creation and diversion effects that was described in the introduction, the sign of the coefficient, α_1, is expected to be positive while α_2 is expected to be negative. The main targets in this study are the trade effects of ACFTA and AJFTA in connection with the international production networks in East Asia. ACFTA has been in force since January 2005, and thus its dummy takes value 1 from 2005, and AJFTA has been in force since December 2008 and its dummy value takes 1 from 2009. In addition, the dummy for AKFTA, AANEFTA, and AIFTA (hereafter AOFTA) is also inserted from 2010 since their FTAs have come into force since January 2010.

To address the FTA-endogeneity bias, the equation includes a bilateral dummy variable between *i* and *j*, D_{ij}. Baier and Bergstrand (2007) argued that the FTA is not an exogenous variable but that it is influenced by considerable unobserved time-invariant heterogeneity among country pairs such as policy-related barriers (that also affect trade volume), and that this omitted variable bias is the major source of endogeneity facing estimation of FTA effects in gravity equations using cross-sectional data. They examined the validity of cross-sectional techniques using instrumental variables and control functions but concluded that these techniques were not reliable enough to provide stable estimates of the FTA effects and that the unobserved time-invariant bilateral variables were best controlled by using bilateral "fixed effects" in the gravity equation using panel data.[5] There would be another potential endogeneity bias created by simultaneity: GDP is a function of net exports. Although the simultaneity bias is considered to be not so large in the literature, the specification (1) has GDPs on the left-hand side.[6]

[5] Baier and Bergstrand (2007) conducted the estimation using first-differenced data as well as fixed effects for robustness analysis and found no significant differences in the estimation outcomes. Thus, we herein only focus on the fixed-effect estimation.

[6] Scaling the left-hand side trade flow by-product of GDPs means imposing the restriction of unitary income elasticities. Baier and Bergstrand (2007), however, showed that imposing the unitary income elasticities had no impact on the FTA coefficient estimate.

The specification (1) includes a bilateral real exchange rate, rex_{ijt}, to take into account the theoretically motivated multilateral time-varying price resistance terms. The gravity trade model proposed by recent formal theoretical developments requires the multilateral price variables. Anderson and van Wincoop (2003) suggested the use of country-specific fixed effects as the method to account for multilateral price terms in cross section. In a panel setting, however, the multilateral price terms would be time-varying. One way to control for price changes is to introduce, similarly to Rose (2000) and Vandenbussche and Zanardi (2010), the bilateral real exchange rate that varies over time and tracks price changes, the coefficient of which is expected to have a negative sign.

Some of the studies on gravity trade model encounter the treatment of zero trade flow values, as Urata and Okabe (2014) applied the Poison pseudo-maximum likelihood model to cope with it. This study, however, deals with aggregated values of trade flows of selected large countries, which do not include zero values.

This study argues the trade effects of ACFTA and AJFTA in connection with the gap between the general tariff rate and the preferential tariff rate for ASEAN in Japan and China in the later Sect. 10.3.4. From the theoretical viewpoint, the Eq. (10.1) should contain the tariff gap as an explanatory variable. Due to the lack of time-series tariff data, however, the tariff gap is not dealt with in the equation but will be discussed as the interpretations of estimation outcomes alternatively.

10.3.3 Data for Gravity Trade Model Estimation

The sample period is from 1993 to 2015. The reason for selecting 1993 as the starting year is that the FTA within ASEAN named AFTA was in force in January 1993, and so after this, we can concentrate solely on the effects of ASEAN-plus-one FTAs.

The sample covers 14 countries/regions: Australia, China, E.U. (28 countries), India, Indonesia, Japan, Korea, Malaysia, New Zealand, Philippines, Taiwan, Thailand, U.S., and the rest of the world (RW). Regarding ASEAN, we focus on Indonesia, Malaysia, Philippines, and Thailand (ASEAN4), since the latecomers such as Cambodia, Lao PDR, Myanmar, and Vietnam have their different schedules of tariff reduction in AFTA.[7] Table 10.1 summarizes the trade flows in the sample countries/regions in 2015. It shows that the exports of China, Japan, and ASEAN4 to the sample countries/regions except RW account for more than sixty percent of their exports to the world.

We then construct panel data for the period between 1993 and 2015 with the trade combinations of 14 countries/regions for the gravity trade model estimation. The trade data comes from RIETI-TID 2015 as stated before. The GDP and the data for

[7] We also exclude Singapore Brunei due to transit-trading and oil producing country, respectively.

Table 10.1 Summary of trade flows in sample countries/regions in 2015

Billion U.S. dollars			
Exporter Importer	China	Japan	ASEAN 4
China		137.1	125.2
Korea	83.5	45.2	24.8
Japan	149.7		67.3
ASEAN 4	111.1	63.5	
Taiwan	41.7	37.2	14.5
U.S.	455.3	126.4	84.1
EU(28)	379.7	75.0	71.5
Australia	42.8	14.2	21.3
New Zealand	6.7	2.3	3.3
India	55.3	9.1	29.1
World	2062.5	672.1	700.8
% of exports to the world			
Exporter Importer	China	Japan	ASEAN 4
China		20.4	17.9
Korea	4.0	6.7	3.5
Japan	7.3		9.6
ASEAN 4	5.4	9.4	
Taiwan	2.0	5.5	2.1
U.S.	22.1	18.8	12.0
EU(28)	18.4	11.2	10.2
Australia	2.1	2.1	3.0
New Zealand	0.3	0.3	0.5
India	2.7	1.4	4.2
Total/World	64.3	75.9	63.0

Source RIETI-TID2015

calculating a bilateral real exchange rate, i.e., consumer prices and bilateral nominal exchange rates, are from World Economic Outlook (WEO) Database (April 2017) and International Financial statistics, by the International Monetary Fund.[8]

[8]See the website: http://www.imf.org/en/data. From the theoretical perspective, the price index for calculating a real exchange rate should be selected according to industries and production stages, considering the supply side of traded goods. Due to data constraints, however, the consumer price index is used to represent the prices regardless of industries and production stages in this study.

10.3.4 Estimation Outcomes and Discussion

Table 10.2 reports the estimation outcomes of the gravity trade model on the trade creation and diversion effects of ASEAN-plus-one FTAs. We herein focus on the trade effects of ACFTA and AJFTA in the context of the international production networks. The other FTA effects are difficult to interpret, since the effects of three FTAs, AKFTA, AANEFTA, and AIFTA, are combined in one dummy's coefficient.

We first concentrate on the results of trade creation effects. Regarding the category of industry total, the trade creation effects of both ACFTA and AJFTA are significantly positive on trade flows as expected in final goods but not in intermediate goods and stage total. When we compare the volume of the effects, the effect of ACFTA is about three times larger than that of AJFTA. The large trade creation effects of ACFTA are consistent with the previous studies of Sheng et al. (2012), Yang and Martinez-Zarzoso (2014), Okabe (2015) and Taguchi (2015). As for the machinery industry, the trade creation effects are significantly positive in ACFTA in both final and intermediate goods, but not (even negative) in AJFTA. On the contrary, for non-machinery industries, the trade creation effects are significantly positive in AJFTA but negative in ACFTA.

Looking at the trade diversion effects, the outcomes are not always significant and even have an opposite (positive) sign. It might be because the imports from outside the FTA members are affected by the trade creation effects in such a way that the trade creation, for instance, induces the additional demands for related capital goods and intermediate goods. As for the price resistance terms, the coefficients of the bilateral exchange rate are significantly negative as expected in all the cases except the case of final goods in non-machinery industries.

We discuss the estimation outcomes above from the perspective of tariff rates. In general, trade flows are affected by tariff elimination and reduction by FTAs in force. The general tariff rate as a benchmark rate is represented by the "Most Favored Nation (MFN) tariff rate". Thus, the gap between the MFN tariff rate and the preferential tariff rate under FTAs could be one of the key elements to give an influence to trade flows. The data of the MFN tariff rate and the preferential tariff rate under FTAs are provided by World Integrated Trade Solutions (WITS).[9]

In the case of ACFTA and AJFTA, the comparison of tariff gaps should be made in the side of China and Japan, since the tariffs on the ASEAN side seem to be common for China and Japan. Table 10.3 describes the MFN tariff rates, the preferential tariff rates for ASEAN under ACFTA and AJFTA and their gaps in China and Japan in 2011, by industry total and machinery industry and by final goods and intermediate goods, based on WITS data. When we focus on industry total, we found that the tariff gaps are larger in final good than in intermediate goods both in China and Japan. This mainly comes from the fact that the MFN tariff rates are larger in final

[9]See the website: https://wits.worldbank.org/WITS/WITS/Restricted/Login.aspx.

Table 10.2 Estimation Outcomes on Trade Effects of ASEAN-Plus-One FTAs

Industry total

Industry total	Stage total	Final goods	Intermediate goods
	exit	*exif*	*exii*
ACFTA: Trade creation	0.159 (1.427)	0.381*** (2.61)	0.155 (1.13)
ACFTA: Trade diversion	−0.051** (−2.05)	−0.362*** (−9.82)	0.122*** (2.84)
AJFTA: Trade creation	0.064 (1.33	0.135*** (2.73)	0.063 (1.09)
AJFTA: Trade diversion	−0.013 (−0.39)	0.157*** (4.57)	0.034 (0.74)
AOFTA: Trade creation	−0.081*** (−2.84)	0.083** (2.49)	−0.189*** (−6.35)
AOFTA: Trade diversion	−0.076*** (−3.51)	0.075*** (2.97)	−0.024 (−1.21)
REX	−0.177*** (−5.90)	−0.470*** (−14.55)	−0.269*** (−22.23)
Constant	9.673*** (69.93)	9.786*** (60.86)	9.348*** (171.0)
Adjusted RR	0.844	0.721	0.849
Observation	4140	4140	4140

Machinery industry

Machinery total	Final goods	Intermediate goods
	exmf	*exmi*
ACFTA: Trade creation	0.629*** (3.29)	0.848*** (3.11)
ACFTA: Trade diversion	−0.359*** (−4.59)	0.127** (2.09)
AJFTA: Trade creation	−0.023 (−0.39)	−0.125** (−2.01)
AJFTA: Trade diversion	−0.176** (−2.44)	−0.253*** (−3.91)
AOFTA: Trade creation	0.295*** (6.83)	0.160*** (4.86)
AOFTA: Trade diversion	0.601*** (13.85)	0.387*** (11.67)
REX	−1.146*** (−15.29)	−0.877*** (−14.65)
Constant	11.944*** (35.34)	10.749*** (39.04)
Adjusted RR	0.691	0.797
Observation	4140	4140

Non-machinery industry

Non-machinery total	Final goods	Intermediate goods
	exif	*exii*
ACFTA: Trade creation	−0.251*** (−2.62)	−0.280*** (−3.00)
ACFTA: Trade diversion	−0.820*** (−12.49)	0.103** (2.27)
AJFTA: Trade creation	0.592*** (8.24)	0.254*** (3.92)
AJFTA: Trade diversion	0.681*** (11.32)	0.184*** (3.33)
AOFTA: Trade creation	−0.086*** (−2.62)	−0.289*** (−7.38)
AOFTA: Trade diversion	−0.251*** (−8.35)	−0.040* (−1.96)
REX	0.159* (1.83)	−0.092*** (−3.27)
Constant	6.122*** (14.71)	8.073*** (65.50)
Adjusted RR	0.624	0.825
Observation	4140	4140

Notes t-statistics are in parentheses. *, **, ***, denotes statistical significance at 10, 5, and 1% level
Source RIETI-TID2015, WEO database(April 2017) and International Financial Statistics

Table 10.3 Gap between MFN Rate and Preferential Rate under ACFTA and AJFTA

% in 2011	MFN tariff rate (a)	Preferential tariff rate for ASEAN (b)	Gap(a−b)
China: Industry total			
Final goods	11.79	0.20	11.59
Intermediate goods	7.69	0.08	7.61
China: Machinery total			
Final goods	8.77	0.20	8.57
Intermediate goods	8.74	0.23	8.51
Japan: Industry total			
Final goods	7.13	2.85	4.28
Intermediate Goods	2.83	0.26	2.57
Japan: Machinery total			
Final goods	0.08	–	
Intermediate goods	0.06	–	

Source World Integrated Trade Solutions (WITS)
See the website: https://wits.worldbank.org/WITS/WITS/Restricted/Login.aspx

goods than in intermediate goods, which is known as "tariff escalation" in general.[10] In the comparison of the tariff gaps between China and Japan, the gaps are much larger in China than in Japan, since the MFN tariff rates are much higher in China than in Japan. When we turn to the machinery industry, the tariff gaps are larger in China both in final goods and intermediate goods, since the MFN rates are still high in China in both categories. On the other hand, in Japan, there seem to be no tariff gaps because the MFN rates themselves are extremely low already in the machinery industry.[11]

The estimation outcomes on the trade creation effects of ACFTA and AJFTA are almost consistent with the structure of the tariff gaps above. First, regarding the category of industry total, the trade creation effects of ACFTA and AJFTA identified not in intermediate goods but in final goods might come from the larger tariff gaps between the MFN rates and the preferential rate for ASEAN in final goods than in intermediate goods, reflecting the structure of "tariff escalation". At the same time, the larger trade creation effects of ACFTA than of AJFTA might generate from the larger tariff gaps in China than in Japan due to the higher MFN rates in China. As for the machinery industry, the trade creation effects are verified on ACFTA probably due to

[10] The tariff escalation is explained by the glossary term by WTO as follows: "Higher import duties on semi-processed products than on raw materials, and higher still on finished products. This practice protects domestic processing industries and discourages the development of processing activity in the countries where raw materials originate."

See the website: https://www.wto.org/english/thewto_e/glossary_e/tariff_escalation_e.htm.

[11] In Japan, since the MFN rates themselves are extremely low already in machinery industry, there are quite limited items as targets for AJFTA.

the large tariff gaps with the still-existing high MFN rates regardless of production stage in China. On the other hand, no trade creation effects are found because of no tariff gaps with almost zero MFN rates in Japan. Concerning non-machinery industries, the trade creation effects identified on AJFTA might be explained by the still-existing high MFN rates in such sectors as agricultural products in Japan. This category should, however, be investigated further by individual industries in connection with tariff rates.

10.4 Concluding Remarks

This article examined the trade creation and diversion effects of ACFTA and AJFTA with focus on production stage and machinery industry by estimating the gravity trade model for the period between 1993 and 2015. The purpose for focusing on the trade flows by production stages (final goods and intermediate goods) and by industries (machinery and non-machinery) was to uncover the effects of ACFTA and AJFTA on the expanding international production networks in East Asia.

The main findings are summarized as follows. First, regarding industry total, the trade creation effects of ACFTA and AJFTA are identified not in intermediate goods but in final goods. This might come from the larger tariff gaps between the MFN rates and the preferential rate for ASEAN in final goods than in intermediate goods, reflecting the structure of "tariff escalation". Comparing the effects of ACFTA and AJFTA, the larger trade creation effects are found in ACFTA than in AJFTA, probably due to the larger tariff gaps with the higher MFN rates in China. As for the machinery industry, the trade creation effects are verified on ACFTA probably due to the large tariff gaps with the still-existing high MFN in China, while no trade creation effects are found because of no tariff gaps with almost zero MFN rates in Japan. In the context of international production networks in East Asia, it can be said that ACFTA rather than AJFAT has had greater influences on vertical production processes in machinery industries.

This study argued the trade effects of ACFTA and AJFTA from the viewpoint of tariff gap. The channels in the trade effects of FTA are, however, not always confined to tariff elimination. As Okabe (2015) discussed, the other FTA measures such as nontariff elimination, coordination of rules of origin and improvement of FTA usability may also give great impacts on trades. It should be noted, thus, that there is still much room to investigate the trade effects of ACFTA and AJFTA from the more comprehensive perspectives.

References

Anderson, J.E. 1979. A theoretical foundation for the gravity equation. *American Economic Review* 69 (1): 106–116.

Anderson, J.E., and E. van Wincoop. 2003. Gravity with gravitas: a solution to the border puzzle. *American Economic Review* 93 (1): 170–192.

Baier, S.L., and J.H. Bergstrand. 2007. Do free trade agreements actually increase members' international trade? *Journal of International Economics* 71 (1): 72–95.

Deardorff, A.V. 1998. Determinants of bilateral trade: does gravity work in a classical world. In *The Regionalization of the World Economy*, ed. J.A. Frankel, 7–22. Chicago: University of Chicago Press.

Frankel, J.A. 1997. *Regional trading blocs*. Washington, DC: Institute for International Economics.

Ghosh, S., and S. Yamarik. 2004. Are regional trading arrangements trade creating? An application of extreme bounds analysis. *Journal of International Economics* 63 (2): 369–395.

Helpman, E., and P. Krugman. 1985. *Market structure and foreign trade*. Cambridge, MA: MIT Press.

Kimura, F. 2006. International production and distribution network in East Asia: Eighteen facts, mechanics, and policy implication. *Asian Economic Policy Review* 1: 326–344.

Kimura, F., Y. Takahashi, and K. Hayakawa. 2007. Fragmentation and parts and components trade: Comparison between East Asia and Euro pe. *North American Journal of Economics and Finance* 18: 23–40.

Okabe, M. 2015. Impact of free trade agreements on trade in East Asia. ERIA Discussion Paper Series, ERIA-DP-2015-01.

Oladi, R., and H. Beladi. 2008. Is regionalism viable? A case for global free trade. *Review of International Economics* 16 (2): 293–300.

Pöyhönen, P. 1963. A tentative model for the volume of trade between countries. *Weltwirtschaftliches Archiv* 90 (1): 93–100.

Rose, A.K. 2000. One money, one market: estimating the effect of common resources on trade. *Economic Policy* 15 (30): 9–45.

Sheng, Y., H.C. Tang, and X. Xu. 2012. The impact of ACFTA on People's Republic of China-ASEAN trade: Estimates based on an extended gravity model for component trade. ADB Working Paper Series on Regional Economic Integration, No. 99.

Taguchi, H. 2015. 'Trade creation and diversion effects of ASEAN-plus-one free trade agreements. *Economics Bulletin* 35 (3): 1856–1866.

Tinbergen, J. 1962. *Shaping the world economy*. New York: Twentieth Century Fund.

Urata, S., and M. Okabe. 2014. Trade creation and diversion effects of regional trade agreements: A product-level analysis. *The World Economy* 37 (2): 267–289.

Vandenbussche, H., and M. Zanardi. 2010. The chilling trade effects of antidumping proliferation. *European Economic Review* 54 (6): 760–777.

Viner, J. 1950. *The customs union issue*. New York: Oxford University Press.

Yang, S., and I. Martinez-Zarzoso. 2014. A panel data analysis of trade creation and trade diversion effects: The case of ASEAN-China free trade area. *China Economic Review* 29: 138–151.

Yi, S.S. 2000. Free trade areas and welfare: An equilibrium analysis. *Review of International Economics* 8 (2): 336–347.

Chapter 11
Analysis of Influential Factors and Spillover Effect on the Regional Economic Disparity in China

Na Wang

Abstract Since the reform and opening-up in 1978, the regional economy in China has implemented regional policies in order to develop the eastern, central, and western regions in turn. However, with the economic development of the eastern coastal areas, the development disparity between the coastal areas and the inland areas began to expand rapidly. This chapter summarizes the evolution process of regional economic development, and through qualitative analysis, the evolution trend of regional economic disparities is examined on the basis of various statistical scales. Using panel data in 31 provinces of China for 1990–2016 years to establish a measurement model, the influencing factors of regional economic disparities are empirically analyzed. Combined with the two-time dividing points in 2000 and 2008, we verify the effect of the spillover effect of the eastern region's economic growth on the regional economic disparity.

Keywords Spillover effect · Regional economic disparity · Theil index · Panel data model

11.1 Introduction

Since the reform and opening-up in 1978, China's regional economy has changed significantly. In the first place, the eastern coastal regions were first developed, and regional policies in the eastern, central and western regions were developed in turn. However, with the economic development of the eastern coastal regions, the development disparity between the coastal regions and the inland regions began to expand rapidly. Therefore, in order to narrow the regional disparity, the government took the balanced development strategy of the regional economy as the priority, and then put forward the policy of promoting labor-intensive industries to inland regions. In March 2003, the strategy of western development was implemented. In October

---

N. Wang (✉)
School of Public Administration, Shandong Normal University, Jinan, Shandong, China
e-mail: wangna@sdnu.edu.cn

T. Ishikawa (ed.), *Locational Analysis of Firms' Activities from a Strategic Perspective*, https://doi.org/10.1007/978-981-13-1684-5_11

2003, the strategy of revitalizing the Northeast was put forward, and the strategy of central China's rise was released in March 2005 (officially launched in April 2007). Since 2006, China Government Ministry of Foreign Affairs started advancing about 1 thousand of the coastal enterprises and overseas enterprises in the Midwest investment "10,000 companies to the west" project within three years. In addition, a number of preferential policies to cooperate with enterprise financing have also been put forward. In September 2008, in order to cope with the world financial crisis, the Chinese government invested 4 trillion yuan of government investment at the end of 2008, most of which invested in the infrastructure construction in the inland region, and promoted the rapid growth of the inland economy.

In the empirical study of the trend of regional economic development and its influencing factors, Baumol (1986) analyzed the Maddison data of 1870–1979 years, and the results showed that the average GDP of the industrialized countries in the market economy had obvious convergence. In other related empirical analysis, Ren and Yang (2010) analyzed the causes of the regional economic disparity from the perspective of capital factors. Zhang and Zhou (2015) analyzed the influence on the regional economic disparity from the perspective of industrial structure and human capital. Chen and Zhang (2017) integrated productive public expenditure into the macroeconomic model and evaluated the effect of fiscal policy on regional economic disparities. For the study of economic spillover effects, Zhang and Felmingham (2002) held that there was a spillover effect on the output of the eastern and central regions to the western region. Groenewold et al. (2007) established VAR model and used 1953–2003 years' data to study the relationship between the three regions in China's eastern and western regions. It is found that the eastern region's economic growth had a strong spillover effect on the central and western regions.

In summary, there are many researches on the factors and causes of regional economic disparities in recent studies. In recent years, the research on spillover effect has also increased, and there are still many shortcomings. For example, in empirical analysis, the object of research is to measure the variables of economic growth, that is, GDP per capita or actual GDP per capita. GDP per capita can prove whether there is a trend of economic convergence, but it cannot better explain the regional economic disparity, so the representative of the research needs to be discussed. In the analysis of the factors affecting the regional economic disparity, there is not a combination of economic spillover effects or only unilateral research.

The purpose of this chapter is to explore the influence factors of regional economic disparity and the regional spillover effect. This chapter analyzes the development trend of regional economic disparities in qualitative, using 1990–2016 years' data to establish a panel data model of 31 provinces, combining the influence factors of regional economic disparities and the economic spillover effect of the eastern region. At the same time, considering the effect of the policy, so it is more practical to consider the effect of a spillover effect on regional economic disparities.

11.2 The Development of Regional Economy Since the Reform and Opening-up

11.2.1 The Division of Three Major Regions

According to the method of regional division used before, China was divided into three major regions. After the western development in 2000, the three regions in the eastern, central, and western regions has changed slightly, and the three regions have been redivided. With the implementation of the strategy of revitalizing the Northeast in 2003, the northeastern regions (Liaoning was selected from the 11 provinces in the eastern region, and Heilongjiang and Jilin were selected from the eight provinces in the central region.) were selected as an independent region from the three regions, and three regions were subdivided into the four major regions. The northeast new four regions contain only three provinces (Heilongjiang, Jilin, and Liaoning), as a separate area is not enough and other areas together to better explain the regional economic disparity, so follow the division of three regions in this chapter, the eastern region includes 11 provinces, the central region includes 8 provinces, and the western region includes 12 provinces. The specific classification and inclusion provinces are as follows.

Eastern (11)	Beijing, Tianjin, Hebei, Liaoning, Shanghai, Jiangsu, Zhejiang, Fujian, Shandong, Guangdong, Hainan
Central (8)	Shanxi, Jilin, Heilongjiang, Anhui, Jiangxi, Henan, Hubei, Hunan
Western (12)	Neimenggu, Guangxi, Chongqing, Sichuan, Yunnan, Guizhou, Xizang, Shanxi, Gansu, Qinghai, Ningxia, Xinjiang

11.2.2 The Development of the Eastern Coastal Regions

During the 3rd Five-Year Plan period (1966–1970), the investment in coastal regions was the lowest level since 1949, and the ratio between coastal regions and inland regions was about 1:3 (Su 2001). During the period from the 4th Five-Year Plan period (1971–1975), that was the planned economy period, the focus of government investment has been transferring to coastal regions, not the pursuit of national economic balanced development, but gave priority to the development of some areas in developed regions to backward regions of economic development strategy as the foundation, to promote the coastal region opening policy. At the same time, the National Planning Commission and the State Bureau of statistics issued "Notice of the division of the coastal and inland regions" in 1982. In this notice, the 11 provinces, municipalities, and autonomous regions of Beijing, Tianjin, Hebei, Liaoning, Shandong, Shanghai, Jiangsu, Zhejiang, Fujian, Guangdong,[1] and Guangxi were divided into coastal region, in addition to the 11 provinces, municipalities, and autonomous regions, 18 provinces[2] and autonomous regions were divided into inland regions.[3]

During the period from 1979 to 1980, four special economic zones in Shenzhen, Zhuhai, Shantou, and Xiamen were set up, and foreign trade activities were actively carried out. Subsequently, 14 coastal ports[4] in the north and south were opened in 1984 as an open coastal zone. In 1985, the Yangtze River Delta, the Pearl River Delta, and the southern Fujian Delta (including 61 cities and counties) were used as open coastal regions. For these areas, the government supports such measures as technical promotion, attracting foreign investment, and processing agricultural products. Instead of entering the cities in the eastern coastal regions, the household contract responsibility system has been carried out at the same time in the rural regions, and the scale of collective ownership of township enterprises has been expanded. In 1990s, the economy of urban and rural regions has achieved a rapid development.

11.2.3 The Development of the Western Regions

The western region is composed of 12 provinces, cities and autonomous regions. By the end of 2016, the area was 6.81 million km^2, accounting for 70.9% of the total area of the country. At the end of the year, the total population was 3.74 million persons, accounting for 27.1% of the total population of the country.[5] The western region has the most extensive area, rich natural resources, and a large number of ethnic groups. In order to narrow the disparity between the eastern and western regions, the government decided to implement the strategy of the western development in 1999. From 2000 to 2007, the state has increased investment in the western region, the cumulative payment of nearly 15,000 billion yuan of fiscal transfer, debt, budget construction funds, and the department of construction funds accumulated about 7300 billion yuan arrangement in the west regions, these measures have effectively promoted the economic development of the western region.[6] The GDP per capita of western regions to 2735 yuan in 2007 increased from 1127 yuan in 2000 (in 1978 as the base period), the average annual growth rate of 13.5%, more than the national

---

[1]The Guangdong province, at that time, also included the present Hainan, which was independent from Guangdong in the province of Hainan in 1988.

[2]At that time, Chongqing was also affiliated to Sichuan. In 1997, it was formally upgraded to a municipality directly under the central government, and it was independent from Sichuan.

[3]The eastern coastal regions are different from those in the East.

[4]From north to south, it is Dalian, Qinhuangdao, Tianjin, Yantai,Qingdao, Lianyungang, Nantong, Shanghai, Wenzhou, Ningbo, Fuzhou, Guangzhou, Zhanjiang, and Beihai.

[5]According to "China Statistical Yearbook 2017".

[6]It is from Wang Zheng's "8 years of West Development: the fastest growing economy and the most benefit of the people" http://www.china.com.cn/aboutchina/txt/2008-10/14/content_16608647.htm. 2008.10.14.

average growth rate of actual GDP per capita[7] in the same period. However, the government has implemented a series of policies, such as infrastructure construction, energy development, ecological environment improvement, development of advantageous industries, poverty reduction, talent attraction, technology development and education. In this series of policies, the policy of "conservation priority and moderate development" of energy saving and emission reduction has become one of the reasons for restraining the industrialization of the western region. In addition, in the western rural regions, the traditional economic foundation was weak, coupled with harsh natural conditions, which delayed the development of infrastructure and the rise of public utilities, so it was hard to narrow the disparity with the eastern region.

11.2.4 The Rise of Central Regions

The area of the central region is 1.03 million km^2, accounting for 10.7% of the total area of the country. At the end of the year, the total population was 4.32 million persons, accounting for 31.3% of the total population of the country. The central region has good traffic conditions and superior geographical position, which connect the eastern coastal regions and the inland regions. In addition, it is well known that the central region has a cheap labor force and rich natural resources. First of all, we should take full advantage of the location advantages of the central region to build a transportation system centered on infrastructure construction and improve their condition as a logistics center. Second, using low-cost labor force to attract foreign capital and improve the competitiveness of labor-intensive industries. In addition, the central region can make use of the production amount as the first in the country and one-thirds of the capital coal sources in Shanxi, which is buried in the country. It can also make use of coal resources in Henan and Anhui and mineral resources in Jiangxi, and vigorously develop related industries such as coal, electricity, metallurgy, and other mineral resources. Following the eastern coastal regions, the government aimed at improving the opening level of the central region and promoted its industrialization, urbanization, and market development.

11.3 The Evolution of Regional Economic Disparities in China

The disparity of regional economy in 1978 after the reform and opening-up was generally divided into three stages to investigate. These three stages mainly refers to the period from the beginning of the reform and opening-up to the period of 1985, the period of 1986–2000, and since 2000.

[7]Calculated according to the annual statistical yearbook data.

11.3.1 Regional Economic Disparities in the Early Stage of Reform and Opening-up

The reform and opening-up began in the 5th Five-Year Plan period (1976–1980) in 1978. Subsequently, the center of national development and construction shifted to eastern regions, and the economy of the eastern coastal regions has developed significantly. During the 7th Five-Year Plan period (1986–1990), the division pattern of the former coastal regions and inland regions has evolved into a new pattern of the eastern, central, and western regions. The dividing pattern of these three major regions has continued until 2000. With the development of the market economy, the disparity between regions was gradually expanding.

As shown in Table 11.1, the economic disparity between the eastern, central, and western regions was evident in the three regions. In 1985, the eastern region accounted for 13.5% of the total area of the country, the largest population accounted for 37.6% of the country, nominal GDP accounted for 51% of the country, was the fastest growing region. In contrast, although the western region accounts for more than half of the country's total population, it was only 28.5% of the country's population. The nominal GDP accounts for only 19.8% of the country's total, and it was most backward in the three regions. In the central region, the population and the nominal GDP were 33.9 and 29.2% in the country, respectively. Although there was an advantage over the western region, the disparity with the eastern region was very large.

11.3.1.1 Regional Economic Disparities Before 2000 Years

As shown in Fig. 11.1, during the 7th Five-Year Plan period (1986–1990) and the 8th Five-Year Plan period (1991–1995), the gross domestic product of each region has increased significantly, and the nominal GDP per capita has also been increasing steadily. Among them, the growth of GDP per capita in the eastern region was the fastest, which has reached 7212 yuan, which was equivalent to 141.8% of the national average. The disparity between the three regions increased rapidly from 1985 to 1995, especially in the eastern and western regions. At the time of 1995, the eastern region had over two times more than the western region.

11.3.1.2 Regional Economic Disparities Since 2000

Since 2000, the government has implemented the western development in succession, after the strategy of the rise of central regions, the economy of the western region and the central region has made great progress, but there was still a certain disparity compared with the eastern region. In particular, the level of economic development in the eastern region was far beyond the national average and was in the leading position in the three regions. As shown in Table 11.2, it showed the economic development

Table 11.1 The development of eastern, central, and western regions (1985)

Regions	Number of regions	Area		Population		Nominal GDP		Nominal GDP per capita	
		Total (ten thousand km^2)	Ratio (%)	Total (ten thousand persons)	Ratio (%)	Total (Billion yuan)	Ratio (%)	Total (yuan)	Ratio (%)
Nationwide	29	960	100.0	103,875	100.0	8614	100.0	829	100.0
Eastern	11	130	13.5	39,021	37.6	4398	51.0	1127	135.9
Central	9	288	30.0	35,209	33.9	2512	29.2	713	86.0
Western	9	542	56.5	29,645	28.5	1704	19.8	575	69.4

Source New China Sixty Years Statistical Data Compilation
Note By the end of 1987, China was divided into 29 provinces, autonomous regions and municipalities directly under the central government (The following is referred to as the province). Hainan was independent of Guangdong in 1988, and the 29 provinces became the 30 provinces. After that, in 1997, Chongqing became one of the municipalities directly under the central government from Sichuan and became the 31 provinces at present

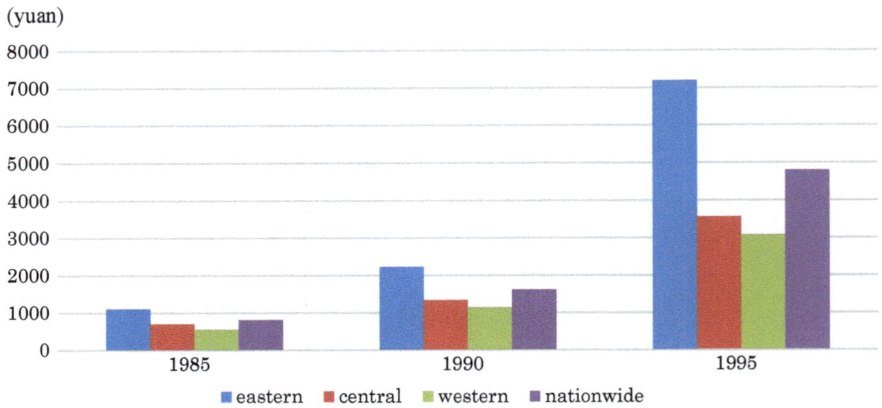

Fig. 11.1 The nominal GDP per capita of the three major regions of China (1985–1995) (*Source* Same Table 11.1)

Table 11.2 Nominal GDP per capita of the three major regions since 2000 (yuan and %)

Regions	2000		2005		2010		2016	
	GDP per capita	Ratio	GDP per capita	Ratio	GDP per capita	Ratio	GDP per capita	Ratio
Nationwide	7937	100.0	15,525	100.0	32,915	100.0	56,533	100.0
Eastern	11,999	151.2	23,548	151.7	45,989	139.7	75,430	133.4
Central	5807	73.2	11,181	72.0	24,979	75.9	44,127	78.1
Western	4893	61.6	9382	60.4	22,476	68.3	41,917	74.1

Source Same Table 11.1

of the three major regions since 2000, and the disparity between the regions and the national average. The nominal GDP per capita level in the eastern region has exceeded the national average, but from 151.2% in 2000 to 133.4% in 2016. The central region and the western region's nominal GDP per capita had varying degrees of increase, the central region increased from 73.2% in 2010 to 78.1% in 2016, the western region increased from 61.6% in 2000 to 74.1% in 2016, we can see that the western region's economic development level has been greatly improved, compared with the western region, the central region economic development was only a slight increase. From the perspective of regional disparities, the regional disparity between the eastern region and the central and western regions has narrowed in 2016 compared with 2000. The regional disparity between the central and western regions showed convergence and convergence trend.

11.3.2 The Evolution Trend of Regional Economic Disparities Based on Various Statistical Scales

11.3.2.1 Regional Economic Disparities Based on Nominal GDP Per Capita

From the change of the regional economic disparity after the reform and opening-up, it is impossible to draw a clear conclusion that the disparity between the three regions was expanding or narrowing. Therefore, the statistical data of nominal GDP[8] was used here to observe the trend of regional disparities in detail.

From Fig. 11.2, the nominal GDP ratio of the three large regions was used to measure the disparity between the eastern and the western region, and the eastern and the central region. It can be seen that the disparity between the eastern and the central region and the disparity between the eastern and the western region almost had the same trend of change, and the regional disparity was first expanded, and then narrowed. Specifically, since 1978, the disparity between the eastern and the western region has widened from 1.8 times and 1.6 times to 2.6 times and 2.1 times the highest point in 2003, and then narrowed down to 1.8 times and 1.7 times in 2016, respectively. In general, the disparity between the eastern and the western region was always higher than that between the eastern and the central region during the period 1978–2016. In recent years, the disparity between the east and the western region, and the disparity between the eastern and the central region had convergent tendency.

11.3.2.2 Regional Economic Disparities Based on Coefficient of Variation

The above is the summary of the regional disparity in the nominal GDP per capita of 31 provinces. Here, we look at the inter province disparity between the nominal GDP by the coefficient of variation.

As shown in Fig. 11.3a and b, the change trend of variation coefficient of disparity represents the nominal GDP per capita between the province and the maximum and minimum ratio of susceptible to nominal GDP per capita in provinces with high impact, therefore will be excluded after the reform and opening-up has been ranked the top three in Beijing, Shanghai, and Tianjin, the three municipalities directly under the central government after investigation. As shown in Fig. 11.3a, the coefficient of variation and the maximum and minimum ratio were all very high. The average GDP disparity between provinces has been shrinking from 1978 to 1990, but from 1990s to 2000s, it has been expanding. From Fig. 11.3b, we can see that in the late 1990s,

[8]China's economic growth rate and inflation rate have risen significantly, and the nominal gap can reflect the change in the rate of inflation.

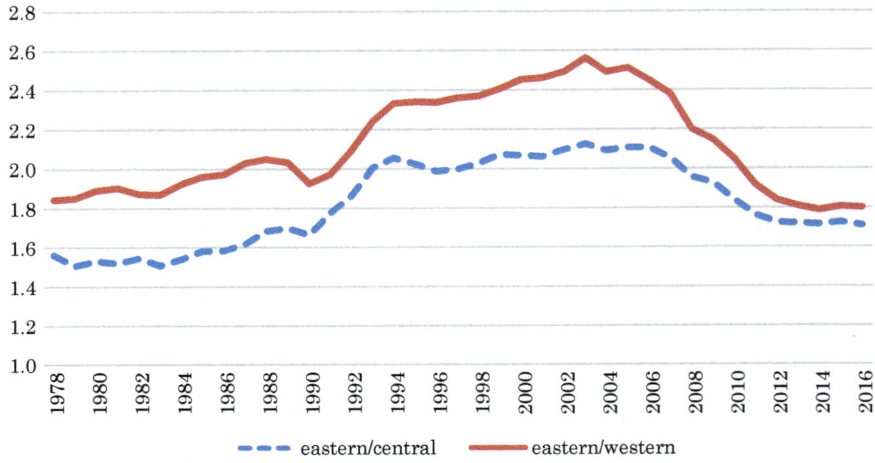

Fig. 11.2 The ratio of GDP per capita in three large regions (*Source* 1978–2003 years' nominal GDP and 1978–2007 years' nominal GDP per capita were compiled according to the "New China Sixty Years Statistical Data Compilation". 2004–2007 years' nominal GDP and 2008–2016 years' nominal GDP per capita were compiled according to "China Statistical Yearbook 2009–2017")

the overall trend was almost the same as Fig. 11.3a. The coefficient of variation and the maximum and minimum ratio both had a significant decrease. The disparity between provinces began to shrink from 1978 to 1982 and then showed an enlarged trend from 1983 to 2006.

11.3.2.3 Regional Economic Disparities Based on Theil Index[9]

In order to further analyze the regional economic disparity in detail, Theil index is used to analyze interregional disparities and intraregional disparities[10] in this chapter.

The definition of Theil index is as follows.

$$T = \sum_{i=1}^{n} (\frac{Y_i}{y} \cdot \ln \frac{Y_i}{y}) \quad (11.1)$$

[9]Theil index is the important index measuring the degree of inequality of income. In all areas, the income share is calculated with the weight of the population on the income share compared with the population share. Here, if the income share of all regions is equal to the population share, the value of the Theil index is 0, and it is completely equal. The higher the value, the higher the unequal degree. According to China's three major regional division methods, we can get the regional disparity between the national overall (T) = the interregional disparity (T_1) + the intraregional disparity (T_2).

[10]According to the data of the provinces, the interregional disparity is calculated based on the data of provinces. The intraregional disparity is the disparity between the provinces in the region, and the intraregional disparity is the weighted average of share in each region.

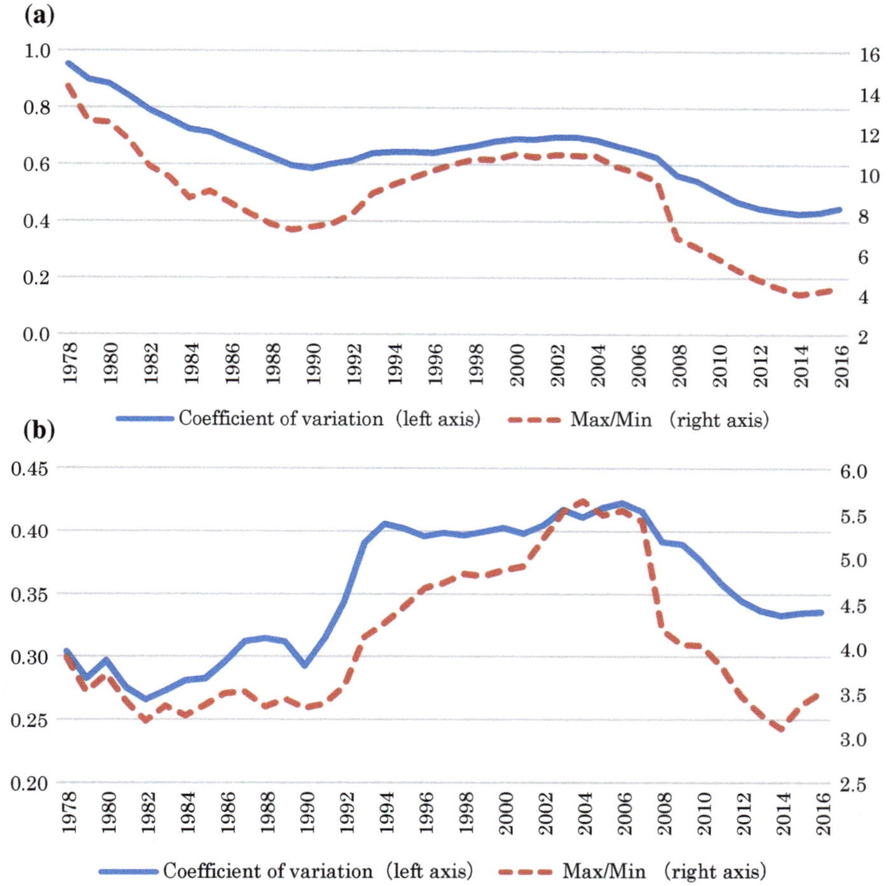

Fig. 11.3 **a** GDP per capita disparity between provinces: Coefficient of variation, maximum, and minimum ratio (1978–2016 years): data of 31 provinces in China (*Source* 1978–2007 year' data was compiled according to "New China Sixty Years Statistical Data Compilation", and 2008–2016 year' data was compiled according to "China Statistical Yearbook 2009–2017". *Note* The coefficient of variation is calculated without considering the number of population. The maximum and minimum ratio is based on the ratio of the maximum and minimum values of the nominal GDP per capita of 31 provinces), **b** GDP per capita disparity between provinces: Coefficient of variation, maximum, and minimum ratio (1978–2016 years): data from 28 provinces in addition to Beijing, Shanghai and Tianjin (*Source* Same Fig. 11.3a)

Here, Y_i represents the total amount of economy in the province of i (represented here with GDP), and Y represents average income.

Theil index can be decomposed using the addition principle. According to the provinces, the national regional disparity = the interregional disparity + the intraregional disparity. The disparity between the three major regions can be divided into three major interregional disparities and three major intraregional disparities that is the interior disparity of the eastern,central, and western.

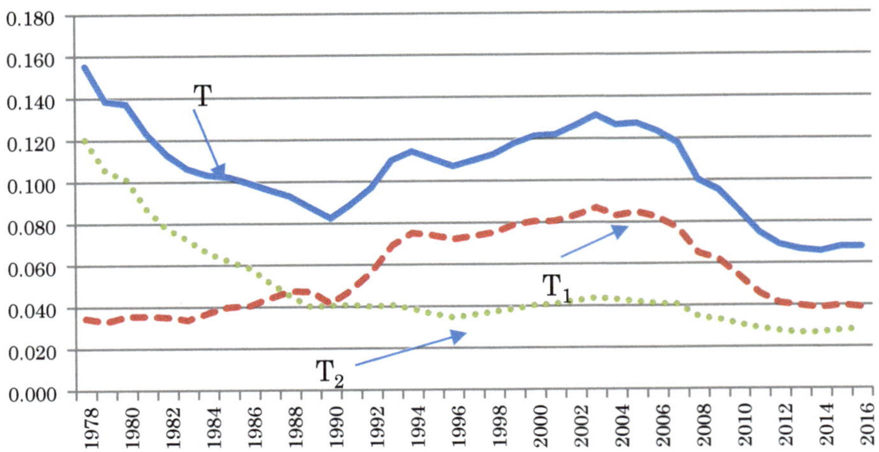

Fig. 11.4 National, interregional, and intraregional disparities based on Theil index (1978–2016) (*Source* Same Fig. 11.3)

The formula for the decomposition of Theil index is as follows.

$$T = T_1 + T_2 = \sum_{k=1}^{m} S_k T_k + \sum_{k=1}^{m} (S_k \cdot \ln \frac{\mu_k}{\mu}) \tag{11.2}$$

T is Theil index obtained according to the province's data, T_1 is the interregional Theil index, and T_2 is the intraregional Theil index. S_k is the income share of the regional k (eastern, central, and western), T_k is Theil index of the regional k, and μ_k is the average income of the regional k.

As shown in Fig. 11.4, Theil index of the national overall was measured for 1978–2016, the trend of three major interregional Theil index and three major intraregional Theil index were measured. The economic disparity between the national overall and the three major inter-area showed a downward trend, while the three major interregional economic disparity was on the rise. From regional economic disparities of the national overall could be seen from 1978 to 1990, the overall regional economic disparity was on the decline, in 1990 0.083 to the lowest point, but the regional economic disparity from 1991 to 2003 on the whole was rising, and in 2003 reached the highest point of 0.131, and then decreased gradually, dropped to 0.066 in 2014. The three major interregional disparity has been almost the same as Theil index of the national overall disparity since 1990. In particular, the three major interregional disparity has risen continuously since 1978, as well as up to 0.087 of the highest value in 2003, and then a downward trend. Theil index of the disparity between the three major intra-area and the national overall was almost the same. It has shown a trend of first decline, and then rise again since 1978.

Figure 11.5 shows the three major intraregional disparity in the eastern, central and western. The interior disparity in the eastern region has been decreasing since

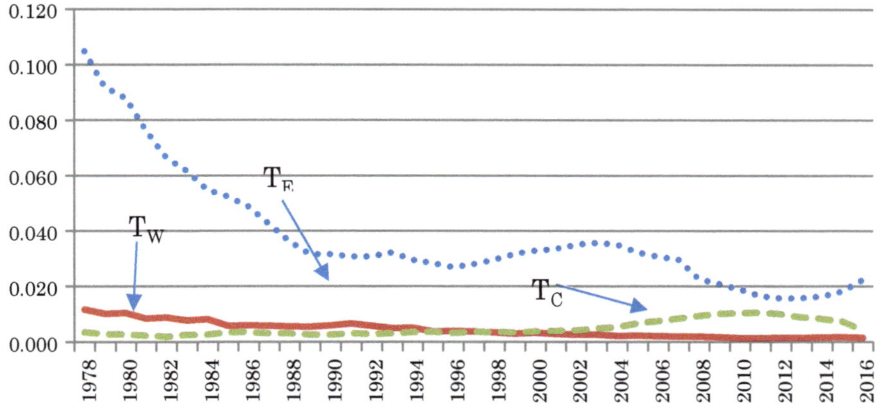

Fig. 11.5 Theil index of the three major intraregional disparity (1978–2016) (*Source* Same Fig. 11.3. *Note* T_E is the interior disparity of the eastern region, T_C is the interior disparity of the central region, and T_W is the interior disparity of the western region)

1978, though it had an upward trend since 1990, and it has increased to 0.036 in 2003, and then decreased again, and then increased again in 2014. However, compared with the 0.105 in 1978, it reached 0.023 in 2016, and the decline was obvious. In contrast, the interior disparity in the central region was steadily declining, down from 0.012 in 1978 to 0.002 in 2016. The trend of the interior disparity in the western region was relatively stable, showing a slight increase from 0.004 in 1978 to 0.011 in 2009. It has decreased again in recent years, and it has dropped to 0.005 in 2016.

Table 11.3 gives the change of the interregional disparity (T_1) and the intraregional disparity (T_2) in the three regions, and the intraregional disparity of the eastern region, central and western, and their contribution to the overall disparity change. Combined with the above chart, we can see that in the 1978–1987 years, the three major intraregional disparity was the main factor affecting the overall regional disparity. Since 1988, the three major interregional disparity has exceeded the intraregional disparity, which has become the main factor affecting the regional disparity. In the three major intraregional disparity, the interior disparity of the eastern region was still narrowing, but it still had the highest contribution to the intraregional disparity. From the decomposition of the regional disparity in 2016, the contribution of the three major inter-area was 57.5%, the contribution of the three major intra-area was 42.5%, while the interior disparity of the eastern, central and western region was 33.3, 2.5, and 6.7%, respectively.

In summary, the regional economic disparity has gone through three stages: during the period 1978–1990, Theil index decreased from 0.156 to 0.083, which was mainly due to the decline of the three major intraregional disparity. During the period 1990–2003, Theil index increased from 0.083 to 0.131, mainly due to the widening of the three major interregional disparity. During the period 2003–2016, Theil index dropped from 0.131 to 0.068, and the decline was due to the simultaneous decline in the disparity between the three major inter-area and the three major intra-area.

Table 11.3 Theil index and contribution rate of the three major inter-area and the three major intra-area

Years	Theil index			Contribution degree (%)				
	T	T_1	T_2	T_1	T_2	T_E	T_C	T_W
1978	0.156	0.035	0.121	22.5	77.5	67.5	7.6	2.4
1980	0.138	0.036	0.102	26.0	74.0	64.1	7.7	2.2
1985	0.103	0.040	0.062	39.2	60.8	51.2	5.9	3.7
1990	0.083	0.042	0.041	50.6	49.4	38.4	7.5	3.5
1995	0.111	0.074	0.037	66.9	33.1	25.8	3.7	3.6
2000	0.122	0.081	0.041	66.4	33.6	27.3	2.9	3.3
2001	0.122	0.081	0.041	66.3	33.7	27.7	2.6	3.5
2002	0.126	0.084	0.043	66.2	33.8	28.0	2.3	3.5
2003	0.131	0.087	0.044	66.5	33.6	27.5	2.2	3.9
2004	0.127	0.083	0.043	65.8	34.2	27.8	2.0	4.4
2005	0.127	0.085	0.042	66.9	33.1	25.6	2.0	5.5
2006	0.124	0.083	0.041	66.7	33.3	25.0	1.9	6.3
2007	0.118	0.077	0.041	65.4	34.6	25.3	1.9	7.4
2008	0.100	0.065	0.035	65.2	34.8	25.9	2.3	10.2
2009	0.096	0.062	0.034	64.9	35.1	25.6	2.1	11.8
2010	0.086	0.054	0.031	63.4	36.6	22.3	1.9	12.4
2011	0.075	0.046	0.029	61.0	39.0	22.3	2.2	14.4
2012	0.069	0.041	0.028	59.5	40.5	23.1	2.6	14.9
2013	0.067	0.040	0.027	59.7	40.3	24.0	2.6	13.7
2014	0.066	0.039	0.027	58.8	41.2	25.4	2.8	13.0
2015	0.068	0.040	0.028	58.8	41.2	27.0	3.0	11.2
2016	0.068	0.039	0.029	57.5	42.5	33.3	2.5	6.7

Source Same Fig. 11.3
Note T_1 is the interregional disparity. T_2 is the intraregional disparity. $T_2 = T_E + T_C + T_W.T_E$ is the interior disparity of the eastern region, T_C is the interior disparity of the central region, and T_W is the interior disparity of the western region

11.4 An Empirical Analysis of Regional Economic Disparities

Through the analysis of the evolution trend of the regional economic disparity, it can be seen that the regional economic disparity in China has a convergence trend. In this chapter, we use the panel data of 31 provinces in China for 1990–2016 years to set up the econometric model, analyze the influencing factors of regional economic disparities, and verify the impact of the spillover effect of the eastern region on the regional economic disparity. The data used are from "New China Sixty Years Statistical Data Compilation", and "China Statistical Yearbook 1991–2017". All data used are based on the latest data.

11.4.1 Variable Description and Data Processing

11.4.1.1 The Influential Factors of Regional Economic Disparities

According to the new classical theory of economic growth, the accumulation of physical capital, labor, and technology level has a significant impact on economic growth, the new economic growth theory thinks that other factors outside the technology also has an effect on economic growth, such as the level of human capital accumulation and market structure and so on. Barro (1990) also incorporated government public expenditure into the endogenous growth model, considering its possible impact on economic growth. After considering the possible effects of various factors on economic growth, this chapter changes the economic growth model into a regional economic disparity model. In previous empirical studies, through empirical research to verify the regional economic disparity, the use of explanatory variables for provincial GDP per capita (Pan 2010; Liu 2011) or GDP per capita growth rate (Liu et al. 2009), or the difference between the regions GDP per capita and GDP per capita of the country (Lu et al. 2012). This chapter uses the relative disparity of regional economy, that is, the ratio of the GDP per capita of each province to the national GDP per capita as the explanatory variable. The variables, as shown in Table 11.4, are calculated for all variables outside the virtual variable to avoid the influence of heteroscedasticity. When considering the explanatory variables that affect the regional economic disparity, it is selected from different perspectives, such as urbanization, industrial structure, human capital, physical capital stock, labor capital, fiscal policy, and market openness. The specific variables include the urbanization rate, the proportion of the secondary industry and the tertiary industry, the level of human capital, the proportion of fixed assets investment, the proportion of urban employees, the proportion of fiscal expenditure and the proportion of import and export trade.

11.4.1.2 Economic Spillover Effect

According to the theory of regional economics, there is a so-called economic spillover and feedback effect between regional economies. The so-called spillover is a region's economic development will play a leading role in other areas and promote the development of other regions' economy. The so-called feedback effect means that the economic development of one region has an impact on the other region after its impact on the other. In order to verify the effect of economic spillover effects on regional economic development, adding variables to the spillover effects of the eastern region on the eastern and the central and western regions in the above measurement model ($east_{it}$, mid_{it}, $west_{it}$). Among them, the value of $east_{it}$ is taken as the average of the average GDP per capita in the eastern provinces except for itself, is that the average actual GDP per capita of the eastern provinces in *t* year, when *i* is a province of the central or western, the value is 0; when *i* is a province of the central, the value of mid_{it} is the average actual GDP per capita of the eastern provinces in *t* year, when

Table 11.4 Variable symbol specification

Variable type	Variable name	Variable symbol	Data processing
Explained variable	Regional disparities	gapr	The ratio of actual GDP per capita to the national average GDP in each province
Explanatory variable	Urbanization rate	urb	The proportion of urban population[a] in each province accounts to the total population[b]
	Proportion of fiscal expenditure	fis	The proportion of financial expenditure in each province to GDP
	Proportion of investment in fixed assets[c]	fci	The proportion of fixed assets investment in each province to GDP
	Proportion of foreign trade	imex	The proportion of import and export trade accounts[d] in each province to GDP
	Proportion of the secondary industry	sec	The proportion of the secondary industry in each province to GDP
	Proportion of the tertiary industry	ter	The proportion of the tertiary industry in each province to GDP
	Proportion of urban employed persons[e]	emp	The proportion of urban employed persons in each province to the total population
	Human capital level[f]	huc	The proportion of college students in each province to the total population
	Spillover effects on the eastern region	east	When it is the eastern province, the average value of the actual GDP per capita in the eastern provinces except themselves for the year, when it is not the eastern provinces, the value is 0
	Spillover effects on the central region	mid	When it is the central province, the average value of the actual GDP per capita in the eastern provinces of the year, when it is not the central provinces, the value is 0
	Spillover effects on the western region	west	When it is the western province, the average value of the actual GDP per capita in the eastern provinces of the year, when it is not the western provinces, the value is 0
	Dummy variable for the western provinces	dwest	When it is the western provinces, the value is 1, when it is the eastern or central provinces, the value is 0

(continued)

Table 11.4 (continued)

Variable type	Variable name	Variable symbol	Data processing
	Dummy variable for 2000	d2000	Before 2000, the value is 0, since 2000, the value was 1
	Dummy variable for 2008	d2008	Before 2008, the value is 0, since 2008, the value was 1

[a]The population data of urban population from 1990 to 1999 separately use census register population data, urban population data of each province are calculated by urban resident population since 2000
[b]The total population from 1990 to 2015 is the ratio of GDP to GDP per capita in each province. The total population of each province in 2016 is the number of the population at the end of each province
[c]Fixed assets investment mainly refers to various cities registered enterprises, institutions, administrative units and individuals in the plan a total investment of 500 thousand yuan and 500 thousand yuan of investment in construction projects. Occurred in the county and the area above the investment, direct leadership, governments at all levels and departments at or above the county-level management of construction projects and enterprises investment, and investment in real estate development
[d]Import and export trade volume is calculated according to equivalent exchange into RMB
[e]Urban employees are different from that of the rural employees. It includes state-owned units, urban collective units, joint stock cooperative units, and continuous battalion units, limited liability companies, Limited by Share Ltd, private enterprises, Hong Kong, Macao and Taiwan investment entities, foreign investment units, and individual businesses
[f]Under normal circumstances, the human capital index using the number of college graduates will be more appropriate, due to the limitation of data, the number of college students used in this chapter

i is not a province of the central, the value is 0; likewise, when i is a province of the western, the value of $west_{it}$ is the average actual GDP per capita of the eastern provinces in t year, when i is not a province of the western, the value is 0. As a measure of economic spillover variables of $east_{it}$, mid_{it}, $west_{it}$ all include 0 values, therefore the three variables are not logarithmic.

In addition, considering the implementation of the western development strategy since 2000, the government slanted from various aspects of policy to the western region. Theoretically, the government's policy tilt strongly supported the infrastructure construction and economic development in the western region, so the policy effect may exceed the economic spillover effect in the eastern region. Therefore, we can take 2000 as a time dividing point to investigate the effect of the eastern region's economic spillover effect on the regional economic disparity since 2000. To this end, a virtual variable d2000 is introduced. The value of the time points before 2000 is 0, and the time points from 2000 to 2016 are all 1. In the panel data model, the interaction between the above economic spillover variables and the virtual variable d2000 is considered ($east_{it} * d2000$, $mid_{it} * d2000$, $west_{it} * d2000$). These three interactions can test the effects of economic spillover effects on regional economic disparities since 2000. Meanwhile, in order to verify whether the western development policy has narrowed the regional economic disparity since 2000, we add the virtual variable dwest in the western provinces to the interaction term of virtual variable d2000 in the model (dwest ∗ d2000). Similarly, in September 2008, in order to cope with the world financial crisis, the government invested 4 trillion yuan of government investment at the end of 2008, most of which invested in the infrastructure construction in the inland region, and promoted the rapid growth of the inland economy. It will be 2008 as a time dividing point, in theory, compared to the eastern coastal regions and the central and western regions, the impact of financial crisis was more serious, therefore, it is necessary to pay special attention to how the eastern region's economic spillover effects on the central and western regions affected the change of regional economic disparities. To this end, the virtual variable *d2008* is introduced. The value of the time points before 2008 is 0, and the time points from 2008 to 2016 are all 1. Similarly, in the panel data model, the interaction of each economic spillover effect variable and the virtual variable d2008 is considered ($east_{it} * d2008$, $mid_{it} * d2008$, $west_{it} * d2008$). These three interactions can test the effects of economic spillover effects on regional economic disparities since 2008. At the same time, in order to verify whether the government investment policy has affected the change of regional economic disparities since 2008, in the model, we add the virtual variable dwest of the western provinces and the interaction term of dummy variable d2000 (dwest ∗ d2008).

11.4.2 Panel Data Model

First, the descriptive statistical analysis of the variables is shown in Table 11.5. The observation data objects, the average value, the standard deviation, the maximum value and the minimum value of the variables are shown, respectively.

Using the variables in Table 11.4, a total of 14 panel data models, such as Tables 11.6 and 11.7, are established. FE (1)–FE (7) in Table 11.6 choose individual fixed effect models,[11] investigate the influencing factors of regional economic disparities, and verify the influence of economic spillovers on regional economic disparities. In the analysis of influencing factors, all models use the same explanatory variables, namely urbanization rate, fiscal expenditure proportion, fixed assets investment proportion, foreign trade proportion, the proportion of the tertiary industry, and human capital index. A model for measuring the spillover effect of the economy, respectively is the spillover effect on its own eastern region (FE (1)), the spillover effect on the central and western region (FE (2)); the spillover effect on its own eastern region (FE (3)), and the spillover effect on the central and western region since 2000 (FE (4)); the spillover effect on its eastern region since 2008 (FE (5)), and the spillover effect on the central and western region (FE (6)), all of the above

[11]The selection of the fixed effect model is the result of Hausman Test. Individual fixed effect model and individual time fixed effect model including the fixed effect model, in the 5% level of significance, through the *F* Test should reject the null hypothesis, establish individual time fixed effect model. Therefore, the choice of the individual fixed effect model is the result of accepting the original hypothesis.

Table 11.5 Descriptive statistical analysis of various variables

Variable	Obs	Mean	Std. Dev.	Min	Max
gapr	837	1.02	0.57	0.30	3.60
urb	837	41.11	17.94	12.30	94.20
fis	837	18.58	15.26	0.56	137.92
fci	837	50.29	23.80	15.27	138.61
imex	837	29.08	38.57	3.20	225.90
sec	837	43.79	8.67	12.90	64.70
ter	837	39.29	8.06	5.60	80.20
emp	837	18.24	9.53	6.00	70.00
huc	837	1.01	0.82	0.10	3.60
east	837	0.39	0.70	0	2.72
mid	837	0.28	0.62	0	2.57
west	837	0.43	0.72	0	2.57
east*d2000	837	0.34	0.71	0	2.72
mid*d2000	837	0.25	0.63	0	2.57
west*d2000	837	0.37	0.74	0	2.57
east*d2008	837	0.25	0.69	0	2.72
mid*d2008	837	0.18	0.59	0	2.57
west*d2008	837	0.27	0.71	0	2.57
dwest*d2000	837	0.63	0.48	0	1
dwest*d2008	837	0.13	0.34	0	1

spillover effects are used to measure the impact on regional economic disparities. FE (7) weighs the impact of policy changes in the western region on regional economic disparities since 2000 and 2008.

However, FE (8)–FE (14) in Table 11.7 all select individual time fixed effect model, investigates the influencing factors of regional economic disparities, and verifies the impact of economic spillovers on regional economic disparities. In the analysis of influencing factors, the same explanatory variables are used in each model, namely urbanization rate, the proportion of fiscal expenditure, the proportion of fixed assets investment, the proportion of the secondary industry and the proportion of urban employees. A model for measuring the spillover effect of the economy, respectively is the spillover effect on its own eastern region (FE (8)), and the spillover effect on the central and western region (FE (9)); the spillover effect on its eastern region (FE (10)), and the spillover effect on the central and western region since 2000 (FE (11)); the spillover effect on its own eastern region since 2008 (FE (12)), and the spillover effect on the central and western region (FE (13)), all of the above spillover effects are used to measure the impact on regional economic disparities. FE (14) weighs the impact of policy changes in the western region on regional economic disparities after 2000 and 2008.

Table 11.6 Panel data analysis results (1)

Variable	ln (gapr)						
	FE (1)	FE (2)	FE (3)	FE (4)	FE (5)	FE (6)	FE (7)
ln (urb)	0.116**	0.097**	0.115**	0.102**	0.112**	0.090**	0.076**
	3.924	3.263	3.852	3.385	3.859	3.170	2.709
ln (fis)	−0.070**	−0.115**	−0.072**	−0.117**	−0.060**	−0.149**	−0.117**
	−3.290	−5.211	−3.364	−5.243	−2.811	−6.635	−5.429
ln (fci)	0.100**	0.084**	0.097**	0.089**	0.112**	0.061**	0.109**
	5.362	3.833	5.016	4.210	6.202	2.909	5.972
ln (imex)	−0.032**	−0.027*	−0.030**	−0.026*	−0.037**	−0.025*	−0.030**
	−2.730	−2.284	−2.584	−2.189	−3.157	−2.186	−2.535
ln (ter)	−0.208**	−0.227**	−0.214**	−0.226**	−0.208**	−0.208**	−0.212**
	−6.549	−7.143	−6.710	−7.109	−6.581	−6.647	−6.743
ln (huc)	−0.035**	−0.048**	−0.033*	−0.053**	−0.043**	−0.032*	−0.028*
	−2.518	−3.337	−2.333	−3.625	−3.103	−2.317	−2.035
east	−0.059**						
	−5.477						
mid		0.044**					
		2.760					
west		0.054**					
		4.089					
east*d2000			−0.047**				
			−4.927				
mid*d2000				0.040**			
				2.919			
west*d2000				0.046**			
				4.034			
east*d2008					−0.048**		
					−6.267		
mid*d2008						0.043**	
						4.104	
west*d2008						0.060**	
						7.099	
dwest*d2000							−0.069**
							−4.190
dwest*d2008							0.103**
							6.085
c	0.145	0.389*	0.178	0.355	0.085	0.538**	0.375*
	0.796	2142	0.973	1.963	0.466	2.992	2.102
Adjusted R-squared	0.9456	0.9446	0.9452	0.9446	0.9462	0.9469	0.9463
Observations	837	837	837	837	837	837	837

Note ** stands for $p < 0.01$, * stands for $p < 0.05$

Table 11.7 Panel data analysis results (2)

Variable	ln (gapr)						
	FE (8)	FE (9)	FE (10)	FE (11)	FE (12)	FE (13)	FE (14)
ln (urb)	0.085**	0.082**	0.084**	0.081**	0.088**	0082**	0.045
	3.176	3.030	3.093	2.968	3.413	3.160	1.784
ln (fis)	−0.222**	−0.223**	−0.221**	−0.222**	−0.231**	−0.234**	−0.213**
	−8.112	−8.108	−8.058	−8.044	−8.581	−8.696	−8.001
ln (fci)	0.115**	0.119**	0.118**	0.121**	0.106**	0.113**	0.171**
	5.291	5.351	5.354	5.370	5.142	5.375	8.638
ln (sec)	0.198**	0.197**	0.206**	0.206**	0.168**	0.160**	0.193**
	5.233	5.162	5.448	5.398	4.540	4.290	5.355
ln (emp)	0.126**	0.126**	0.124**	0.124**	0.134**	0.136**	0.151**
	4.914	4.887	4.838	4.800	5.343	5.403	6.043
east	−0.043**						
	−3.521						
mid		0.036*					
		2.379					
west		0.044**					
		3.384					
east*d2000			−0.032**				
			−2.968				
mid*d2000				0.027*			
				2.043			
west*d2000				0.032**			
				2.839			
east*d2008					−0.056**		
					−6.413		
mid*d2008						0.044**	
						4.095	
west*d2008						0.061**	
						6.623	
dwest*d2000							−0.118**
							−6.671
dwest*d2008							0.139**
							7.694
c	−1.322**	−1.364**	−1.360**	−1.386**	−1.188**	−1.194**	−1.468**
	−8.324	−8.772	−8.576	−8.847	−7.740	−7.840	−9.938
Adjusted R-squared	0.9557	0.9555	0.9554	0.9554	0.9572	0.9573	0.9586
Observations	837	837	837	837	837	837	837

Note ** stands for $p < 0.01$, * stands for $p < 0.05$

11.4.3 Analysis of Panel Data Results

11.4.3.1 The Influencing Factors of Regional Economic Disparities

According to the panel data analysis of the fixed effect model (1)–(14). The following conclusions are obtained.

First, from the model (1)–(7), during the study period, the changes in the ratio of urbanization and the proportion of investment in fixed assets have a significant positive effect on regional economic disparities, the coefficient of urbanization rate exceeds that of the proportion of fixed assets investment. That is to say, the increase of urbanization level and the increase of material capital stock expand the regional economic disparity, and the changes in the level of urbanization have a greater impact on the regional economic disparity. While the proportion of fiscal expenditure, the proportion of foreign trade, the proportion of the tertiary industry and the level of human capital have a significant negative impact on regional economic disparities. The coefficient of the proportion of the tertiary industry before more than other variables coefficient. In other words, the increase of local government fiscal expenditure, the deepening of market opening, the increase of the proportion of the tertiary industry and the improvement of human capital level are all conducive to the narrowing of the regional economic disparity. The change of the proportion of the tertiary industry has a stronger effect on narrowing the regional economic disparity.

Second, from the model (8)–(14), during the study period, the changes in the ratio of urbanization and the proportion of investment in fixed asset, the proportion of the secondary industry and the proportion of urban employed persons have a significant positive effect on regional economic disparities, the coefficient of the proportion of the secondary industry before more than other variables coefficient. That is to say, the improvement of urbanization level, the increase of material capital stock, the increase of the proportion of the secondary industry and the increase of urban employees have expanded the regional economic disparity. The change of the proportion of the secondary industry has a greater impact on the regional economic disparity. The change of the proportion of the fiscal expenditure has a significant negative impact on the regional economic disparity, that is, the increase in the local government's fiscal expenditure has narrowed the regional economic disparity.

In summary, the estimated results of the explanatory variables are basically in line with the explanation of the economic growth model.

First of all, from the perspective of narrowing the regional economic disparity, it is mainly influenced by the level of human capital, industrial structure, market openness and financial expenditure. Human capital had a significant positive impact on economic growth, which was conducive to narrowing the regional economic disparity. The better the development of service industry was, the more reasonable the industrial structure was. The technology-intensive industry in the tertiary industry was more conducive to increase the income of residents than the labor-intensive industries in the secondary industry, and the development of the tertiary industry was conducive to narrowing the regional economic disparity. The higher the maturity of foreign trade was, the higher the openness of the market was, the more conducive to attracting foreign investment, the better the development of regional economy, and then the narrowing of the regional economic disparity. Although there were many studies in advance, the larger the scale of fiscal expenditure was, the more serious the government intervention was. The excessive government intervention was often proved to be harmful to the economy, which often lead to the distortion of resource allocation (Liu et al. 2009). However, as a whole, government intervention was still beneficial to the regional economic disparity during the period 1990–2016.

Second, from the perspective of expanding the regional economic disparity, it is mainly influenced by the level of urbanization, the proportion of urban employed persons, the stock of physical capital and the proportion of the secondary industry. The urbanization level of a region reflected the degree of population centralization. However, under the misunderstanding and policy intervention for a long time,[12] there were many distortions in China's urbanization. The level of urbanization lags behind the industrialization process in China, city system and city layout was not reasonable, the income disparity between urban and rural was still large, and the social division of the interior of the city was becoming increasingly prominent (Lu 2017), which affect the further development of the regional economy, there was no better to narrow the economic disparity between regions. The government used administrative means to reduce the speed of urbanization,at the same time, it also restricted the free allocation of labor elements in urban and rural regions and between regions. The increase in the proportion of urban employed persons did not promote the aggregation effect of the size of the population in the city, but it was not conducive to the reduction of regional economic disparities. The input of physical capital had already appeared a decreasing trend of scale return of factor input in various regions. The increase of capital investment would not bring more large-scale economic effect. That is, the economic mode which relied on extensive input was no longer able to meet the goal of economic growth. Its pressure on the economic and social environment would only hinder the further development of the regional economy but expand the regional economic disparity. In terms of industrial structure, due to the different economic development centers of different provinces, the economic disparity between provinces and regions dominated by the development of the secondary industry and the tertiary industry development was bound to exist. The positive role of the development of the tertiary industry in economic growth was better than that of the secondary industry, which was consistent with the above analysis. The development of the tertiary industry would narrow the regional economic disparity, while the development of the secondary industry would expand the regional economic disparity.

[12]In the aspect of city system adjustment, the government's policy orientation was the focus of development to promote the development of small towns, big city limits, reflected in the city the population scale and the household registration system, "12th Five-Year Plan" proposed: Megacities should control population size rationally. Mega and medium-sized cities should strengthen and improve population management and continue to play an important role in attracting foreign population. Small and medium-sized cities and small towns should relax their settlement conditions according to actual conditions.

11.4.3.2 The Influence of Economic Spillover Effect on Regional Economic Disparities

The conclusion of the economic spillover effect is based on the panel data analysis of the fixed effect models (1)–(14).

First, during the period 1990–2016, the actual GDP per capita of other provinces except for their own provinces in the eastern region increase by 1 units, the spillover effect on the eastern region reduce regional economic disparities by 0.059 units (FE (1)), and the actual GDP per capita of the eastern region increase by 1 units, the spillover effects on the central and western regions, respectively, expand regional economic disparities by 0.044 and 0.054 units (FE (2)). During the period 2000–2016, the actual GDP per capita of other provinces except for the eastern itself increase by 1 units, the spillover effect on the eastern region reduce regional economic disparities by 0.044 units (FE (3)), and the actual GDP per capita of the eastern region increase by 1 units, the spillover effect on the central and western regions, respectively, expand regional economic disparities by 0.040 and 0.046 units (FE (4)). Similarly, during the period 2008–2016, the actual GDP per capita of other provinces except for the eastern itself increase by 1 units, the spillover effect on the eastern region reduce regional economic disparities by 0.048 units (FE (5)), and the actual GDP per capita of the eastern region increase by 1 units, the spillover effect on the central and western regions, respectively, expand regional economic disparities by 0.043 and 0.060 units (FE (6)). In addition, it is verified that the western development has a significant negative impact on the regional economic disparity since 2000. It can be explained that the western development policy helped the regional economic convergence since 2000. However, the investment policy of the government has a significant positive impact on the regional economic disparity since 2008. It can be concluded that the government investment policy did not achieve the desired effect on the western region, but expanded regional economic disparities since 2008(FE (7)).

Second, during the period 1990–2016, the actual GDP per capita of other provinces except for their own provinces in the eastern region increase by 1 units, the spillover effect on the eastern region reduce regional economic disparities by 0.043 units (FE (8)), and the actual GDP per capita of the eastern region increase by 1 units, the spillover effects on the central and western regions, respectively, expand regional economic disparities by 0.036 and 0.044 units (FE (9)). During the period 2000–2016, the actual GDP per capita of other provinces except for the eastern itself increase by 1 units, the spillover effect on the eastern region reduce regional economic disparities by 0.032 units (FE (10)), and the actual GDP per capita of the eastern region increase by 1 units, the spillover effect on the central and western regions, respectively, expand regional economic disparities by 0.027 and 0.032 units (FE (11)). Similarly, during the period 2008–2016, the actual GDP per capita of other provinces except for the eastern itself increase by 1 units, the spillover effect on the eastern region reduce regional economic disparities by 0.056 units (FE (12)), and the actual GDP per capita of the eastern region increase by 1 units, the spillover effect on the central and western regions, respectively, expand regional economic disparities by 0.044 and 0.061 units (FE (13)). It is also verified that the western development policy to help the western region has promoted regional economic convergence since 2000. However, government investment policy has expanded regional economic disparities by helping the western region since 2008(FE (14)).

In summary, the following conclusions are obtained on the effect of economic spillover effect on regional economic disparities with the time dividing point.

First, to measure the impact of economic spillover effect on regional economic disparities, the economic growth of other provinces except for their own provinces in the eastern region, its spillover effect on the eastern region has promoted the convergence of regional economic disparities, while the spillover effect of the eastern region's economic growth to the central and western regions has enlarged regional economic disparities. Most of the eastern provinces were economically developed regions. Based on the high-tech industries in the tertiary industry, vigorously developing the service industry and the advantageous geographical location advantages were conducive to attracting foreign investment and expanding the market openness. The resulting economies of scale have attracted more talents and enterprises to gather further. Therefore, the economic spillover effect of the eastern region has played an active role in the convergence of the intraregional economic disparity in the eastern region. On the other hand, the spillover effect of the eastern provinces' economic growth on the central and western regions was not as expected to drive the economic development of the central and western regions, and the economic disparity of three major intraregional disparities in the eastern, central, and western tended to expand.

Second, the policy effect exceeded the economic spillover effect of the eastern region, which impacted on regional economic disparities since 2000. The implementation of the western development policy has played a positive role in promoting the convergence of regional economic disparities since 2000. Through investment in physical capital and infrastructure, the government strengthened investment drive mechanism, narrowed the disparity of the infrastructure level between the western region and the eastern and central regions, and then narrowed regional economic disparities between the western region and the eastern and the central regions. From the perspective of economic spillover effect, the economic spillover effect of the eastern region's economic growth on the central and western regions has not increased significantly and has not further expanded the three interregional economic disparity since 2000. It can be said that the strong effect of the government policy has weakened the economic spillover effect of the eastern region.

Third, the economic spillover effect of the eastern region covered the policy effect, which impacted on regional economic disparities since 2008. The government of the western region investment policy has eased the negative effects of the financial crisis to a certain extent, but not fundamentally changed the western region of the extensive economic growth mode, and strengthened the intangible capital to human capital as the representative of the investment, relying solely on physical capital investment on economic growth was weak since 2008. Therefore, the policy effect on the west not only failed to narrow the economic disparity between the western region and the eastern and central regions but also expanded regional economic disparities. From the perspective of economic spillover effect. Under the world financial crisis and the impact of economic growth in eastern regions were strongly influenced by the external environment in 2008. Therefore, the interior disparity of the whole eastern region tended to be balanced, its economic spillover effect on the central and western regions has made the economic disparity of the three major inter-area significantly expanded.

11.5 Conclusions

This chapter summarizes the evolution process of regional economic development, and through qualitative analysis, the evolution trend of regional economic disparities is examined on the basis of various statistical scales. Using panel data in 31 provinces of China for 1990–2016 years to establish a measurement model, the influencing factors of regional economic disparities are empirically analyzed. Combined with the two-time dividing points in 2000 and 2008, we verify the effect of the spillover effect of the eastern region's economic growth on the regional economic disparity and draw the following conclusions.

First, based on the observation of nominal GDP per capita, the disparity between the eastern and the western region was always higher than that between the eastern and the central region during the period 1978–2016. In recent years, the disparity between the east and the western region, and the disparity between the eastern and the central region had convergent tendency. Based on the coefficient of variation, the average GDP disparity between provinces also tended to converge since 2007.

Second, based on the trend of Theil index, the economic disparity between the national overall and the three intra-area had a downward trend, while the economic difference of the three inter-area showed an upward trend. At the same time, in terms of the contribution of the disparity between inter-area and intra-area to the regional economic disparity, during the period 1978–1987, we can see that the three major intraregional disparity was the main factor affecting the overall regional disparity. Since 1988, the three major interregional disparity has exceeded the intraregional disparity, which has become the main factor affecting the regional disparity.

Third, the following conclusions are drawn from the analysis of the factors affecting the regional economic disparity by the panel data model. From the perspective of narrowing the regional economic disparity, it is mainly influenced by the level of human capital, industrial structure, market openness, and financial expenditure. However, from the perspective of expanding the regional economic disparity, it is mainly influenced by the level of urbanization, the proportion of urban employed persons, the stock of physical capital and the proportion of the secondary industry.

Fourth, from the economic spillover effect of the eastern region on regional economic disparities can be found based on the analysis of panel data model. It is that the economic growth of other provinces except for their own provinces in the eastern region, its spillover effect on the eastern region has promoted the convergence of regional economic disparities, while the spillover effect of the eastern region's economic growth to the central and western regions has enlarged regional economic disparities.

Fifth, taking 2000 and 2008 as the time dividing point, we can see that: The implementation of the western development strategy promoted the convergence of regional economic disparities, and its policy effect exceeded the economic spillover effect of the eastern region, which impacted on regional economic disparities since 2000. The government's policy support to the western regions widened regional economic disparities, the economic spillover effect of the eastern region concealed the policy effect, which impacted on regional economic disparities since 2008.

References

Barro, R.J. 1990. Government spending in a simple model of endogenous growth. *Journal of Political Economy* 98 (5): 103–125.

Baumol, W.J. 1986. Productivity growth, convergence, and welfare: What the long-run data show. *American Economic Review* 76 (5): 1072–1085.

Chen, K., and F. Zhang. 2017. Productive public expenditure, spatial spillover effect and regional economic disparities: Based on multi-regional DGE model. *China Population, Resources and Environment* 27 (4): 58–67. (in Chinese).

Groenewold, N., L. Guoping, and A. Chen. 2007. Regional output spillovers in China: Estimates from a VAR model. *Papers in Regional Science* 86 (1): 101–122.

Liu, S., Y. Wang, and A. Hu. 2009. The effect of western development program and regional economic convergence in China. *Economic Research Journal* 9: 94–105. (in Chinese).

Liu, Q. 2011. China's regional disparity, linkage and analysis of spillover and feedback effect. Master thesis, Tsinghua University. (in Chinese).

Lu, M. 2017. *The power of space: Geography, politics and urban development*, 25–26. Shanghai: Gezhi Press. (in Chinese).

Lu, H., F. Zheng, and S. Jia. 2012. Frontier technical development, technical efficiency and regional disparity. *China Population, Resources and Environment* 22 (5): 120–125. (in Chinese).

Pan, W. (2010). The Economic Disparity between Different Regions of China and Its Reduction—An Analysis from the Geographical Perspective. *Social Sciences in China, 1*, 72–84.

Ren, J., and G. Yang. 2010. Analysis of China's regional economic development of the differences and their cause. *Economic Geography* 30 (5): 784–789. (in Chinese).

Su, S. 2001. Research on the economic development gap between the eastern coastal and inland regions in 1950s–1970s. *Journal of Zhongnan University of Finance and Economics* 1: 1–12. (in Chinese).

Zhang, L., and L. Zhou. 2015. Does industrial transfer Narrow regional inequality—Empirical study from Western China. *Finance and Economics* 2: 80–88. (in Chinese).

Zhang, Q., and B. Felmingham. 2002. The role of FDI exports and spillover effects in the regional development of China. *Journal of Development Studies* 38 (4): 157–178.

Chapter 12
Spatial Dimensions of Expenditure Inequality in India: With Attention to the Roles of Education and Social Classes

Mitsuhiro Hayashi and Kaliappa Kalirajan

Abstract Based on the 1999/2000 and 2011/12 NSS data, this study examines inequality in household expenditure in India from spatial perspectives and analyzes the factors causing spatial disparity, using three decomposition methods: (1) a conventional Theil index decomposition by population subgroups; (2) an alternative Theil index decomposition proposed by Elbers et al. (2008), which addresses problems with the standard method, by comparing observed between-group inequality with the maximum attainable between-group inequality; and (3) the Blinder–Oaxaca decomposition. In India, the expansion of economy and rise in income levels have been accompanied by an increase in inequality. Spatial decomposition of expenditure inequality in India by six regions shows that the level of inequality within the six regions is higher than that of inequality between the six regions and the major portion of overall inequality can be attributed to intra-regional differences. Urban–rural decomposition of expenditure inequality in India as a whole and each of the six regions, respectively, indicates that inequality within urban and rural areas is more significant than inequality between urban and rural areas. Overall, inequality in urban areas increases, disparity in rural areas increases, the gap between urban and rural areas increases, and inequality at the national level increases. The share of between-area inequality is relatively lower than that of within-area inequality, when using the conventional Theil decomposition method. However, the gaps between urban and rural areas have become noticeable and are not necessarily small enough to ignore their impact. Using the alternative Theil decomposition, the share of inequality between urban and rural areas increases substantially. The result of decomposition of urban and rural inequalities by educational attainment level and social classes

Mitsuhiro Hayashi is grateful to the Japan Society for the Promotion of Science for financial support (Grant-in-Aid for Science Research No. 26380317 and 17K03714). Hayashi is also grateful to Chuo University for its financial support (Grant for Special Research).

M. Hayashi (✉)
Faculty of Economics, Chuo University, Hachioji, Tokyo, Japan
e-mail: mhayashi@tamcc.chuo-u.ac.jp

K. Kalirajan
Crawford School of Public Policy, The Australian National University, Canberra, Australia

T. Ishikawa (ed.), *Locational Analysis of Firms' Activities from a Strategic Perspective*, https://doi.org/10.1007/978-981-13-1684-5_12

indicates that within-group inequalities are more significant than between-group inequalities, in both urban and rural areas. At the same time, however, within urban areas, educational differences appear to have played an important role in expenditure inequality. The Blinder–Oaxaca decomposition analysis reveals that differences in educational, social class, and job sector endowments appear to have been determinants of urban–rural disparity. This study found that the influence of between-area inequality may be more significant than we measured using the conventional Theil decomposition approach. Education could have a large impact on reducing inequality between urban and rural areas as well as inequality within urban and rural areas. Social classes and job sector would also be related to the gaps between urban and rural areas.

Keywords Blinder–Oaxaca decomposition · India
Roles of education and social classes · Spatial inequality · Theil decomposition

JEL classification O5 · O8 · R12

12.1 Introduction

Lagging behind China by more than 10 years, India has launched its economic reforms in the early 1990s and promoted economic growth since then. India has achieved remarkable economic growth for 12 years between 2000 and 2012, with an average real GNI growth rate of 7.2% per annum and an average real GNI per capita growth rate of 5.5% per annum. There is a possibility that along with the acceleration of economic growth, problems with spatial disparities would arise in India, similar to China.[1]

In fact, while China has adopted the reform and market-opening policy since the end of the 1970s and achieved rapid economic development through the transition to market-oriented economy, it has faced various kinds of distortions accompanied with high growth. According to Akita and Kawamura (2001), in China, since the 1980s, income inequality between the eastern region and the other three regions (the western, central and northeast regions) has expanded and, in parallel, intra-province inequalities of Guangdong and Jiangsu, with rapid growth, in the eastern region have become noticeable. This regional income inequality is a major impediment to sustainable economic development in China and one of the most important issues to be solved.

Sen and Himanshu (2005) point out that, in India, in the 1990s after the implementation of economic reforms, the top 20% earners increased their expenditure, while the bottom 80% earners could not take advantage of economic liberalization

[1] Mukhopadhaya et al. (2011) and Pal and Ghosh (2007) summarize the situation of inequality in India, based on the existing research outcomes.

and could not fully increase their expenditure. They emphasize the widening of household expenditure inequality, particularly between urban and rural areas.

Cain et al. (2008) observed inequality and poverty in India in 1983, 1993, and 2004. According to their findings, expenditure inequality has not largely changed and remained stable between 1983 and 1993, but the disparity has grown between 1993 and 2004. Based on their analysis, one reason behind the widening gap in urban areas would be the fact that since the demand for jobs requiring high expertise, high technological capabilities, and advanced management skills has been increasing in urban areas, highly educated people who have the abilities to meet such requirements can enjoy high income, while those who do not have such abilities can earn only low income.

This chapter is intended to examine expenditure inequality in India, from spatial perspectives and identify factors causing regional disparity.[2] It uses nationwide household survey data in 1999/2000 and 2011/12, adjusts household expenditures temporally and spatially, and analyzes expenditure inequality through three decomposition approaches. More specifically, this study examines how much inequality within location groups (within urban and rural areas) and inequality between location groups (between urban and rural areas), respectively, cause spatial inequality in per capita household expenditure, using a conventional Theil index decomposition by population subgroups and an alternative Theil index decomposition proposed by Elbers et al. (2008). Furthermore, our study clarifies how important the roles of social factors (e.g., educational attainment and social classes) are to inequality within urban and rural areas and inequality between urban and rural areas, using the Blinder–Oaxaca decomposition method, in addition to both conventional and alternative Theil index decomposition methods.

In general, decompositions of inequality have tended to find little evidence of significant between-group inequality. According to Elbers, et al. (2008), this tendency has been generated from using total inequality as an inappropriate benchmark when calculating the contribution of the conventional between-group inequality. Total inequality can be considered as the between-group inequality that would be observed if every household in the population constituted a separate group. Calculating the contribution of the between-group inequality in a conventional way is equivalent to comparing observed between-group inequality across a few groups against an extreme benchmark including perhaps millions of groups.

A new method, the maximum between-group inequality, proposed by Elbers et al. (2008), uses an alternative benchmark as the denominator instead of total inequality and thus attempts to overcome the problem of the extreme benchmark as mentioned above (for details on this method, see Sect. 12.2). This alternative approach can give us a complementary perspective on the question of how effective a particular partition of the population is for an assessment of inequality in a country. Kanbur (2000) points out that a relatively small contribution by between-group inequality to overall inequality does not necessarily mean that between-group inequality is less

[2]In Hayashi et al. (2014), the author undertakes a study on regional inequality in Indonesia, with similar purposes, frameworks, and methods.

important than within-group inequalities. Our study seeks to confirm his statement in the context of spatial disparity in India, using Elbers' alternative decomposition approach.

Spatial disparity can be intertwined with various factors such as gender, ethnicity, education, and labor market conditions (OECD 2011). ADB (2007) analyzes the impact of various household characteristics such as age, location, gender, education, social classes, and production sector on national inequality in per capita expenditure in several Asian economies, by using the regression-based decompositions.[3] The results reveal that education of the household heads was the most important observable household feature in India, accounting for around 54% of explained inequality in 2004. The report also finds that in Indonesia and the Philippines, as in India, educational attainment, among observable household features, made the largest contribution to inequality in 2002–03.

India has a large population with large land area and there are more than 30 states with several union territories (see Fig. 12.1). Analysis of spatial inequality in such a large country requires appropriate classifications of the whole country into coherent regional groups based on similarities of economic, social, and/or geographical features. However, it does not seem that, in India, there are common regional groupings, apart from urban–rural location. To cope with that, a geographical demarcation of the six councils in India is used as a regional classification in this study (see Table 12.1).[4]

The chapter is organized as follows. Section 12.2 describes the data and methods used in this study. Sections 12.3–12.5 report the results of decomposition analyses. In these sections, the factors causing spatial inequality, with special attention to education and social classes, are examined. Finally, Sect. 12.6 presents the main findings with some policy implications.

12.2 Data and Method

12.2.1 Data

This study uses the National Sample Survey (NSS) data on expenditure, compiled by the National Sample Survey Office (NSSO) under the Indian Ministry of Statistics and Programme Implementation, to analyze the spatial distribution of economic

[3]This methodology is based on Fields (2003).

[4]The Indian government has established the following five Zonal Councils and one council as coordinating bodies for regional development: (1) Northern Zonal Council; (2) Central Zonal Council; (3) Eastern Zonal Council; (4) Western Zonal Council; (5) Southern Zonal Council; and (6) North Eastern Council. For their purposes, roles, activities, etc., see the Indian Ministry of Home Affairs' Home Page (https://mha.gov.in/division_of_mha/zonal-council). Lakshmana (2013) also uses the same regional classification as our study.

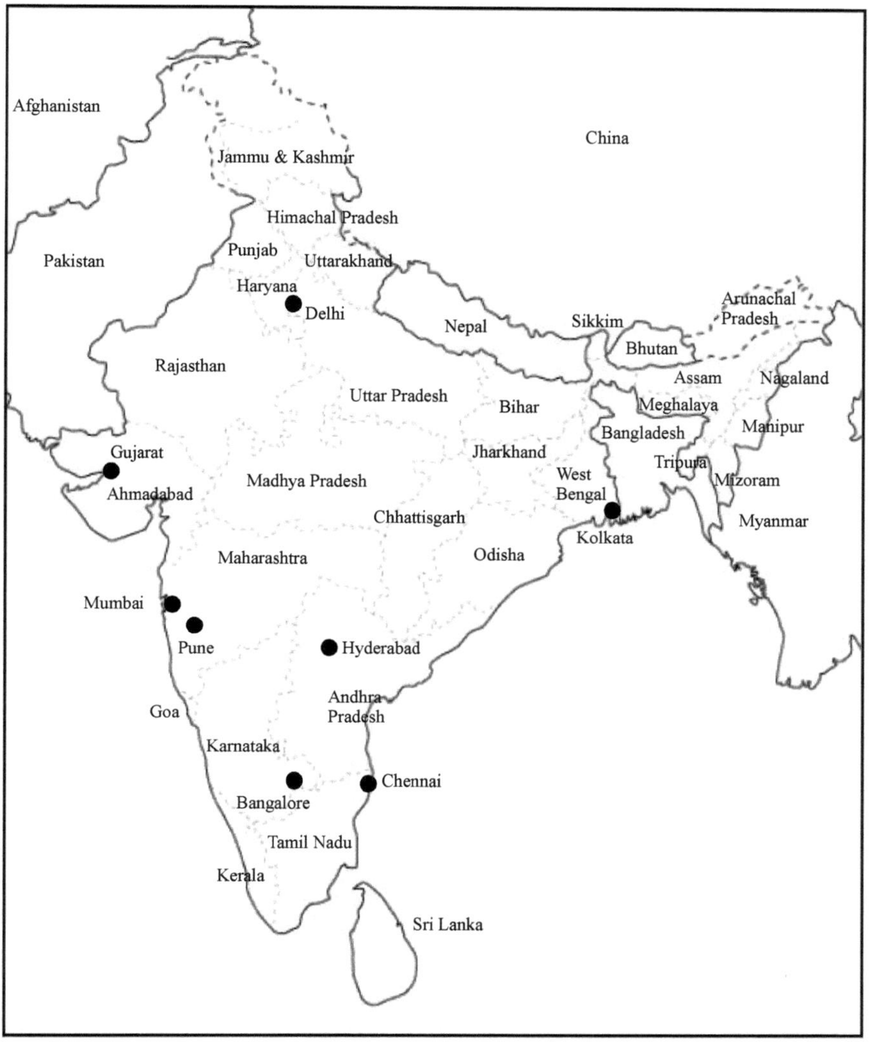

Fig. 12.1 Outline Map of India. *Note* In India, there are areas where the borders have not been confirmed, and the borders with other countries are drawn for the sake of convenience. The names of Union Territories, except for National Capital Territory of Delhi, are not described. Island areas such as Andaman and Nicobar Islands and Lakshadweep are not drawn in this map

Table 12.1 Regional classification and states in India

Regional classification and states/union territories	
Northern region	
1	Haryana
2	Himachal Pradesh
3	Jammu & Kashmir
4	Punjab
5	Rajasthan
6	Delhi
7	Chandigarh
Central region	
8	Madhya Pradesh (including Chhattisgarh)
9	Uttar Pradesh (including Uttarakhand)
Eastern region	
10	Bihar (including Jharkhand)
11	Odisha (Orissa)
12	West Bengal
Western region	
13	Goa
14	Gujarat
15	Maharashtra
16	Daman & Diu
17	Dadra & Nagar Haveli
Southern region	
18	Andhra Pradesh
19	Karnataka
20	Kerala
21	Tamil Nadu
22	Puducherry (Pondicherry)
23	A & N Island
24	Lakshadweep
North Eastern region	
25	Assam
26	Arunachal Pradesh
27	Manipur
28	Tripura
29	Mizoram
30	Meghalaya
31	Nagaland
32	Sikkim

Note Regional classification here is based on a geographical demarcation of the six councils (five zonal councils and one council) in India
Source Planning Commission (2014)

well-being in India.[5] Specifically, the study uses the NSS 55th Round Survey (July 1999–June 2000) and 68th Round Survey (July 2011–June 2012). The NSO datasets in those two rounds include around 102,000–120,000 households, of which about 40% are in urban areas and 60% are in rural areas. The shares of urban households estimated using sampling weights are roughly 27% in 1999/2000 and 31% in 2011/12.[6]

To adjust for spatial differences in prices at a point in time and spatial differences in inflation rates, this study converts current price expenditures into constant price expenditures by using current price provincial urban and rural poverty lines in 1999/2000 and 2011/12.[7] Based on the poverty line in the urban area of Delhi (National Capital Territory) in 2011/12, per capita household expenditure at 2011/12 constant prices with consideration of spatial differences is calculated and used.[8]

Table 12.2 presents figures on mean monthly per capita household expenditure and the shares of population and expenditure by different categories such as region, urban and rural areas, educational attainment, and social group in 1999/2000 and 2011/12. Among the six regions, the levels of mean per capita expenditure in 1999/2000 and 2011/12 are significantly higher in the northern, southern, and western regions than in the central, eastern, and northeastern regions. This reflects the fact that there exist Delhi, as the capital of India, in the northern region, Chennai, Bangalore, and Hyderabad in the southern region, and Mumbai and Pune in the western region, which are large cities and function as the center of politics and administration, manufacturing industry, and service industry. On the other hand, the remaining three regions have a large population in rural areas, with agriculture-dependent economic structure.

In Table 12.2, urban and rural areas for each region and India as a whole indicate a similar trend. Urban areas have higher mean expenditure per capita than rural areas without exception. Also, the population share is larger in rural areas than in urban areas. The majority of the country's population resides in rural areas. However, between 1999/2000 and 2011/12, the shares of population and consumption expenditure have been shifting from rural to urban areas in the country as a whole and six regions, particularly the southern and western regions with large-scale cities of vital economic activities. This implies the advancement of dynamic urbanization in India.

[5]As for the history, implementation method and problems of NSS, see Mukhopadhaya et al. (2011) and Tsujita (2006).

[6]All calculations in this study use sampling weights in order to adjust over- or underestimation of sections of the population.

[7]Cameron (2002) notes that the BPS official figures and most studies in the literature do not control the regional cost of living differences when calculating the inequality figures. According to her, spatial differences in prices are taken into account in different official poverty lines used in urban and rural areas by province, although the urban poverty line tends to be inflated relative to the rural poverty line.

[8]Poverty lines in 2011/12 were calculated using only Tendulkar methodology, and those in 1999/2000 were only Lakdawala methodology. However, poverty lines in 2004/05 were calculated using both methodologies. Due to this, based on poverty lines in 2011/12, those in 1999/2000 are adjusted by connecting both series in 2004/05.

Table 12.2 Mean per capita expenditure and the shares of population and expenditure by groups

	1999/2000 (NSS 55th round)			2011/2012 (NSS 68th round)		
	Mean p.c. expend[a]	Population share %[b]	Expend share %[c]	Mean p.c. Expend[a]	Population share %[b]	Expend share %[c]
Region						
Northern region	1,989	11.6	14.0	2,606	12.1	13.8
Central region	1,511	23.0	21.0	1,970	22.3	19.2
Eastern region	1,344	21.3	17.3	1,870	21.6	17.6
Western region	1,806	15.1	16.6	2,507	15.3	16.8
Southern region	1,818	25.8	28.5	2,719	25.3	30.0
North Eastern region	1,326	3.2	2.6	1,738	3.4	2.6
Total	1,649	100.0	100.0	2,290	100.0	100.0
Urban and rural areas in each region						
Northern region						
Urban	2,524	33.6	42.6	3,364	36.3	46.8
Rural	1,718	66.4	57.4	2,175	63.7	53.2
Total	1,989	100.0	100.0	2,606	100.0	100.0
Central region						
Urban	1,995	22.4	29.6	2,844	24.1	34.8
Rural	1,371	77.6	70.4	1,693	75.9	65.2
Total	1,511	100.0	100.0	1,970	100.0	100.0
Eastern region						
Urban	1,946	18.7	27.0	2,934	19.9	31.2
Rural	1,206	81.3	73.0	1,607	80.1	68.8
Total	1,344	100.0	100.0	1,870	100.0	100.0
Western region						
Urban	2,364	37.9	49.6	3,231	46.2	59.6
Rural	1,466	62.1	50.4	1,884	53.8	40.4
Total	1,806	100.0	100.0	2,507	100.0	100.0
Southern region						
Urban	2,323	30.9	39.4	3,478	37.8	48.4
Rural	1,592	69.1	60.6	2,257	62.2	51.6
Total	1,818	100.0	100.0	2,719	100.0	100.0
North Eastern region						
Urban	1,920	15.2	22.0	2,514	16.4	23.7
Rural	1,219	84.8	78.0	1,586	83.6	76.3
Total	1,326	100.0	100.0	1,738	100.0	100.0
Urban and rural areas						
Urban	2,236	27.2	36.9	3,205	31.3	43.8
Rural	1,430	72.8	63.1	1,873	68.7	56.2
Total	1,649	100.0	100.0	2,290	100.0	100.0

(continued)

Table 12.2 (continued)

	1999/2000 (NSS 55th round)			2011/2012 (NSS 68th round)		
	Mean p.c. expend[a]	Population share %[b]	Expend share %[c]	Mean p.c. Expend[a]	Population share %[b]	Expend share %[c]
Educational attainment in urban and rural areas						
Urban						
Below primary	1,524	31.6	21.6	1,890	23.7	14.0
Primary	1,764	11.6	9.1	2,261	10.8	7.6
Junior secondary	1,897	14.2	12.0	2,469	14.5	11.1
Senior secondary	2,534	26.0	29.5	3,414	30.4	32.4
Tertiary	3,740	16.6	27.8	5,421	20.6	34.9
Total	2,236	100.0	100.0	3,205	100.0	100.0
Rural						
Below primary	1,271	65.1	57.9	1,610	52.7	45.2
Primary	1,486	11.4	11.8	1,802	13.2	12.7
Junior secondary	1,605	11.1	12.5	1,982	15.1	16.0
Senior secondary	1,946	9.9	13.5	2,390	15.4	19.7
Tertiary	2,456	2.5	4.3	3,292	3.6	6.4
Total	1,430	100.0	100.0	1,873	100.0	100.0
Social group in urban and rural areas						
Urban						
Scheduled castes	1,567	13.8	9.7	2,338	14.2	10.4
Scheduled tribes	1,721	3.5	2.7	2,474	3.6	2.7
Other backward classes	1,974	30.1	26.5	2,789	40.6	35.3
Others	2,597	52.6	61.1	3,970	41.6	51.6
Total	2,236	100.0	100.0	3,205	100.0	100.0
Rural						
Scheduled castes	1,240	21.2	18.4	1,649	21.2	18.7
Scheduled tribes	1,117	10.9	8.5	1,429	11.4	8.7
Other backward classes	1,417	37.1	36.7	1,892	44.2	44.6
Others	1,686	30.8	36.4	2,259	23.2	28.0
Total	1,430	100.0	100.0	1,873	100.0	100.0

Notes [a]The average monthly per capita expenditures for each group at 2011/12 constant prices (rupee). [b]The population share for each group. [c]The expenditure share for each group

Source Calculated based on National Sample Survey (the 55th and 68th rounds)

Mean per capita household expenditure increases monotonically with education in both urban and rural areas. However, there is a striking contrast between urban and rural areas in educational attainment level. The proportion of households whose heads have received higher education is considerably larger in urban areas than in rural areas. Also, mean per capita household expenditure is higher in urban areas than in rural areas even in the same educational attainment level, and such a tendency appears clearly in the groups of highly educated people.

In both urban and rural areas, the levels of per capita household expenditure are lower in the discriminated social classes than in those without discrimination. In rural areas, in comparison with urban areas, there is a tendency that the shares of households in discriminated social classes such as scheduled castes, scheduled tribes, and other backward classes are larger and the levels of per capita expenditure by such discriminated classes are remarkably lower.

12.2.2 Theil Index and Its Decomposition by Population Groups

As described below, since the Theil T index is additively decomposable, this study uses it as the main inequality measure.[9] Unlike the Theil T, the Gini index cannot be decomposed into within and between components, but the figures of the Gini coefficient are also added in most of the tables in our study, for reference purposes.

Suppose that there are n households in a population, which are classified into m mutually exclusive and collectively exhaustive groups in accordance with a certain categorical variable, such as location (for example, urban and rural areas, states, and regions), gender, age, education, occupational sector, social class, etc. Let μ, n_i, μ_i, and y_{ij} be the mean per capita expenditure of all households, the number of households in group i, the mean per capita expenditure of households in group i, and the per capita expenditure of household j in group i, respectively. Overall inequality in per capita household expenditure is then measured by the Theil T index as follows (Anand 1983; Fields 2001):

$$T = \frac{1}{n}\sum_{i=1}^{m}\sum_{j=1}^{n_i}\left(\frac{y_{ij}}{\mu}\right)\log\left(\frac{y_{ij}}{\mu}\right) \tag{12.1}$$

The Theil T index belongs to the generalized entropy class of inequality measures and satisfies several desirable properties as a measure of inequality.[10] Furthermore,

[9]This paper does not present the figures measured by another Theil index, the Theil L index, known also as the mean log deviation measure because the results computed by Theil T and Theil L show similar trends.

[10]Desirable properties as a measure of inequality here are: (1) anonymity; (2) income homogeneity; (3) population homogeneity; and (4) the Pigue-Dalton principle of transfers. For details, refer to, for example, Chap. 6 in Haughton and Khandke (2009).

it can be additively decomposed, as a conventional approach, into the within-group inequality component (T_W) and the between-group inequality component (T_B) as follows (Shorrocks 1980):

$$T = \sum_{i=1}^{m} \left(\frac{n_i}{n} \frac{\mu_i}{\mu} \right) T_i + \sum_{i=1}^{m} \left(\frac{n_i}{n} \frac{\mu_i}{\mu} \right) \log \left(\frac{\mu_i}{\mu} \right) = T_W + T_B \qquad (12.2)$$

where T_i is the Theil T index for the within-group inequality of group i.

12.2.3 Theil Decomposition and the Maximum Between-Group Inequality

As explained earlier, Elbers et al. (2008) proposed an alternative measurement approach for the contribution of the between-group inequality component. As shown in Eqs. (12.2), the between-group component depends on the number of groups, the relative sizes of the groups, and differences in mean per capita expenditures among the groups. Care should therefore be taken to compare decomposition results based on different spatial groupings, for example, urban and rural areas, south and north regions, states, etc., although any finer nested partitions, for example, partitions of regions into subregions such as states and districts, will not decrease between-group inequality (Shorrocks and Wan 2005). Even when the same spatial grouping is used, decomposition results would not be comparable if the relative sizes of the groups are different.

In order to rectify the problem, Elbers et al. (2008) suggested that between-group inequality should be assessed against the maximum between-group inequality attainable given the number and relative sizes of the groups, rather than against the overall inequality that is used in the conventional approach for the contribution of the between-group inequality component. In our study, between-group inequality is evaluated not only against overall inequality but also the maximum between-group inequality that is obtained based on the observed ranking of the groups in mean per capita household expenditures. Specifically, given the number and relative sizes of the groups under consideration, all households are reclassified in an ascending order of per capita household expenditure into groups that are nonoverlapping and preserve the ranking of the original groups. The maximum between-group inequality can be obtained based on these nonoverlapping and rank-preserving groups.

The contribution of observed between-group inequality to the maximum attainable between-group inequality, as measured by the Theil T index, is denoted by

$$\overline{CT_B} = T_B / T_B^{\max} \qquad (12.3)$$

as opposed to $CT_B = {}^{T_B}/_{T}$, which denotes the contribution of observed between-group inequality to overall inequality used in the conventional decomposition method.

This study calculates the figures of the between-group inequality based on this maximum between-group inequality method, in addition to giving the figures measured by the conventional Theil decomposition method.[11]

12.2.4 Blinder–Oaxaca Decomposition

In order to explore the determinants of the urban–rural disparity in mean per capita expenditure, this study performs a Blinder–Oaxaca decomposition, which was popularized by Blinder (1973) and Oaxaca (1973).[12]

Let Y_U and Y_R be the natural log of per capita expenditure of urban and rural households, respectively. Given the linear regression model,

$$Y_k = \boldsymbol{X}'_k \boldsymbol{\beta}_k + e_k \quad E(e_k) = 0 \quad k = U, R$$

where $\boldsymbol{X}_k$ is a vector of explanatory variables, $\boldsymbol{\beta}_k$ includes the parameters associated with $\boldsymbol{X}_k$, and e_k is the error term, which contains unobserved factors, we let $\hat{\boldsymbol{\beta}}_k$ be a vector of the least-squares estimates for $\boldsymbol{\beta}_k$ ($k = U, R$), obtained separately from the urban and rural samples and $\bar{\boldsymbol{X}}_k$ be the estimate for $E(\boldsymbol{X}_k)$. Then, the estimated urban–rural difference in mean per capita expenditure is expressed as (twofold decomposition)

$$\hat{D} = \bar{Y}_U - \bar{Y}_R = (\bar{\boldsymbol{X}}_U - \bar{\boldsymbol{X}}_R)'\hat{\boldsymbol{\beta}}^* + \left(\bar{\boldsymbol{X}}'_U(\hat{\boldsymbol{\beta}}_U - \hat{\boldsymbol{\beta}}*) + \bar{\boldsymbol{X}}'_R(\hat{\boldsymbol{\beta}} * - \hat{\boldsymbol{\beta}}_R)\right) \quad (12.4)$$

where $\hat{\boldsymbol{\beta}}^*$ is a vector of the least-squares estimates for the slope parameters and the intercept which are obtained from the pooled sample of urban and rural households (Neumark 1988). The first term in Eq. (12.4) is the part of the urban–rural difference in mean per capita expenditure that is explained by urban–rural differences in the explanatory variables (endowments or quantity effect) and the second term is the unexplained part. Based on Eq. (12.4), this study decomposes difference in mean per capita household expenditure between urban and rural areas into several components, including educational differences.

[11]As pointed out by Elbers et al. (2008), this alternative measure is not the result of a statistical decomposition exercise for any inequality measure of a certain class. Thus, it does not seem that the conventional decomposition method can be fully replaced by Elbers' decomposition method.

[12]For a comprehensive review of the Blinder–Oaxaca decomposition method and its applications, please see Jann (2008).

12.3 Spatial Decomposition of Expenditure Inequality

Table 12.3 shows the results of spatial decomposition of expenditure inequality in India by six regions (northern region, central region, eastern region, western region, southern region, and northeastern region) in 1999/2000 and 2011/12. As measured by the Theil *T*, overall inequality in per capita household expenditure is 0.205 in 1999/2000 and 0.246 in 2011/12. These figures indicate an upward trend in inequality in India as a whole over the period. This coincides with a rising trend in our estimate of the Gini coefficient from 0.317 to 0.351 between the same two time points.

Looking at the six regions, the major part of inequality in per capita household expenditure arises from the disparity within regions. Differences in the distribution of per capita household expenditure are very large within the six regions. All regions have shown an increase in within-region inequality between 1999/2000 and 2011/12. Within-region inequality can explain around 95% of overall inequality. In particular, the southern region with large-scale cities representing India such as Chennai, Bangalore, and Hyderabad contributes the most to per capita expenditure inequality. With its high within-region inequality, the southern region accounts for more than 30% of the overall inequality in India.

Table 12.3 Inequality decomposition by region

	1999/2000 (NSS 55th round)			2011/2012 (NSS 68th round)		
	Theil *T*		Gini	Theil *T*		Gini
	Value	Contribution %[a]		Value	Contribution %[a]	
Region						
Northern region	0.164	11.2	0.297	0.213	12.0	0.332
Central region	0.175	17.9	0.301	0.248	19.3	0.344
Eastern region	0.170	14.3	0.284	0.195	14.0	0.308
Western region	0.212	17.1	0.333	0.253	17.3	0.357
Southern region	0.239	33.3	0.325	0.250	30.6	0.356
North Eastern region	0.119	1.5	0.254	0.139	1.4	0.270
Within-region	0.195	95.3		0.233	94.6	
Between-region (A)[b]	0.010	4.7		0.013	5.4	
Total	0.205	100.0	0.317	0.246	100.0	0.351
Between-region (B)[c]	0.010	5.9		0.013	7.5	
Max between-region[d]	0.164	100.0		0.177	100.0	

Notes [a]The percentage contribution of each inequality component to overall inequality
[b]Between-region inequality is assessed by using a conventional approach (see text Sect. 12.2)
[c]Between-region inequality is assessed by using an alternative approach (see text Sect. 12.2)
[d]This is obtained as the maximum between-region inequality attainable given the numbers and relative sizes of the groups (see text Sect. 12.2)
Source Calculated based on National Sample Survey (the 55th and 68th rounds)

Conversely, although between-region inequality measured by the Theil T increases from 0.010 in 1999/2000 to 0.013 in 2011/12, it accounts for only around 5% of overall inequality. Even when using the alternative measure $\overline{CT_B}$ (Between-region (B) in Table 12.3), its contribution hardly increases, signifying that there are large overlaps in the distribution of per capita expenditure among the six regions. To sum up, inequality within the six regions is more significant than inequality between the six regions and the major portion of overall inequality can be attributed to intra-regional differences.

This study further disaggregates the six regions into urban and rural areas. Table 12.4 indicates urban–rural decomposition of expenditure inequality in each of the six regions in 1999/2000 and 2011/12, respectively. In all regions, the value of the Theil T index is considerably higher in within-area inequality than in between-area inequality, and the contribution of within-area inequality to total within-area inequality is also remarkably larger than that of between-area inequality.

Broadly speaking, urban inequality is more significant than rural inequality. In all regions, urban inequality is higher than rural inequality, as measured by the Theil T. With some exceptions, the contribution of urban inequality to total within-region inequality is larger than that of rural inequality. Excepting the southern region, inequality in urban areas has risen between 1999/2000 and 2011/12. Over this period, the western region contributes the most to total within-region inequality.

As observed above, between-area inequality relative to within-area inequality is low, ranging from 0.014 in the central region to 0.036 in the eastern and western regions, as measured by the Theil T. Using the conventional measure CT_B (between-area (A) in Table 12.4), its contribution is less than 19% to total inequality in each region. However, with the exception of the northeastern region, per capita expenditure inequality between urban and rural areas has risen and its contribution to total inequality in each region has increased for the 12 years from 1999/2000 to 2011/12.

Using an alternative measure $\overline{CT_B}$ (Between-area (B) in Table 12.4), the contribution increases remarkably. In the eastern and western regions, particularly, the contribution rises to around 29–31%, which is 12–15 percentage points larger than the contribution using the conventional measure. This means that there is no large overlap in the distribution of per capita expenditures between urban and rural areas in the eastern and western regions. To a lesser extent, in the other four regions, there is also an increase in the contribution of between-area inequality, when using the alternative measurement approach. This suggests a possibility that the contribution of urban–rural inequality is larger than we thought it was when based on the conventional Theil decomposition approach.

Table 12.5 examines urban and rural areas nationally and presents the result of urban–rural decomposition of per capita expenditure inequality in 1999/2000 and 2011/12. Nationally, inequality within urban and rural areas is more prominent than inequality between urban and rural areas, in terms of both value and contribution measured by the Theil T. In 1999/2000 and 2011/12, around 86–89% of overall inequality is attributed to inequality within urban and rural areas. Urban areas have a higher

Table 12.4 Inequality decomposition by urban and rural areas in each region

	1999/2000 (NSS 55th round)			2011/2012 (NSS 68th round)		
	Theil *T*		Gini	Theil *T*		Gini
	Value	Contribution %[a]		Value	Contribution %[a]	
Northern region						
Urban	0.193	50.3	0.331	0.252	55.2	0.372
Rural	0.111	38.9	0.248	0.136	33.9	0.270
Within-area	0.146	89.2		0.190	89.1	
Between-area (A)[b]	0.018	10.8		0.023	10.9	
Total	0.164	100.0	0.297	0.213	100.0	0.332
Between-area (B)[c]	0.018	17.9		0.023	19.4	
Max between-area[d]	0.099	100.0		0.120	100.0	
Central region						
Urban	0.231	39.1	0.353	0.346	48.6	0.429
Rural	0.131	52.9	0.266	0.151	39.8	0.278
Within-area	0.161	92.0		0.219	88.4	
Between-area (A)[b]	0.014	8.0		0.029	11.6	
Total	0.175	100.0	0.301	0.248	100.0	0.344
Between-area (B)[c]	0.014	13.3		0.029	19.4	
Max between-area[d]	0.105	100.0		0.148	100.0	
Eastern region						
Urban	0.247	39.3	0.347	0.282	45.2	0.388
Rural	0.113	48.4	0.240	0.103	36.5	0.239
Within-area	0.149	87.7		0.159	81.7	
Between-area (A)[b]	0.021	12.3		0.036	18.3	
Total	0.170	100.0	0.284	0.195	100.0	0.308
Between-area (B)[c]	0.021	22.7		0.036	30.7	
Max between-area[d]	0.092	100.0		0.116	100.0	
Western region						
Urban	0.230	53.8	0.351	0.249	58.8	0.361
Rural	0.138	32.9	0.274	0.169	27.0	0.285
Within-area	0.184	86.7		0.217	85.8	
Between-area (A)[b]	0.028	13.3		0.036	14.2	
Total	0.212	100.0	0.333	0.253	100.0	0.357
Between-area (B)[c]	0.028	23.3		0.036	28.9	
Max between-area[d]	0.121	100.0		0.124	100.0	

(continued)

Table 12.4 (continued)

	1999/2000 (NSS 55th round)			2011/2012 (NSS 68th round)		
	Theil *T*		Gini	Theil *T*		Gini
	Value	Contribution %[a]		Value	Contribution %[a]	
Southern region						
Urban	0.324	53.4	0.361	0.261	50.5	0.376
Rural	0.157	39.7	0.282	0.195	40.3	0.305
Within-area	0.222	93.1		0.227	90.8	
Between-area (A)[b]	0.017	6.9		0.023	9.2	
Total	0.239	100.0	0.325	0.250	100.0	0.356
Between-area (B)[c]	0.017	13.6		0.023	16.4	
Max between-area[d]	0.121	100.0		0.141	100.0	
North Eastern region						
Urban	0.150	27.7	0.298	0.193	32.8	0.334
Rural	0.089	58.6	0.222	0.100	54.5	0.231
Within-area	0.103	86.3		0.122	87.3	
Between-area (A)[b]	0.016	13.7		0.017	12.7	
Total	0.119	100.0	0.254	0.139	100.0	0.270
Between-area (B)[c]	0.016	25.8		0.017	21.5	
Max between-area[d]	0.063	100.0		0.082	100.0	

Notes [a]The percentage contribution of each inequality component to overall inequality
[b]Between-area inequality is assessed by using a conventional approach (see text Sect. 12.2)
[c] Between-area inequality is assessed by using an alternative approach (see text Sect. 12.2)
[d]This is obtained as the maximum between-area inequality attainable given the numbers and relative sizes of the groups (see text Sect. 12.2)
Source Calculated based on National Sample Survey (the 55th and 68th rounds)

within-group inequality than rural areas. Between 1999/2000 and 2011/12, inequality in both urban and rural areas is rising, but the contribution of urban inequality to total inequality increases to almost 50%, while that of rural inequality decreases to 37%.

As stated above, urban–rural inequality is not so remarkable as compared to urban and rural disparity. Over this observation period, however, as measured by the Theil T, the value of between-area inequality rises from 0.022 to 0.035 and its contribution to total inequality increases from 11 to 14%. In addition, an alternative measure $\overline{CT_B}$ (between-area (B) in Table 12.5) indicates that, in 2011/12, inequality between urban and rural areas accounts for 24% of the maximum attainable between-area inequality given the current distribution of per capita household expenditures, the relative sizes of urban and rural areas, and their ranking in terms of mean per capita expenditure.

In the six regions as well as India as a whole, inequality within urban and rural areas is more conspicuous than inequality between urban and rural areas during the study period. In particular, urban disparity is noticeable. Also, there is a possibility that inequality between urban and rural areas is more significant than we thought it was through the conventional Theil decomposition approach.

Table 12.5 Inequality decomposition by urban and rural areas

	1999/2000 (NSS 55th round)			2011/2012 (NSS 68th round)		
	Theil *T*		Gini	Theil *T*		Gini
	Value	Contribution %[a]		Value	Contribution %[a]	
Urban and rural areas						
Urban	0.258	46.4	0.354	0.275	49.0	0.385
Rural	0.139	42.7	0.270	0.162	37.0	0.285
Within-area	0.183	89.1		0.211	86.0	
Between-area (A)[b]	0.022	10.9		0.035	14.0	
Total	0.205	100.0	0.317	0.246	100.0	0.351
Between-area (B)[c]	0.022	19.2		0.035	24.0	
Max between-area[d]	0.116	100.0		0.143	100.0	

Notes [a]The percentage contribution of each inequality component to overall inequality
[b]Between-area inequality is assessed by using a conventional approach (see text Sect. 12.2)
[c]Between-area inequality is assessed by using an alternative approach (see text Sect. 12.2)
[d]This is obtained as the maximum between-area inequality attainable given the numbers and relative sizes of the groups (see text Sect. 12.2)
Source Calculated based on National Sample Survey (the 55th and 68th rounds)

12.4 Urban and Rural Inequalities: Decomposition by Educational Attainment Levels and Social Classes

The result of the above Theil decomposition analysis shows that the major part of disparity in India comes from within-area inequality, particularly urban inequality. Also, as indicated earlier, the existing literature on inequality decomposition in Asian developing countries finds that differences in educational attainment levels and social classes have played an important role in accounting for overall inter-household inequality.[13] This study thus focuses on differences in educational attainment levels and social classes as the major determinants of inequality and conducts a Theil decomposition analysis of urban and rural inequalities, respectively, with respect to the educational attainment level of household heads and social class of households.

In the NSS dataset, households are classified into 12–13 groups according to educational attainment levels. These groups in the NSS 68th Round Survey (2011/12) are: not literate; EGS (Education Guarantee Scheme)/NFEC (Non-Formal Education Courses)/AEC (Adult Literacy Centers); TLC (Total Literacy Campaign); others; below primary; primary; middle; secondary; higher secondary; diploma/certificate course; undergraduate; and postgraduate and above.[14] In our study, these 12–13

[13]As for studies that relate inequality with the attributes of households including education, see, for example, ADB (2012) and OECD (2011).

[14]In the NSS 55th Round Survey (1999/2000), educational attainment levels after higher secondary are classified into the following groups: undergraduate/above in agriculture; undergraduate/above in engineering/technology; undergraduate/above in medicine; and undergraduate/above in other fields.

groups are aggregated into five groups to conduct a decomposition analysis: (1) no education (no schooling and incomplete primary school); (2) primary education; (3) junior secondary education; (4) senior secondary education ((higher) secondary education and diploma/certificate course); and (5) tertiary education (undergraduate education and postgraduate education).

As indicated in Table 12.2, in both urban and rural areas, mean per capita household expenditure increases as the level of education that household heads have attained rises. However, in 2011/12, more than 50% of urban households are headed by those with the completion of at least junior secondary education, while more than 50% of rural households are led by those without primary education. This shows a large education gap between urban and rural areas.

Table 12.6 shows the result of decomposition of urban and rural inequalities, respectively, by educational attainment level. In both urban and rural areas, within-group inequality is more significant than between-group inequality in terms of value and contribution measured by the Theil T.

However, in urban areas, between-group inequality measured by the Theil T rises from 0.056 in 1999/2000 to 0.074 in 2011/12, and its contribution to total urban inequality, based on the conventional measure, increases from 22 to 27% in the same period. Furthermore, using an alternative measure $\overline{CT_B}$ (between-group (B) in Table 12.6), its contribution increases from 30% to nearly 36% over the period. This suggests that educational differences are an important factor in creating urban inequality. In rural areas, relative to urban areas, the influence of educational differences on expenditure inequality is not large.

In urban areas, the pattern of expenditure inequality in each education group has considerably changed for 12 years from 1999/2000 to 2011/12. In 1999/2000, among the five education groups, the group without primary education (including incomplete primary education) records the highest level of inequality in per capita expenditure (0.296 by the Theil T) and the largest contribution (nearly 25%) to total urban inequality. On the other hand, in 2011/12, unlike the pattern in 1999/2000, the tertiary education group which occupies around 20% of households (see Table 12.2) has the highest within-group inequality in urban areas. By the Theil T, its contribution to total urban inequality amounts to almost 30%, which is the largest among the five education groups. The senior secondary education group registers the second highest within-group inequality and the second largest contribution to total urban inequality. These tertiary and senior secondary education groups together account for nearly 55% of total urban inequality in 2011/12.

In rural areas, in both 1999/2000 and 2011/12, although the higher education groups tend to have higher values of the Theil T, a greater part of within-group inequality comes from the lower education groups. The lower education groups (the primary and below primary education groups) explain more than 40% of total rural inequality in 2011/12.

As already indicated in Table 12.2, while educational levels of household heads have increased in India as a whole over the observed 12 years, the gap between urban and rural areas in educational attainment has remained conspicuous. Under such a situation, expenditure inequalities between education groups and within higher

Table 12.6 Decomposition of urban and rural inequality by educational attainment level[a]

	1999/2000 (NSS 55th round)			2011/2012 (NSS 68th round)		
	Theil *T*		Gini	Theil *T*		Gini
	Value	Contribution %[b]		Value	Contribution %[b]	
Urban						
Below primary	0.296	24.7	0.305	0.154	7.8	0.288
Primary	0.227	8.0	0.286	0.129	3.6	0.271
Junior secondary	0.138	6.5	0.279	0.170	6.9	0.302
Senior secondary	0.166	19.0	0.299	0.214	25.2	0.341
Tertiary	0.186	20.1	0.322	0.234	29.6	0.362
Within-group	0.202	78.3		0.201	73.1	
Between-group (A)[c]	0.056	21.7		0.074	26.9	
Total	0.258	100.0	0.354	0.275	100.0	0.385
Between-group (B)[d]	0.056	30.4		0.074	35.9	
Max between-group[e]	0.184	100.0		0.207	100.0	
Rural						
Below primary	0.110	45.8	0.240	0.109	30.5	0.243
Primary	0.117	9.9	0.253	0.144	11.3	0.264
Junior secondary	0.134	12.1	0.266	0.151	14.9	0.277
Senior secondary	0.159	15.4	0.298	0.181	22.0	0.303
Tertiary	0.162	5.1	0.308	0.228	9.1	0.340
Within-group	0.123	88.3		0.142	87.8	
Between-group (A)[c]	0.016	11.7		0.020	12.2	
Total	0.139	100.0	0.270	0.162	100.0	0.285
Between-group (B)[d]	0.016	14.5		0.020	14.7	
Max between-group[e]	0.111	100.0		0.134	100.0	

Notes [a]Educational attainment level of household head
[b]The percentage contribution of each inequality component to overall inequality
[c]Between-group inequality is assessed by using a conventional approach (see text Sect. 12.2)
[d]Between-group inequality is assessed by using an alternative approach (see text Sect. 12.2)
[e]This is obtained as the maximum between-group inequality attainable given the numbers and relative sizes of the groups (see text Sect. 12.2)
Source Calculated based on National Sample Survey (the 55th and 68th rounds)

education groups have been more significant in urban areas than in rural areas. This suggests that, in addition to problems with differences in educational attainment, urban inequality is associated with differences in the quality of education within higher education, and rural inequality is linked with differences in the quality of education within lower education.

Table 12.7 presents the result of decomposition of urban and rural inequalities, respectively, by social classes. The Theil decomposition analysis is carried out with

Table 12.7 Decomposition of urban and rural inequality by social group

	1999/2000 (NSS 55th round)			2011/2012 (NSS 68th round)		
	Theil T		Gini	Theil T		Gini
	Value	Contribution %[a]		Value	Contribution %[a]	
Urban						
Scheduled castes	0.160	6.0	0.299	0.198	7.4	0.331
Scheduled tribes	0.209	2.2	0.333	0.241	2.4	0.362
Other backward classes	0.321	33.0	0.340	0.238	30.6	0.354
Others	0.221	52.4	0.346	0.277	51.8	0.392
Within-group	0.241	93.6		0.254	92.2	
Between-group (A)[b]	0.017	6.4		0.021	7.8	
Total	0.258	100.0	0.354	0.275	100.0	0.385
Between-group (B)[c]	0.017	13.6		0.021	14.2	
Max between-group[d]	0.122	100.0		0.151	100.0	
Rural						
Scheduled castes	0.119	15.8	0.242	0.118	13.7	0.251
Scheduled tribes	0.102	6.2	0.242	0.112	6.0	0.248
Other backward classes	0.129	34.1	0.258	0.151	41.8	0.274
Others	0.141	37.1	0.278	0.188	32.5	0.306
Within-group	0.129	93.2		0.152	94.0	
Between-group (A)[b]	0.010	6.8		0.010	6.0	
Total	0.139	100.0	0.270	0.162	100.0	0.285
Between-group (B)[c]	0.010	9.8		0.010	8.4	
Max between-group[d]	0.096	100.0		0.116	100.0	

Notes [a]The percentage contribution of each inequality component to overall inequality
[b]Between-group inequality is assessed by using a conventional approach (see text Sect. 12.2)
[c]Between-group inequality is assessed by using an alternative approach (see text Sect. 12.2)
[d]This is obtained as the maximum between-group inequality attainable given the numbers and relative sizes of the groups (see text Sect. 12.2)
Source Calculated based on National Sample Survey (the 55th and 68th rounds)

respect to the following four social classes based on the categories used in NSS: (1) scheduled castes; (2) scheduled tribes; (3) other backward classes; and (4) others (nondiscriminatory class). In both urban and rural areas, inequality within social classes tends to be larger than inequality between social classes, in terms of both value and contribution measured by the Theil T.

In urban areas, in 1999/2000 and 2011/12, considerably high expenditure inequalities exist within scheduled tribes, other backward classes and nondiscriminatory classes, respectively, and the contribution of such within-group inequalities to total urban inequality is noticeably large. Specifically, other backward classes and nondiscriminatory classes account for around 30–33% and more than 50%, respectively, of urban inequality.

However, during the period of 1999/2000–2011/12, inequality between social classes rises from 0.017 to 0.021, as measured by the Theil T, and its contribution to urban inequality increases from 6 to 8%. The level and influence of inequality within social classes have increased in urban areas. Furthermore, when using the alternative Theil index decomposition, the share of inequality between social classes almost doubles. This implies that there are differences in the distribution of per capita household expenditures between social classes.

On the other hand, in rural areas, relative to urban areas, the level of disparity within social classes is not high. The values of the Theil T are relatively low in expenditure inequalities within scheduled castes and scheduled tribes over the period. The contribution of those two social groups to total rural inequality is also not relatively large. In addition, between-group inequality accounts for around 6–7% of total rural disparity in 1999/2000 and 2011/12. Even when using the alternative measure $\overline{CT_B}$ (between-region (B) in Table 12.7), its contribution does not increase substantially, suggesting that there are large overlaps in the distribution of per capita consumption expenditures among four social class categories.

12.5 Urban–Rural Disparity: Blinder–Oaxaca Decomposition

According to Table 12.2, the urban-to-rural ratio in mean per capita expenditure increases from 1.56 in 1999/2000 to 1.71 in 2011/12. Also, as already seen in Table 12.5, the contribution of urban–rural inequality to overall inequality in India by the Theil T increases from 10.9% in 1999/2000 to 14% in 2011/12. There is an increase in this contribution by around 8–10 percentage points, when using the alternative measurement approach. These indicate an upward trend in urban–rural disparity during the observed period and a possibility for a larger influence of urban–rural inequality on overall inequality than it looks. The Blinder–Oaxaca decomposition method, as explained above, is adopted here to examine the determinants of the urban–rural inequality in India.

This study decomposes difference in mean per capita household expenditure between urban and rural areas into the following components:

(1) *gender* (gender of household head: female = 0; male = 1);
(2) *age* (age of household head);
(3) *square of age* (square of age of household head);
(4) *years of education* (years of education of household head);[15]

[15] Based on Cain et al. (2008), the number of years of education is calculated according to the following: (1) illiterate = 0 years; (2) literate through nonformal schooling (i.e., NFEC (Non-Formal Education Courses), AEC (Adult Literacy Centers), EGS (Education Guarantee Scheme), TLC (Total Literacy Campaign), and others) = 1 years; (3) literate, but incomplete primary education = 3 years; (4) primary education = 5 years; (5) middle schools/lower secondary education = 8 years; (6) secondary education = 10 years; (7) higher secondary education = 12 years; (8) diploma/certificate

(5) *job sector* (job sector of household head: primary sector = 0; non-primary sector = 1); and
(6) *social classes* (scheduled castes = 0; scheduled tribes = 1, other backward classes = 2; others = 3).

Table 12.8 presents the result of the Blinder–Oaxaca decomposition in 1999/2000 and 2011/12.

In our sample, the mean of the natural log of per capita expenditure in 1999/2000 is 7.535 for urban households and 7.203 for rural households, yielding an urban–rural expenditure gap of 0.332. Similarly, these figures in 2011/12 are 7.748 for urban households and 7.508 for rural households, yielding an urban–rural expenditure gap of 0.240. In Table 12.8, the expenditure gap is divided into two parts. The first part, i.e., the explained part (endowments or quantity effect), reflects the increase in mean per capita expenditure if rural households had the same endowments as urban households, assuming that urban and rural households have the same coefficients, obtained from the pooled sample of urban and rural households. The second part is a residual or unexplained part that captures all potential effects of differences in unobserved variables. The increases of 0.253 in 1999/2000 and 0.160 in 2011/12 indicate that differences in endowments (gender, age, education, job sector and social classes) as a whole account for 76% and 67%, respectively, of the urban–rural expenditure gap.[16]

In the explained part, the components related to gender and age have only a marginal role. On the other hand, most noticeable is the education component, which is followed by the social class and job sector components. Educational differences measured by years of education of the household head are the largest contributor to differences in mean per capita household expenditure between urban and rural areas. This education component accounts for around 55% of the urban–rural expenditure gap in 1999/2000 and 2011/12.

Differences in social classes also explain 8–9% of the gap during the period. As indicated in Table 12.2, the ratio of population classified into scheduled castes or scheduled tribes is higher in rural areas than in urban areas. The differences in the proportion of such discriminated population could be one of the factors for gener-

courses = 12 years; (9) undergraduate education = 15 years; and (10) postgraduate education = 17 years). For the details of education system in India, refer to NSSO (2015).

[16]The estimated urban–rural difference in mean per capita expenditure can also be decomposed into the three terms as follows (threefold decomposition):

$$\hat{D} = \bar{Y}_U - \bar{Y}_R = (\bar{\mathbf{X}}_U - \bar{\mathbf{X}}_R)'\hat{\boldsymbol{\beta}}_R + \bar{\mathbf{X}}_R'(\hat{\boldsymbol{\beta}}_U - \hat{\boldsymbol{\beta}}_R) + (\bar{\mathbf{X}}_U - \bar{\mathbf{X}}_R)'(\hat{\boldsymbol{\beta}}_U - \hat{\boldsymbol{\beta}}_R) \text{ or}$$

$$\hat{D} = \bar{Y}_U - \bar{Y}_R = (\bar{\mathbf{X}}_U - \bar{\mathbf{X}}_R)'\hat{\boldsymbol{\beta}}_U + \bar{\mathbf{X}}_U'(\hat{\boldsymbol{\beta}}_U - \hat{\boldsymbol{\beta}}_R) - (\bar{\mathbf{X}}_U - \bar{\mathbf{X}}_R)'(\hat{\boldsymbol{\beta}}_U - \hat{\boldsymbol{\beta}}_R).$$

The first term reflects the mean increase in rural households' per capita expenditures if they had the same characteristics as urban households (endowments effect), while the second term presents the increase in rural households' per capita expenditures when applying the urban households' coefficients to the rural households' characteristics. The third component is the interaction term. According to the result of our calculation, differences in endowments as a whole account for 54–67% of the urban–rural expenditure gap, while differences in coefficients account for nearly 10% in 1999/2000 and 2010/12. As in the result in Table 12.8 based on the twofold decomposition, differences in educational attainments, social classes, and job sector play an important role in the urban–rural gap.

Table 12.8 Blinder–Oaxaca decomposition of urban–rural differences in mean per capita expenditure[a]

	1999/2000 (NSS 55th round)			2011/12 (NSS 68th round)		
	Coefficient	Z-score[b]	Contribution %[c]	Coefficient	Z-score[b]	Contribution %[c]
Prediction (urban)	7.535	2,789.05		7.748	2,418.94	
Prediction (rural)	7.203	3,931.81		7.508	3,615.17	
Difference (urban–rural)	0.332	101.70	100.0	0.240	62.79	100.0
Explained	0.253	94.34***	76.3	0.160	71.70***	66.8
Gender[d]	0.001	3.35***	0.2	0.003	8.64***	1.2
Age[d]	0.004	4.78***	1.1	0.006	6.58***	2.4
Square of age[d]	-0.009	-9.44***	-2.6	-0.007	-7.33***	-3.0
Years of education[d]	0.186	99.56***	56.2	0.130	70.83***	54.3
Job sector (primary vs. non-primary sectors)[d]	0.045	21.38***	13.5	0.006	5.44***	2.7
Social classes (scheduled castes, scheduled tribes, other backward classes, and others)	0.026	40.19***	7.9	0.022	33.06***	9.2
Unexplained	0.079	21.81***	23.7	0.080	22.18***	33.2

Notes [a]The Blinder–Oaxaca decomposition technique used here is a "twofold" decomposition method (see text in Sect. 12.2)
[b]Z-score is used here as a test of statistical significance for coefficient. *indicates significant at the 1% level
[c]The percentage contribution of each factor to the urban–rural expenditure gap
[d]Characteristics of household head
Source Calculated based on National Sample Survey (the 55th and 68th rounds)

ating the urban–rural expenditure gap. Nearly 14% of the urban–rural expenditure gap in 1999/2000 can be attributed to differences in job sector of household heads. Nonagricultural jobs and off-farm opportunities in rural areas would have an effect on reducing the gap between urban and rural areas.[17] This result suggests that urban–rural disparity is largely associated with educational attainments, social classes and job sectors.

12.6 Conclusions

Based on the data from the NSS 55th Round Survey in 1999/2000 and 68th Round Survey in 2011/12, this study examines inequality in household expenditure in India from spatial perspectives and analyzes the factors causing spatial disparity, using three decomposition methods: (1) a conventional Theil index decomposition by population subgroups; (2) an alternative Theil index decomposition proposed by Elbers et al. (2008), which addresses problems with the standard method, by comparing observed between-group inequality with the maximum attainable between-group inequality; and (3) the Blinder–Oaxaca decomposition. The summary of our analytical results and implications drawn from this study are as follows.

While India has achieved remarkable economic growth for 12 years between 2000 and 2012, with an average real GNI growth rate of 7.2% per annum and an average real GNI per capita growth rate of 5.5% per annum, overall inequality in per capita household expenditure over the same period rises from 0.205 to 0.246 as measured by the Theil T and from 0.317 to 0.351 as measured by the Gini coefficient. In India, the expansion of economy and rise in income levels have been accompanied by an increase in inequality.

The result of spatial decomposition of expenditure inequality in India by six regions in 1999/2000 and 2011/12 shows that the level of inequality within the six regions is higher than that of inequality between the six regions and the major portion of overall inequality can be attributed to intra-regional differences. Within-region inequality can explain around 95% of overall inequality. In particular, the southern region, with its high within-region inequality, accounts for more than 30% of the overall inequality in India.

Urban–rural decomposition of expenditure inequality in India as a whole and each of the six regions, respectively, over the observed period indicates that inequality within urban and rural areas is more significant than inequality between urban and rural areas, in terms of both value and contribution measured by the Theil T. In 1999/2000 and 2011/12, approximately 86–89% of overall inequality is attributed to inequality within urban and rural areas. Looking at inequality within areas, urban inequality is significantly higher than rural inequality, accounting for around 46–49%

---

[17] The contribution of job sector component to the urban–rural expenditure gap drops to around 3% in 2011/12. This change could also be explained by a recent increase in nonagricultural jobs and off-farm business opportunities in rural areas.

of overall inequality. Among the six regions, southern, western, and northern regions, respectively, have recorded significant urban inequalities, which explain more than half of total within-region inequality in each region. Overall, inequality in urban areas increases, disparity in rural areas increases, the gap between urban and rural areas increases, and inequality at the national level increases.

As described above, the share of between-area inequality is relatively lower than that of within-area inequality, when using the conventional Theil index decomposition method. However, the gaps between urban and rural areas at the national level and in each of the six regions have become noticeable for these 12 years and are not necessarily small enough to ignore their impact. Furthermore, when using the alternative Theil index decomposition, the share of inequality between urban and rural areas increases substantially. In 2011/12, the contribution of urban–rural inequality jumps to 24% for India as a whole and around 30% for eastern and western regions, which is clearly larger than the contribution we measured using the conventional Theil index decomposition. This observation suggests that there are notable differences in the distribution of per capita household expenditures between urban and rural areas. It is thus useful to use an alternative approach such as Elbers' decomposition as a supplementary tool for the conventional decomposition approach.

The result of decomposition of urban and rural inequalities by educational attainment level and social classes indicates that within-group inequalities are more significant than between-group inequalities, in both urban and rural areas. Looking at educational attainment level, especially in urban areas, expenditure inequalities within higher education groups are very salient. At the same time, however, within urban areas, educational differences appear to have played an important role in expenditure inequality. In 2011/12, expenditure disparity due to educational differences explains around 27% of urban inequality, as measured by the Theil T. When using the alternative approach, the contribution increases to 36%.

The Blinder–Oaxaca decomposition analysis reveals that, in 1999/2000 and 2011/12, differences in educational endowments appear to have been a key determinant of urban–rural disparity, by accounting for around 55% of the urban–rural expenditure gap. Differences in social classes also explain 8–9% of the gap during the period. In addition, to a lesser extent, differences in job sector (primary sector vs. non-primary sector) contribute to the expenditure gap. Differences between urban and rural areas in access to opportunities including education and employment would be the main determinants of expenditure inequality between urban and rural areas.

The above findings suggest that the influence of between-area inequality may be more significant than we measured using the conventional Theil index decomposition approach. This implies that the Indian government needs to pay attention to urban–rural disparity, in addition to urban inequality. Education could have a large impact on reducing inequality between urban and rural areas as well as inequality within urban and rural areas. Social classes and job sector would also be related to the gaps between urban and rural areas. In order to narrow spatial inequality in India, the government is required to expand the quantity of education, improve the quality of education, ameliorate social class systems, and develop better environment for creating non-primary-sector jobs with higher value added and productivity.

References

Akita, T., and K. Kawamura. 2001. *Regional income inequality in China, ERINA report*, vol. 40. Niigata: Economic Research Institute for Northeast Asia.

Anand, S. 1983. *Inequality and poverty in Malaysia: Measurement and decomposition.* New York: Oxford University Press, World Bank Research Publication.

ADB (Asian Development Bank). 2007. *Key indicators 2007*. Manila: ADB.

ADB (Asian Development Bank). 2012. *Asian development outlook 2012: Confronting rising inequality in Asia*. Manila: ADB.

Blinder, A.S. 1973. Wage discrimination: Reduced form and structural estimates. *Journal of Human Resources* 8 (4): 436–455.

Cain, J.S., R. Hasan, R. Magsombol, and A. Tandon. 2008. Accounting for inequality in India: Evidence from household expenditures. ERD Working Paper Series No. 117. Asian Development Bank, Manila.

Elbers, C., P. Lanjouw, J.A. Mistiaen, and B. Ozler. 2008. Reinterpreting between-group inequality. *Journal of Economic Inequality* 6 (3): 231–245.

Fields, G.S. 2001. *Distribution and development*. Cambridge: MIT Press.

Fields, G.S. 2003. Accounting for income inequality and its changes: A new method with application to the distribution of earnings in the United States. *Research in Labor Economics* 22: 1–38.

Haughton, J., and S. Khandker. 2009. *Handbook on poverty and inequality*. Washington D.C: World Bank.

Hayashi, M., M. Kataoka, and T. Akita. 2014. Expenditure inequality in Indonesia, 2008–2010: A spatial decomposition analysis and the role of education. *Asian Economic Journal* 28 (4): 389–411.

Jann, B. 2008. The Blinder-Oaxaca decomposition for linear regression models. *The STATA Journal* 8: 453–479.

Lakshmana, M. 2013. Population, development, and environment in India. *Chinese Journal of Population Resources and Environment* 11 (4): 367–374.

Mukhopadhaya, P., G. Shantakumar, and B. Rao. 2011. *Economic growth and income inequality in China, India and Singapore: Trends and policy implications*. Oxford, UK: Routledge.

Neumark, D. 1988. Employers' discriminatory behavior and the estimation of wage discrimination. *Journal of Human Resources* 23 (3): 279–295.

NSSO (National Sample Survey Office). 2015. *Status of education and vocational training in India: NSS 68th round.* Ministry of Statistics and Programme Implementation, Government of India. http://mospi.nic.in/sites/default/files/publication_reports/nss_report_no_566_21sep15.pdf. Retrieved 30 Mar 2017.

Oaxaca, R. 1973. Male-female wage differentials in urban labor markets. *International Economic Review* 14 (3): 693–709.

OECD. 2011. *Divided we stand: Why inequality keeps rising*. Paris: OECD.

Pal, P., and J. Ghosh. 2007. Inequality in India: A survey of recent trends. DESA Working Paper No. 45. United Nations (Department of Economic and Social Affairs), New York.

Planning Commission. 2014. Report of the expert group to review the methodology for measurement of poverty, Government of India. http://planningcommission.nic.in/reports/genrep/pov_rep0707.Pdf. Retrieved 25 Feb 2017.

Sen, A., and H. Himanshu. 2005. Poverty and Inequality in India: Getting closer to the truth. In *The great Indian poverty Debate,* ed. A. Deaton, V. Kozel. Delhi: Macmillan.

Shorrocks, A. 1980. The class of additively decomposable inequality measures. *Econometrica* 48 (3): 613–625.

Shorrocks, A., and G. Wan. 2005. Spatial decomposition of inequality. *Journal of Economic Geography* 5 (1): 59–81.

Tsujita, Y. 2006. "Hinkon Sakugen Program no Genjyo to Kadai" (Current situation and challenges in poverty reduction program). In *Yakudo suru India Keizai: Hikari to Kage (Dynamic economy in india: light and shade)*, ed. S. Uchikawa. IDE-JETRO: Tokyo.

MIX
Papier aus verantwortungsvollen Quellen
Paper from responsible sources
FSC® C105338

If you have any concerns about our products,
you can contact us on
ProductSafety@springernature.com

In case Publisher is established outside the EU,
the EU authorized representative is:
Springer Nature Customer Service Center GmbH
Europaplatz 3, 69115 Heidelberg, Germany

Printed by Libri Plureos GmbH
in Hamburg, Germany